RECOLLECTIONS
OF A
MIDWEST M.D.

By
HARRY Y. GREELEY, M.D.

THE ROSEN PUBLISHING GROUP, Inc.
New York

To James Dreher, My heart and soul are in this book. Sincerely, Harry Y. Greeley M.D.

Published in 1984 by The Rosen Publishing Group, Inc.
29 East 21st Street, New York City, New York 10010

First Edition
Copyright 1984 by Harry Y. Greeley

Library of Congress Cataloging in Publication Data

Greeley, Harry Y. (Harry Yerkes), 1915–
    Recollections of a midwest M.D.

    1. Greeley, Harry Y. (Harry Yerkes), 1915–
2. Physicians—Middle West—Biography.   I. Title.
R154.G7667A37 1983   610'.92'4 [B]   83-21203
ISBN 0-8239-0630-2

Manufactured in the United States of America

A Christian physician with uncommon compassion for his fellow man, Harry Yerkes Greeley has a great ability to inspire confidence in his judgments. His singleness of purpose is evidenced by his leaving home after high school and achieving admirable medical and personal success.

He has been the major physician force in the development of the Dreyer Medical Clinic of Aurora, Illinois, over the past thirty years. His travels have carried him to most major countries of the world. The achievements of his children and lovely wife attest to the character of this fine friend of forty years.

William H. Blackburn, M.D.
Aurora, Illinois

Dedication

—to my father, without whose encouragement and faith in me I could never have become a doctor.

—to my wife, Violet, who put up with my being gone seventy hours a week for thirty-eight years and who was the stellar performer in raising our children.

Special Appreciation

—to Helen Wullbrandt, whose untiring efforts in deciphering my rambling tapes made it possible to put this book together.

—to all the wonderful people who were my patients during my thirty-eight years of practice.

—to my medical colleagues in Aurora, who were of more help to me than they will ever know.

Prologue

Friday, June 6, 1941, dawned bright and clear. The long-awaited day when I was to graduate from the University of Illinois Medical School had finally arrived. I could hardly believe it. This was the culmination of eight long, hard years of work and study, and at last I had achieved my goal. Graduation exercises were to be held at the Civic Opera House on Wacker Drive in Chicago at 10 A.M. I made the trip from Waterman, Illinois, with my sisters and their families and with my fiancée, Violet Schoeppel.

The graduates of the schools of medicine, dentistry, and pharmacy filled the auditorium, each group seated in its own section in alphabetical order to facilitate the handing out of diplomas. I sat in the middle of the medical school section, and as I looked around at my classmates a dreadful thought crossed my mind: suppose this is just a dream and soon I will awake to find that this day is just like any other day and graduation is still in the distant future. I pinched myself to make sure it was real.

I thought about the two letters I had received the day before—one from my father, in which he wrote:

> "It makes one have a feeling of satisfaction to have completed a hard program. You have finally completed your course. Of course you have a pull ahead of you yet, but you feel that you are nearly ready to step out in your profession. I hope that you will make the right turns as you continue to advance—that you will be a blessing to the people you meet and that you will always be an honor to your profession."

Simple words, but oh, so sincere! The other, from my mother, said she was sorry I had gone to medical school, that the field of medicine was overcrowded and I would starve to death if I tried to go into practice—I should come home and work on the farm. I had come too far to turn back now, and I was happy with the decision I had made.

The chairman made some brief announcements and complimented the classes that were to graduate. He then introduced the man who was to deliver the commencement address. Although the speaker talked for about an hour, I didn't hear a word he said. As he started to speak, it was as if I were in a trance. My whole life up to that moment flashed through my mind. Memories of my childhood and school days appeared in a steadily developing pattern. I would like to share with you the sequence of events up to the day of my graduation.

I/My Arrival

Date: March 9, 1915
Time: 8:00 A.M.
Place: Arenzville, Illinois

I was born on that date and at that hour in the upstairs bedroom of a ten-room farmhouse. The labor was very difficult, and I was what is called a "blue baby," not breathing at birth. Dr. J. M. Swope, the family doctor, delivered me, and thanks to his persistence and knowledge of what to do in such cases, I was able to survive. He worked on me for over an hour before I was breathing satisfactorily so that he felt it was safe to leave. It shows how fragile is the thread on which one's life hangs. If he had not been so persistent or had had a little less know-how, my whole life's history would never have occurred and I would not be here to write this story.

I was the fifth in a family of seven children—three older sisters, an older brother, and two younger brothers. My eldest sister, Rose, was given responsibility for my care and stayed out of school frequently to help when I was an infant. This established a closeness between us that has lasted all our lives.

It seemed that from the start there was friction between my mother and me. As I later grew into adolescence and she could not mold me according to her pattern, she said many times that she almost wished I had not survived my birth. I never had any trouble getting along with my father or my sisters and brothers, but it seemed that I was always rebellious against my mother. If she wanted me to do one thing, sure as heck I would want to do just the opposite. I apparently was a rather assertive child, since I walked at the age of nine months and was able to learn quite rapidly from the start.

Our early home life was basically happy, although there was always a certain amount of friction between my mother and us children. My maternal grandfather, George Crum, lived with us as long as I can remember and was like one of the family. My grandmother had died in 1910 of diabetes. Her death precipitated the move of my parents from Duluth, Minnesota, where my father had a dental practice, to Arenzville to take over the family farm in 1910.

[1]

II/Family History

My parents respected tradition and always included family names in the names of their children. My middle name is Yerkes, my grandmother's maiden name on my father's side.

In the history of my father's family, Andrew Greeley came to the New World in 1640, and practically all of the Greeleys in the United States can be traced to him. For instance, Horace Greeley was on a different branch of the same family tree and can be traced accurately back to Andrew. In later years I was given a "Greeley book," which was compiled by my father's cousin George Hiram Greeley. In this book are ten thousand names of people who are descendants of Andrew Greeley. There is also a branch of the family that can be traced directly to a Mayflower passenger, Edward Fuller.

In the early eighteen hundreds my mother's family, the Crums, came to the Midwest, where my great grandfather homesteaded land for which he paid $1.25 an acre. He had twelve children, and before he died he was able to give each a farm, one of the farms being the one on which I was born. There were many Crums throughout central Illinois, but I never became well acquainted with many of them. They were an industrious and successful family, but my mother for some reason did not associate with them much. She was very conscious of our long family history on both sides, especially my father's, and she felt that we were a step above everybody else in the neighborhood. This attitude resulted from the fact that we had a family history dating back to 1620 and also that the Greeley family was by most standards an academic family, which tried to ensure that all the children had good educations.

My father's parents moved from New York and settled on a farm in Waterman, Illinois, about 1850 but later moved to Minnesota about 1884 because of my uncle Clarence's poor health. Eventually they moved back to Waterman. My father worked his way through Valparaiso University and then through dental school at Northwestern University. His twin brother, Henry, attended medical school and became an M.D. Another of my father's brothers, Uncle Liston, also worked his way through medical school and practiced in Duluth. Uncle Clarence was ill and unable to go further than high school. In looking back, there were many Greeleys who were well educated and made names for themselves in the professions, including teaching.

The Crum side of the family was also well educated. Although my grandfather was born in 1848 and raised on a farm, he went on to medical school and had an M.D. degree. He was unable to practice medicine because of alcoholism. Although he took a "cure," which was successful, he never tried to go back into medicine because he was afraid it might result in a recurrence of his alcohol problem. Instead, he farmed in central Illinois.

III/The Family Home

My earliest memories of our home are very pleasant. The house, built in 1848, had ten rooms and a porch all the way around it. This elegant and well-kept home had a large yard with many shrubs and maple and pine trees. The grass in the lot between the yard and the road was kept short by grazing horses. My grandfather kept the lawn mowed, the shrubbery neatly trimmed, and the weeds pulled. It was a beautiful homestead, one of the show places of the neighborhood.

The house had no plumbing, no running water, and no heat other than wood and coal stoves. There were four bedrooms upstairs and one downstairs, a parlor, living room, dining room, sitting room, and kitchen. We had no electricity and used kerosene lamps. The kitchen stove was wood-fired, as were the stoves in the dining room, sitting room, and downstairs bedroom. The parlor had a coal-fired stove. There were registers in the ceilings that let a little heat rise into the upstairs bedrooms. The house was not insulated in any way, and it was a real project to try to keep it warm in the winter. Every year we had to spend half the winter months cutting wood from our fifteen-acre woodlot, sawing it, and splitting it up into stove lengths so it would be ready for the next year. Usually fires would go out during cold nights and have to be rebuilt in the morning after we took out the ashes.

Our outside toilet, with its five holes, was the finest in the neighborhood, but we still used pages from old Sears Roebuck and Montgomery Ward catalogues in lieu of tissues. When it was snowing and ten degrees below zero outside, our toilet facilities were not only inconvenient but deathly cold. Water for washing, bathing, and laundering was provided by a cistern. An open well on the porch was fed by a spring at the bottom. This spring water was drawn up in a bucket for drinking. Although the well had a cover, occasionally a rat or cat would get into it and drown. We wouldn't be aware of it until the water became pungent. Then we would draw out many buckets of water until we reached fresh water again.

When my grandfather became too old to work, and my mother spent more and more money until she couldn't get any more, the house began to deteriorate, as did our family structure. The depression came and the bank took over the farm, on which it already had a second mortgage, and then we worked for the bank instead of ourselves. The house and grounds were not kept up. The window screens disintegrated to nothing, and the house was practically taken over by flies from the nearby barns. Many times we would have to shoo the flies off our food before we could eat.

Our house became so filthy and the food so unsanitary that when threshing crews came to our farm they would refuse to stay for dinner, preferring to go home to eat and then come back to finish their work. We didn't have a refrigerator or an icebox. The only way we could keep food cool was to lower it into the well, which was only a little cooler than the air outside. Our more efficient neighbors stored ice from the ponds in sawdust in their icehouses to be used in their iceboxes through the summer. In spite of our dirty house, unsanitary food, poorly balanced diet, and the flies, we managed to stay healthy most of the time.

IV/My Mother

To write about one's parents is very difficult. A person's portrayal of them cannot help but be colored by his own feelings, his own experiences, and his own contacts. It is hard to be objective, and I am sure that what I say about my mother and my father is not what my brothers and sisters would say. Nevertheless, I will express my own feelings.

My mother, Cora Crum Greeley, was a small woman, five feet tall, well filled out but not fat, with dark brown to blackish hair so long it reached her thighs. She wore her beautiful hair in two braids and tied them into a knot on top of her head. She had never had it cut until she was fifty years old. When the fashion for short hair developed around 1930, she had it bobbed quite short. I always thought she looked much better with long hair, but she never let it grow again because she said it felt so much better. My mother had very straight features and a medium complexion, and when she was dressed up she was quite beautiful. In later years she lost some of this beauty, as we all do when we grow older.

She was one of two sisters, raised by very proud parents who instilled in her the idea that she was better than anybody who was not educated and did not have money. She always felt that her neighbors were not good enough for her to associate with closely; she had few, if any, close friends. Neighbors who lived nearby would visit, but she remained aloof. She was brought up in an environment where she did not have to work since her family always had servants. She could not understand or cope with the responsibilities and hard work of farm wives.

After her preliminary education, Mother had attended Valparaiso University, where she majored in music and piano. She became an accomplished musician and played better than anybody I have ever heard. After coming back to the Arenzville farm, she continued to take music lessons at a conservatory in Jacksonville, Illinois. She drove to Jacksonville in a horse and buggy every week for her lesson as long as she could afford to pay for it. My mother wanted her daughters to learn the piano also and gave them all lessons for years. My youngest sister played more than the others, but none of the girls had the musical ability of their mother. As Mother always favored the girls, she didn't really care much about teaching the boys. The boys resented her and did not want to learn to play, but we loved to hear her music.

[6]

As long as I can remember, I had it drilled into me by my mother that girls were smarter than boys, did better in school, got into less trouble, and made better citizens. When I went to school, I fully expected all the girls to be better. I was pleasantly surprised to find that, at least in grade school and high school, I never found a girl that I couldn't beat academically. As I matured, I finally came to my own conclusion that it was not sex that determined mental acuity but that both boys and girls can be very intelligent.

It was at Valparaiso University that my mother and father met. Father was working his way through college and had ambitions to go to dental school. They had a few dates and corresponded some as my father went through dental school at Northwestern University in Chicago, and they were married about the time of his graduation.

My mother had some characteristics that were very difficult for her family. She was always late. Whether it was going to church, getting the children ready for school, or just the ordinary daily routine of getting the meals, she was never on time. I found that the only way I could get to school on time was by secretly setting the clock ahead fifteen or twenty minutes so my mother didn't know what time it really was. This worked quite well, although occasionally she would find that the clock was fast and set it back. The next day the clock would be set ahead again, if not by me, by one of my sisters or brothers.

To get farm work done, it is essential to have meals on time. While Mother slept late every morning, my father would get up early, do all the chores, and then come in and get breakfast for the family and, of course, would be late getting out to the fields to work. At noon, it was the same thing. He would come in at twelve o'clock and the meal was not ready until one or one-thirty, so he would lose valuable time in the fields. At night he would finish his field work, do the chores, and come in at seven or seven-thirty to find that supper wasn't even started. Supper was always after eight and sometimes as late as nine. This habit of lateness made a strong impression on me, and I vowed that when I grew up I was going to be on time. Mother was prompt only when she went to Jacksonville for her music lesson: she knew that if she were late her teacher would cancel her lesson.

My mother was always a big spender and wanted to have more material things than her neighbors. During World War I and for several years afterward, our farmhouse and buildings were the finest in the community. To keep up this pretense of affluence, my mother went into debt for as much as she could borrow. She spent wildly on furniture, books, and unnecessary items. All our neighbors knew about our fancy toilet with its five holes of different sizes. I suppose it was not so all the children could use them at the same time, but so that they could graduate from one size to the next as they grew older.

While many of our books were not practical and were never read, others were invaluable not only to our family but also the schools and the neighbors, who would come to borrow them. This was one expenditure for which we children could be thankful. Our home library was an asset to us in furthering our education. Our father had instilled in us the love of good books, and we were all avid readers.

Even before the depression, we were completely broke because my mother had used up all her credit and owed practically everybody in Arenzville. The neighborhood and the local educational facilities were never good enough for her. For this reason, she sent my two oldest sisters to Jennings Seminary, a private boarding high school for girls, in Aurora. This was expensive and was done with borrowed money.

My mother's housework habits and other day-to-day activities left much to be desired. She had difficulty organizing her household tasks. As clothes became dirty, they were piled in the clothes room adjacent to the kitchen and left until they were moldy. Eventually, she put them in tubs and washed them by hand with a scrub board and hand wringer. She hung them on the clothesline, and when they were dry we wore them without ironing. Our clothes were never very clean, and we wore them for weeks at a time. It must have been unpleasant for people to be around us, but nobody ever mentioned it. Had it not been for our father's insistence that we take a bath every Saturday night, we would have been much dirtier. Bath consisted of standing in a washbasin and dabbing water over us the best we could. Mother never got around to mending our clothes, so we wore them with buttons off and holes; we looked like ragamuffins. I will never forget my chagrin when I had to wear my sisters' middie blouses because I had no shirts.

Our house was always dirty and there was never any attempt to clean the place or to redecorate. My mother was like a packrat, and several of the rooms were piled full of old magazines that she saved for years and years.

She was a strict disciplinarian. She demanded prompt obedience, and whatever she told us boys to do had to be carried out to the letter or we were punished. Very rarely were my sisters punished for their disobedience, because they were female, but we boys experienced a lot of physical punishment. Because I was the most rebellious, I was switched more often than any of my brothers. A green switch was especially favored because it had more sting to it than a stiff, dry branch or wooden paddle. When I did something Mother didn't like, she would order me to come and bend over her knee and then would switch me hard five or six times. We found that if we cried loudly, she wouldn't switch us as hard or as long. I was determined not to cry when she punished me, and perhaps that is one reason I was switched harder than the other boys. Sometimes, though, I hurt so much that I couldn't help crying. My brother Clarence was next in number of switchings and George was least. George, because of his poor health, never crossed anything our mother said and did everything she asked without argument. George was a fine person and probably more like our father than the rest of us.

[8]

My mother tried to dominate all the people with whom she came in contact. Nobody could cross her without getting a tongue lashing. She completely dominated my father as long as I can remember. I suppose at some time their relationship might have been on an equal basis, but somewhere along the line he gave up the fight, and from then on she got her way no matter what the circumstance. Occasionally he tried to reason with her, but she made life so miserable and went into such tantrums that he would give in to have peace. She even dominated his decisions about the farm; if he had good reason to plant corn in a certain field and she wanted him to plant something else, she raised such a fuss that he finally gave in and put in the crop she wanted, even though it was not in the best interest of the farm. It was a frustrating and impossible situation. She often physically abused my father, but he never retaliated. Few men would have put up with the verbal and physical abuse he endured in order to keep the family together.

My mother was basically a good cook. When she had the time and put herself to it, she could bake excellent cakes, pies, and other things. The problem was that she never got around to doing it, and the family suffered immeasurably because of this. Our school lunches were always the most inadequate of any of the school children. As we became poorer, they got worse. When I went to high school, I used to walk five miles and carry my lunch in a little tin pail lined with newspaper. Usually it consisted of three cold biscuits with honey dripped on them as a filling—no butter. The honey soaked through into the newspaper, and sometimes I had to scrape the newsprint off the bottom of the biscuits before I could eat them. All of the other boys and girls had nice lunches with bread, butter, and meat sandwiches, cake or a can of peaches for dessert, and maybe a thermos bottle of milk or cocoa. I was so ashamed of my lunch that I sat a little way from the others and held my bucket between my knees, tipped up, so that they could not see what I had. Then I sneaked a bite of biscuit, trying not to be seen. After all, I did need the calories, so I ate my three biscuits and wondered what was fair about this world that I had to be so poor and others so well off. Sometimes other children felt sorry for me and offered me something from their lunch buckets, but I never took it—I was too proud. I would say, "No, I'm really not very hungry." I can remember many times at home when we children did not have enough to eat. During one two-week period in the middle of the summer, when we were working hard in the fields, all we had was skim milk, corn bread, and baked beans. I wondered if I would ever grow up to be healthy and if times like this would ever end.

My mother always blamed my father for everything, saying that he did not make enough money and therefore our family situation was his fault. She always forgot that she spent all the money my father earned, plus all she could borrow. As our resources became less and less, she became more bitter and harder to live with. She could never understand that it was her fault my father couldn't get his work done because he had to get his own breakfast and wait hours for a late lunch and an eight-thirty to nine o'clock dinner. It affected his crop yields and livestock and depressed his earning power.

My mother always believed that sons of a farmer were there to work. She felt very rich in that she had three boys who would be able to take the place of hired men as they grew up and would make the farm pay. The farm came ahead of everything else. Education would be possible only if there were money to pay a hired man. At one time, we had a hired man who lived in a tenant house. As the depression came on and we became poorer, we could no longer hire a man, so we boys did the work. None of us was ever paid a nickel, and none of us ever had an allowance.

In spite of my mother's deficiencies, she did have many good points, and I am sure that she really loved us children very much. Having grown up in an environment where money was no object and help was plentiful, she had difficulty adjusting to the responsibilities of a large family and a household where money was in short supply. If she had been able to hire the help she needed and to have generous amounts of money with which to raise her children and provide them with an education, she might have been a very lovable mother. She did have one characteristic that was good in some respects: she never gave up. Long after everyone knew that the bank owned our farm, she insisted that some day she was going to get it back. If this tenacity had been teamed with the ability to judge events more logically, it would have made her an entirely different person. There was no question that she was unhappy with the situation in which she lived, much of which she had created. When she saw that her children were not returning her love and saw the respect and trust they had for their father, it probably was very frustrating to her.

It must have been apparent to her that all her children resented her and wanted to get away from home as soon as possible, yet she was unable to change and make our home life more bearable. My sister Rose went into nurse's training after graduation from high school and only came home for short visits after that. Cynthia eloped when she was a senior in high school. She lived close by and was able to be of help to the family, but at the same time was away from the scene of an unhappy existence. My sister Avis went to Chicago, where she entered nurse's training. Clarence left home but came back for a few years to help when our father was sick. He then went into the service for four years, after which he returned only for short visits. I left home when I was seventeen, determined to get an education. George and Wilcox remained on the farm, since their physical and mental disabilities left them no alternative.

On the other side of the ledger, my mother had a soft heart for anyone in need. If a tramp stopped at our door and asked for food or a night's lodging, he was invited to share whatever food we had. Sometimes a tramp would be asked to cut wood or do other work as payment. The neighbors not only refused to help transients but would sic their dogs on them. My mother would literally give someone the clothes off her back if she thought the person needed them. I know this does not seem consistent with her other attributes, but she was a complex individual. Even though our personalities clashed, I always felt that I could understand what had caused her to be what she was. Down deep, I loved her very much, and I know she loved me and was proud of my accomplishments, but it was difficult for her to admit it.

V/My Father

To describe my father is much more difficult. He was mild-mannered, absolutely honest, not particularly aggressive, and deeply religious, but he did not flaunt his religion. He was five feet ten inches tall and weighed about 170 pounds. He was a good-looking man, with straight features and a friendly smile. He was not capable of putting on airs and was always the same despite the emotional trauma caused by my mother. If we children had problems, he always had time to listen, and he was the best tutor in the world. Of his many interests in life, he loved most his family, animals, flowers, and people. No matter what he tried, he could do it well. The problem was that he liked to do so many things that he did not concentrate on any one. His main weakness was that he was not aggressive and dominant enough to counteract my mother's strong-willed personality.

My father came from a hard-working farm family, four boys and one adopted girl. During his boyhood, he lived in Minnesota in a log cabin. The family survived many hardships there. About 1894 they returned to their northern Illinois farm. My father worked his way through North-western Dental School. After graduation, he and Cora Crum were married and moved to Duluth, Minnesota, where he practiced dentistry for six years. He had built up a good practice but following the death of my grandmother was persuaded by my mother and grandfather to move to Arenzville to run the family farm. While he enjoyed dentistry, he also liked farming, so he obliged.

When Father was in undergraduate school, he especially enjoyed botany. His classified collection of leaves and plants, which he preserved by pressing in books, was later given to the State Museum in Springfield, Illinois. Although they had been collected around 1900, they were still in good condition years later. I loved to walk in the woods with my father, who could name every flower, weed, tree, and animal. In the spring, we would go looking for mushrooms because he knew which ones were poisonous and which were edible. I have many fond memories of those walks.

Whereas most farms concentrated on raising hogs, cattle and, perhaps, chickens, my father had a few of everything. We had guineas, ducks, geese, turkeys, horses, cows, ponies, pigs, dogs, cats, and, at one time, a pet skunk and a possum. He knew their habits and feeding patterns and took good care of them, but it took so much of his time that he was often late in getting his farm work done. His many interests made him an inefficient farmer but a good teacher of growing children.

I often wonder why my father did not lose patience with me, as I was not the easiest child to manage and was very mischievous. I sat at his right side at the dining table. He always asked the blessing before meals as we all bowed our heads. Sometimes the temptation was too great and we children would throw bread balls or beans across the table at each other. I especially liked to throw them at Avis because she got so upset. Then Clarence would join in the fun, and the first thing we knew we were all punished. My father's favorite way of punishing me was to pull my ears. Everyone kidded me, saying I would have the longest ears of anyone in the family because they were pulled so much. Once we were punished or reprimanded, our father forgave us and never mentioned the incident again. He had the ability to see the good in all of us.

All of us boys loved to work with our father, to husk corn or shock corn or wheat; whatever work there was to be done was a pleasure whenever he was along. For this reason, I probably worked harder than I would have otherwise. He was an industrious worker and never asked any of us boys to do anything he wouldn't do. In summer, from the time I was ten years old, we always got up at four o'clock to get the horses in and harnessed, milk the cows, and get out in the field. In the wintertime, when we were going to school, we were expected to get up at five o'clock and do all the chores first. We could hardly wait until Sunday, when we were able to sleep until 5:30. That was a real treat!

My father taught me many things—how to get the horses in and care for them, how to teach them to respond to our whistle, and how to call the cows and milk them. A different type of voice was used to call the pigs. I learned to do everything on the farm—how to bed down the old sows so they wouldn't lie on their baby pigs and kill them, and how to avoid the old boars and bulls, which were especially mean to young boys. I helped to vaccinate our pigs and to castrate the males.

At the age of ten, I was taught how to plow a straight furrow with the gang plow and sulky plow, how to disc, how to run the corn planter and set the wire at each end so that the rows would be straight, and how to plow corn with two horses and a one-row cultivator. I knew farming well, and I enjoyed it. If circumstances had been different, I probably would have been a farmer instead of a doctor.

It was a treat to go threshing. In those days, the wheat and oats were cut with a binder and the bundles shocked. A threshing crew consisted of about ten neighbors who owned a threshing machine together and went from farm to farm until the wheat and oats were all threshed. My first job in this operation was "water boy." With a horse and buggy, I would go around at least once an hour with cold drinking water for the men who were pitching bundles and running rack wagons. All the men, including some who chewed tobacco, drank out of the same jug, and no thought was given to its being unsanitary. I learned the unique skill of drinking out of the jug balanced on the shoulder just like the men.

When I was twelve, my father taught me to run a grain wagon. All the wheat that was threshed had to be hauled to Arenzville, five miles away, so it took about ten or twelve grain wagons to keep ahead of the threshing machine. Although this was not a hard job, it was a responsible one in that sometimes when going into the elevator to dump the grain, the horses would become nervous and upset and try to run away, especially if a train came whistling by. As I grew older, I learned to run a rack wagon, to load the bundles about ten feet high on the wagon, and then pitch them into the threshing machine. Pitching the bundles onto the rack wagons was the hardest job of all. It was a killer! When I was fifteen and George was seventeen, we pitched all the bundles for the whole threshing run. I certainly didn't have any fat on me in those days, but I had a lot of muscle and was as thin as a rail.

Another thing that I liked to do with my father was put up hay. We would load hay on the rack wagon with a hay loader, bring it to the barn, set the hayfork, and drive the horse to pull the fork full of hay into the loft and drop it. We would then spread the hay around the loft so it was properly packed. This was very hard work, but it was satisfying because I was doing it with my father.

When I was twelve years old, and George and Clarence and I had worked hard through the spring, my father said, "When the main summer work is done in August, we will all go into Jacksonville and have a big picnic in the park." All of us thought that would be the most wonderful celebration we could ever imagine. We planned on it all summer. After all, we didn't have cars and we didn't get to do a lot of things that the other boys did, but this would be a climactic end to a season of hard work. Finally the day was set about the time of Father's birthday on August 15 and George's on the sixteenth. The day came and we all went in a spring wagon with a team of horses into Jacksonville. In those days, there were still places where one could tie horses in the parking areas. We roamed through the park, looking at the animals and the swimming pool. We all wanted to go swimming, but none of us had swimming suits. Our picnic lunch wasn't very good—it was mostly biscuits—but it was eating it there together that made it one of the most delicious lunches we ever had. We didn't get home until late that night. We talked about that day for the next year; in fact, we all still look back on it with pleasure. We really didn't do much on that picnic. What made it such a happy occasion was our father.

Our father had great influence over all of us that is difficult to explain. If we were tempted to do something of which he would not approve, we wouldn't do it. This pattern followed me throughout my life. I found myself thinking—What would my father say if he knew I was doing this? More than any one thing, this helped me to be a decent person. When I felt I had to leave home, I was afraid he would not approve. Again and again in our quiet moments together he had told me that I would have to strike out someday on my own and would have to get my education by myself, that he would never be able to help me. I think if he had taken a stand and said, "Harry, you have to stay here and help us on the farm. We need you and just can't do without you," I probably would have stayed. I loved my father that much. However, he never put me in that position, so when I left home I knew that he would be proud of whatever I did that was good.

VI/The Twig Is Bent

From the standpoint of my education, I was very fortunate to have had the type of parents that I did. My father, especially, was a private tutor for me from the time I can remember. As soon as I was able to learn at all, he taught me the ABCs, to read and write, and the multiplication tables, so that by the time I went to school, I knew everything there was to learn in the first grade. In those days, in the country school that I attended, the teacher would advance a student to a higher grade if she thought he deserved it. I started the second grade on my sixth birthday, and in two months I had completed everything that the second graders had accomplished for the year. I read and studied and did arithmetic at home that summer, and by September I knew as much as if I had finished the third grade. When I went back to school, the teacher was going to put me in the fourth grade. However, my mother intervened because she felt that six was too young an age to be in the fourth grade, and I was returned to third grade.

In a one-room schoolhouse with one teacher for nine grades, a student can easily fail, but I was so far advanced in my class that I would get my lessons by the first recess. Then the rest of the day I would spend my time listening to the upper classes recite, so that I was almost always a year or two ahead of my grade level. I owe all this to my father. My teachers never had to spend much time with me because I always knew my lessons and didn't require any special attention. In addition to my father's tutoring, my grandfather Crum was especially good to me and read to me by the hour. He took great pride in all his grandchildren, and he was greatly loved in return. My father and grandfather spent a great deal of time with each of the children, especially from three to six years of age, and I think that their tutelage probably was the basis for my being able to do well in school in later years.

My parents were very religious people, and from the time I can remember we had Bible devotions every night. We all gathered in the bedroom, usually after we had undressed for bed, and my father read a chapter in the Bible. Following this, we all got down on our knees while he prayed. His prayer was usually fairly long, but we always ended by saying the Lord's Prayer together. These devotions continued all the time I was at home; I am sure they had a profound effect on my later life.

When I was very young, I didn't understand what my father was reading in the Bible, but as I grew older and the chapters were repeated, I received quite a religious education.

My father was absolutely honest and lived his religion. My mother professed to be just as religious, but sometimes she didn't live it as well. She could quote Scripture all day long to support almost anything she said. She used it as a weapon to try to make us children behave. It worked for some of my brothers and sisters, but for me it fostered a sort of rebellion and had an opposite effect. We were not supposed to question anything that was in the Bible. One of the Ten Commandments that my mother used over and over was, "Honor thy father and thy mother, that thy days may be long upon the land which the Lord thy God giveth thee." My mother always used that commandment as a club, saying that if we didn't honor our father and mother and do everything they said, we would have a short life. For a young boy, this could be quite frightening. After all, if you were going to believe the Bible at all, you had to believe the Ten Commandments, and if the Ten Commandments said you were not going to live a long life unless you did everything your folks said, it really put you in a spot.

In addition to our religious training, prayers, and Bible readings, we were always encouraged to attend church. There was a Methodist church in Arenzville, five miles away, but it was difficult for us to get the chores done, change clothes, and get to church on time when our only means of transportation was horse and buggy. However, we did go there from time to time. There was a country church about one and one-half miles from us, called the Union Church, near the country school that I attended. My father and Charles Ater, a neighbor, would start services at this church in the spring and continue them every Sunday until fall. The attendance was usually only fifteen to forty. This local church did establish a place where the young people and a few of the older folks could go to services and have some semblance of worship. Mr. Ater was a self-styled preacher of hellfire and brimstone and was quite sincere about it. He had two sons, who were about the same age as my brother George and me, and we often played together in school and visited back and forth in our homes.

When we went to church, we had to hitch up the horse and buggy, drive the one and one-half miles, and then tie the horse to a fence while the services were going on. We had a short session of Sunday School in which my father and Mr. Ater each taught a class. Following that was a church service, which began with the singing of hymns. There was an out-of-tune piano in the church but frequently no one to play it. Then Mr. Ater rose in the pulpit and prayed and delivered his hellfire and brimstone sermon for about a half hour, following which we had another song and a prayer to complete Sunday School and church for the week. Although it wasn't a very well-structured program, it was the only one that served a considerable community of mostly poor people.

Although we were not considered poor at that time, we still did not have a car and were the only family to come to church by horse and buggy. The Greeley boys had quite an inferiority complex because they lacked the modern conveniences that their neighbors had. My mother would not go to the country church; she disliked the Aters because of some imagined grievances. We children could never understand why, as the rest of us got along fine and the Ater boys were among our favorite playmates. This church was continued for many years as we were growing up. I think it was probably disbanded when we were in high school.

When my brother George was seven and I was five, something happened that greatly changed my brother's life. George had always been a good child, easygoing and hard-working, and always wanted to help even when he was very small. He would help with dishes, rake the yard, or do anything he could do without hesitation. One day in August of his seventh year, he developed a fever and headache. He was seen by Dr. A. S. Streuter, who at first thought he had just a cold or flu and prescribed aspirin or something of that nature. The next day, George tried to get out of bed and fell flat on his face. He could not get up by himself and called for help. My folks helped him back into bed and noticed that he could not move his right leg or right arm very well. Dr. Streuter was called and came out to see him again. This time he told my parents what they had feared, that George had infantile paralysis (poliomyelitis) and at this stage it was impossible to tell whether he would be paralyzed or not. George was in bed for several weeks, following which he was helped into a chair. He began, gradually, to use his right arm and right leg and regained the entire function in his arm. The function in his leg came back quite well later and he was able to walk, but he always had a definite limp after that time. I am sure this handicap affected his life, as he could no longer keep up with the other boys in running or playing. Being of the nature he was, he never complained but accepted it as part of God's plan. George was very religious and believed that everything was planned for us and that there was nothing anybody could do about it.

In looking back, I think I probably had poliomyelitis at that time. I had a headache and was sick for two or three days, but I never suffered any weakness or paralysis; I probably had a nonparalytic polio. Every summer after that, when the polio season came around, we were apprehensive that somebody else in the family would get the disease, but nobody did. I carried this fear of polio on through grade school, high school, college, and medical school, never knowing for sure whether I did or did not have it as a child.

As I grew into my school years, I developed a trait that has been of great help throughout my life but also at times has been a liability—I became an avid competitor. My father, like all farmers of that day, counted on his boys to do a lot of work on the farm. As soon as we were old enough, he taught us to milk cows, harness horses, plant corn, help with the garden, and do whatever needed to be done. I always wanted to learn to do everything that George did, even though I was two years younger and really not old enough. I was not satisfied just doing the things George did—I wanted to do them faster and better.

When I was six or seven, we had a large herd of cows and I wanted to learn to milk. My father said, "Fine." There was one cow that was gentle enough for me, but most of them didn't want an inexperienced little kid pulling on their teats, and I was kicked over into the manure trench more than once. At first, milking was sort of fun, but when my father found out that I could really do it, he gave me a regular job of milking and then it was drudgery. I found that if I had a sore finger, my father wouldn't make me milk, so one time I managed to have a sore finger for about three months. He finally called my bluff and I had to get back on the job again.

Milking was fun in that I could squirt this nice, warm milk into my mouth; also, I could squirt milk at the cats and they would lap it up. The worst part was the flies. In the summer we sprayed the cows before we milked them, but the flies still swarmed. The cows, trying to knock them off, would swing their tails around and knock off our hats or hit us in the face. If we tied their tails down so they couldn't switch us, that was their cue to kick instead. Most of the cows didn't kick maliciously, but there were always one or two that did. For those, we had hobbles to prevent them from kicking so that we could milk them without trouble.

We took the milk in buckets up to the house, where we strained out the dirt and then ran it through a cream separator. We boys always had the job of turning the separator, the last chore of the day. In those days there was usually a creamery in every small town, and we took the cream there about twice a week and got what little money we could for it. We never could use the cream for butter at home because my mother felt that we needed the money too badly. We were practically raised on skim milk.

When I was about six years old, my sisters were in their latter years of high school and were dating brothers whom they had met at Arenzville High School. Their beaus came twelve miles out to the farm every Sunday afternoon or evening in their Model-T Ford and stayed until ten or eleven o'clock, when my mother insisted that they go home. Although I didn't understand the ways of young people in love, I was completely fascinated by the way they talked and acted. I was so curious that I often hid behind the davenport in the parlor, unbeknownst to the young lovers, and when they came in from outdoors and closed the parlor door to be separated from the rest of the family, I knew I was in for an enjoyable evening. Eventually, when the hour grew late and it was necessary for me to reveal myself, my sisters were very upset and I was severely reprimanded. Sometimes they sat out in the Model-T and talked, and I hid underneath the car and listened. There was no danger of my getting run over: cars in those days had no self-starters and had to be cranked, in which case I could scramble out from underneath in a hurry. I am sure I was quite a nuisance to my sisters during their courting, but it was part of my education.

One day when my sister Cynthia's boyfriend, Phillip Rice, came to the farm, I had caught a half-grown rabbit and was sitting with it on the porch swing. Phillip admired my catch and then very seriously said, "Harry, if you just talk to that rabbit long enough, it will die." I believed him, so I started talking. I talked and talked, a steady stream of chatter— though what I said I can no longer recall. At the end of forty-five minutes, lo and behold! the rabbit toppled over, gave a long shudder, and breathed its last. Phillip came around the corner of the house just in time to see me jump up and down and shout excitedly, "I did it! I did it!" Phillip's mouth dropped open and he peered at the rabbit in amazement. "You actually talked that rabbit to death?" he asked. I nodded my head, proud of my accomplishment. Neither of us knew the real reason for the rabbit's demise, and even to this day, when Phillip reminds me of the episode, we speculate as to what I could have said that packed such a wallop. Phillip, incidentally, married Cynthia, and the two of them never let me forget what a menace I was during their courtship days.

When I was about nine or ten, I wanted very badly to have some spending money. There were so many things I wanted that my folks were unable to buy for me. I wondered what I could do to earn some money, and I got the idea of trapping animals and selling their fur. Some of the boys at school did that and seemed to make out quite well. Using some of my father's spring-type traps, which he used for rats, I established a line of traps in the woods, and every morning before school I checked them to see if I had caught anything. I made my way into the fifteen acres of dense woods each morning just as the sun was beginning to come up. The hooting of the owls and the stirring of animals gave me an eerie feeling, but my dog, Ring, was the best protection a boy could have. He would fight any other dog or animal without hesitation if I said the word, so I felt reasonably safe. I kept my traps for several years and was able to catch one or two skunks, some possum, and a few muskrats each winter. I sold the furs and was able to buy a few things; however, my mother frequently took the money and I never got it back.

When I was fourteen, I got the idea that I could earn a little money by growing popcorn. There was a small unused patch of land by one of the creeks, and I asked my father if I could plant it in popcorn. He agreed that if I did all the work I could have the money from what I sold. I plowed this land with a walking plow, planted it, and cultivated the corn by myself. In the fall when it came time to harvest, I husked it and put it in one of the upstairs rooms to dry out. I had a small corn sheller with which I shelled about twenty bushels of popcorn. I then went into Jacksonville to a Greek place that always sold popcorn and asked the proprietor if he would like to buy my crop. He agreed to buy the lot. I loaded it into sacks and took it into Jacksonville in the spring wagon one day, and he paid me the grand sum of thirty dollars. That was more money than I had ever seen. I was elated. All the work I had done seemed worthwhile when I thought of all the things I could buy now. I decided that I would put the money in the bank and spend it little by little so that it would last. When I arrived home and my mother found out that I had thirty dollars, she said I would have to lend it to her because there were bills that had to be paid, and that she would pay it back sometime. That was quite a blow. Here I had worked and worked all summer plowing, planting, cultivating, husking, shelling, selling it, delivering the corn, and collecting the money, and now it was gone! I didn't get a dime for all my work, as the money was never repaid. I think that if I hadn't come home with the thirty dollars, the family would have gotten along some way without it.

VII/Education, the Key to All Things

High school was a brand-new experience for me. I had gone through eight grades in a country school with one teacher and had done well. My father had always encouraged me in my homework, and nobody could do better in his studies than I. My sisters had the privilege of driving a horse and buggy to high school, but by the time we boys attended it was necessary for us to walk. The girls had driven to Arenzville and left the horse at Niestradt's livery stable for the day. Mr. Niestradt fed the horse the food we provided and had it harnessed and hitched to the buggy when the girls returned from school. For this service, he charged fifteen cents a day. When our bill reached thirty-five dollars and my mother was unable to pay, Mr. Niestradt refused to keep the horse anymore. Consequently, we boys had to walk.

My high school years were difficult. I got up at five o'clock every morning, helped with the chores, packed my lunch bucket with biscuits, and walked five miles to school. By cutting across the fields, I could walk that distance in about an hour and ten minutes. When school was over at four o'clock, I walked home, did the chores again, ate a nine o'clock supper, went to bed, and then was up at five in the morning to begin the same routine. I did most of my studying by kerosene light and often thought how nice it would be to have electricity.

I had good rapport with my teachers and made straight A's in everything but English. I adjusted to my classes very well, but my social life was limited because I had no car, no money to spend on dates, and frequently had to stay out of school to work on the farm. In May of my freshman year my brothers and I had to stay out of school to get the crops in. After I had missed three weeks straight, I was so far behind in my assignments that I became discouraged and told my father I thought I would be a farmer and forget about school, that I was sure I could make the farm pay if given the chance. This was one time my father sat down with me and was very stern and adamant. He said, "Harry, you are in a rut. There is nothing more satisfying than education. You have just scratched the surface. Education is the key to all things. By all means, make up your studies and go back to school in the fall." I knew he was right, and because he had faith in me, I did what he said. It meant hard work, and many times I didn't know how it was all going to turn out, but I always remembered what he said about education being the key to all things.

My sophomore year was a little easier. I enjoyed the sociability of the other boys and girls. I had fewer material things than any of the other students but was respected for my ability to learn and was always at the top of the class. I particularly liked acting and had the leading part in a series of plays, including the junior class play during my sophomore year. I had to hurry home after school to help with the chores, eat quickly, and then ride a horse back to Arenzville for play practice. Although it was extra work, it was very important for my ego to be able to excel in whatever I undertook. The following year, I had the lead in my junior class play.

I stayed out of school to work on the farm between my junior and senior years. George, who was two years ahead of me in school, had stayed out between his junior and senior years and now would return to finish his senior year and graduate with my class. I had spent three years with the same eighteen students, and not being able to graduate with them seemed, at that time, to be a great tragedy of my life; but I had to make the sacrifice because George deserved an education and it was only fair that I take my turn. I was sixteen years old when I started this year of farm work. I had full charge because my father had severe arthritis and wasn't able to work very much, although he did help some with the chores. Since we had no tractor, I farmed the two hundred acres with six horses and limited equipment. It required a lot of work and planning, but I did, basically, a very good job. I got up early and worked late, but I enjoyed it. I husked three thousand bushels of corn by hand during the winter of 1931, scooping the corn into an overhead crib. I worked the entire year without even a nickel of pay, and all the money the farm earned went into the bank to pay past debts. That was one year when the Greeley farm was run efficiently; our crops were in on time and were good.

During that year, the teacher of the one-room schoolhouse that I had attended, but who had never been my teacher, asked me to be the hero in a play she was producing. She was to play the part of the heroine even though she was ten years older than I. She got together a number of young men and girls, and we rehearsed at night at the schoolhouse. Afterward, we and another couple would go out in her car to a quiet area and practice some more. You can imagine what this did to a young, virile male of sixteen. It was a new experience for me, and it turned me on with a vengeance. The situation could easily have gotten out of hand and spoiled my whole life but for my father's influence. In the back of my mind were the questions: What would my father do? What would my father say? Because of that, I kept our practice on a safe plane. I'll admit, it was fun, but it went no further than that. We gave the play several times and everyone did well.

In the latter part of December, we had just given the play for the last time when I contracted a severe case of measles. I didn't have the corn quite all husked, and it had to wait until after the first of the year when I was sufficiently recovered to get back in the field. I had a high fever for a number of days before I broke out, and as I look back on it, I was really in quite a bit of danger, as mine was a much more severe case of measles than the average. I didn't get any solace from my mother. She blamed my running around nights, practicing and putting on the play, for my being so sick. My father, in his usual good manner, sympathized and comforted me during my illness.

The school year came to an end, and I was still working hard to put in the new crops of corn, oats, and wheat. George graduated with my class and immediately contracted tuberculosis and was unable to work. My mother said, "Harry, you will have to stay out of school another year. We can't take care of the crops without you." I worked hard all summer, and as school approached I told my mother, "I think I can make it if I can go to school two or three days a week and work the rest of the week on the farm." My teachers knew my family situation and were very good to me. One teacher, especially, did everything she could to help me get through another year of school. At the end of the first six weeks, I did well on exams, but I was working so hard and such long hours that I realized I couldn't go through the winter like this. Clarence was getting older and was able to help with the chores, but he was also in school. As October went by, I became more and more convinced that I was going to ruin my health if I tried to keep on; something had to give. The farm had been taken over by the bank, and I felt there was no future for me there as I was now working for the bank instead of my folks.

I had been corresponding with my sister Rose and cousin Paul Greeley, a doctor, in Waterman, Illinois. Their letters were sent through the teacher who had been so kind to me, rather than direct to our mailbox, as my mother would have read them and I would never have received them. Cousin Paul and Rose thought that if I came to Waterman and established a residence there, perhaps George could also come up and go to a TB sanitarium in DeKalb County. In retrospect, that was not really feasible, but it was one of the reasons for my decision to leave home. It was a very difficult decision to make, and many times I have looked back and wondered if I did the right thing. If my father had said, "Harry, you had better stay here, we need you," I would have stayed. When I told him I was thinking about leaving, he said, "We will get along somehow." And that is what they did; they got along somehow. It wasn't good.

VIII/Leaving Home

Monday, November 1, 1932, in the middle of the depression, I told my father I was going to leave. He asked me if I would stay another day to help get the potatoes dug. On the morning of November 2, I told my mother for the first time that I was going to leave home. She was very upset and didn't believe me. She yelled and screamed at me, but I told her it was no use because I was not going to be there any more. I put some biscuits in my tin lunch bucket, put on my old red sweater, and got ready to leave. When she finally realized that I was going, she gave me two dollars. That was the only money I had, and I have been very grateful to her ever since. I don't know what I would have done if I had not had the money to get a room that night and breakfast the next morning. I suppose I would have stayed in a jail somewhere.

I will have to admit, as I walked down the road that morning, that I was a very scared young man. The future was unknown. I had never hitch-hiked before. I knew that I had to travel two hundred miles to get to my sister's home in Waterman. Through the letters we had exchanged, she knew I was coming and what day I was leaving home. Rose didn't have much in those depression years, but she was willing to share what she had to help me. She lived with Uncle Clarence in a very small house with one small bedroom downstairs, which was Uncle Clarence's, a small living room, and dining room with a daybed. Up a narrow stairs, in the attic, was a double bed which Rose and her husband, Jim Phelps, shared when he came home weekends from his traveling job.

I walked the first two miles, and then two girls from Virginia High School, whom I knew, gave me a ride to Virginia. There, I went out to the highway and tried to thumb a ride. It didn't take long, and I was able to ride for forty miles. As the day went on, I got a number of rides, but as evening approached it was obvious that I would never make it to Water-man that night. Naive as I was, I thought if I stopped at some farmer's house and offered to cut wood or do some other work for a night's lodging, he would be glad to oblige. I thought of how many times my folks had helped somebody who needed a place to spend the night. About two miles from Tonica, I turned in at a farmhouse and was greeted by a big dog. When the farmer answered my knock on the door, I asked if I could stay all night if I worked for my lodging. In a surly manner, he warned, "Get out, or I will sic my dog on you." That was quite a letdown; I hadn't expected such a reception.

I walked on to Tonica and asked at the jail if there was any place I could get a room for the night, that I had two dollars. I was directed to a house near the railroad, where the people were very nice to me and said I could stay all night for a dollar and they would give me breakfast for another twenty-five cents. I didn't sleep much that night. To begin with, the trains went roaring by at various hours; second, I was a rather apprehensive young man, but I felt sure I was doing the right thing. I was willing to work and was confident that I could make my way if given the chance.

The next morning I started out again and was able to get rides to approximately ten miles from Waterman. Then it seemed that every car went right on by, and I walked the rest of the way. When I reached Waterman, I stopped at the post office and asked where Mrs. Phelps and Clarence Greeley lived. Their home was only a block away, but I think that was the longest block I ever walked. As I neared the house, I thought: What if they don't want me? What if, after I have come this far, they just turn me around and send me home again? I finally got up enough courage to knock on the door. I was completely unprepared for the reception I received. Rose came to the door crying. She threw her arms around me and said, "Harry, I didn't sleep all night last night, worrying about you. I wondered where you were and if you were safe." She then called Uncle Clarence, who greeted me with enthusiasm and made me feel welcome. By then, I was starved; the biscuits with which I had started out were long gone, and I had had a very light breakfast. After Rose gave me a good meal, I felt better.

Rose then telephoned Cousin Paul, the doctor, who had his own small hospital in Waterman. He rushed over immediately to welcome me. Since I didn't have much in the way of clothes, he brought some of his old suits. They were rather baggy on me, but I was able to wear them. Then he sent me to the store to get a couple of shirts and some underwear. Within an hour he had taken me to the high school, where he introduced me to the high school principal. Evidently the principal was expecting me, because he had the answers to all my questions; they would get my records from Arenzville and I could start to school the next day. That night my cousin Carl Greeley came to see me and said if I wanted to work Saturdays cutting wood on his farm, I could earn a little extra money. I just couldn't believe that all these nice things were happening to me.

Waterman High School had a good reputation and, although it was small, had an excellent basketball team, and the whole town was basketball crazy. The year before, they had gone to the state finals but had lost the first game to Beardstown, a town not far from Arenzville. I had always liked athletics but was not eligible to play at Waterman, so the coach gave me a job helping with the equipment. By selling pop to the fans, I was able to get free passes to the games. As the season ended and we came to the last game, there was still a large number of bottles left to sell. I closed all the windows so the temperature in the gym became very warm, and when the fans became hot and thirsty I sold every bottle of pop we had.

Academically, Waterman rated quite well with other schools of its size in the area. There were twenty-five in the senior class, nineteen boys and six girls. I adjusted to this new group of students rapidly. They were all nice to me, and I tried to reciprocate. They evidently had heard tales of how I got there and how poor I was, but they never made any disparaging remarks about my situation. By the end of my senior year, I felt almost as if I belonged in Waterman instead of Arenzville. I did well in my studies and graduated third in my class.

I became more and more determined that I was going to go to college somehow. I knew I couldn't do it the following September because I didn't have any money, but I thought if I could get a job and work a year I could save enough to go to school again. I was burning with ambition but didn't have any resources with which to back it up. I didn't go to our high school graduation because I didn't feel that I belonged to this group yet. I felt that the diploma was a stepping-stone to something better and that I should get on with it.

Rose couldn't have been nicer to me that winter. I managed to earn a little money by doing odd jobs. I caught mice, for which I was given three cents apiece. I worked for the neighbors for ten cents an hour. I did janitor work at the school for ten cents an hour and frequently on Saturdays went out to Cousin Carl's farm and split wood for ten hours for a dollar. I kept track of everything. Below is part of my record of expenses and income for that first year.

Example of my financial accounting in the days just after high school.

IX/To College at Last

After graduation, I started working immediately on Cousin Carl's farm for twenty dollars a month, and the whole next year can be described in one word—work. I helped him shingle his barn that summer, worked a short time for another farmer, and then returned to work for Cousin Carl when another job opened up on his farm. To give you an idea of prices in the depression years, I cite the following: Rose had been very good to me, and I thought I should do something for her. In the fall of 1933 I was working on a farm in Waterman and bought a two-hundred-pound pig from the farmer. This pig cost four dollars per hundred pounds, or eight dollars. I butchered it myself, cut it up, and gave it to Rose to help repay her for the many things she had done for me. I had learned how to slaughter a hog and cut it up from my father as I was growing up.

As the year went on, I tried desperately to save every dime and nickel I could, hoping to have enough money to enter college in the fall of 1934. Although the University of Illinois was by far the cheapest school to attend, I made the mistake of being afraid of a big school, thinking it would be very difficult for me and that I would have no personal attention. I later regretted that I didn't go there. I was accepted at Illinois Wesleyan at Bloomington, and though I got a half-scholarship that helped a good deal, it was still expensive for one making only twenty dollars a month. My goal was to save $150 with which to start college.

That summer, the World's Fair was in Chicago. I wanted very much to go but didn't want to spend the money. I rode a milk truck to Chicago, which didn't cost me anything, and stayed all night at the YMCA on Wabash Avenue for fifty cents. I paid admission to the fair with a quart of chinch bugs that I had caught and brought with me. During the depression, people were more cautious about spending money, and the publicity people had devised this gimmick to increase attendance. I spent about a dollar and a half altogether, which included a few hot dogs and rides. After spending a day and night in Chicago, I came home on the milk truck again, and my total expense for the fair was about two dollars.

When one is waiting and planning for something, time seems to pass very slowly. I was very anxious to start college and thought I would be able to make it when September rolled around at last. The day before I went to Wesleyan, I quit my job, packed everything I had in an old cardboard suitcase, and hitchhiked to Bloomington, arriving there in the late afternoon. I didn't have a place to stay and was completely ignorant of how to go about getting one. The president of Illinois Wesleyan found me a bed for the night, and the next morning I started out to look for a place to live and a job for my board. Sometimes it seems that God is with us and things happen that are unexplainable unless one believes in a divine being. I went six blocks north, just the other side of Brokaw Hospital in Normal, turned on Healy Street, went one block and turned in at the second house. Why I took this route, I will never be able to explain unless it was divine providence. I asked the Roeders, who lived there, if they wanted a student for room and board, and they said yes, they would be glad to have me. The Roeders were wonderful to me, and it seemed that it was more than by chance that I met them. They were the first people I visited and were not very close to the campus.

After I had registered, I still did not have a job. I started at the north end of Main Street in Normal and visited every business establishment through Normal and Bloomington on each side of the street, a distance of two miles, asking for any kind of work that was available. This took several days, and I found absolutely nothing. I was beginning to get discouraged when Mr. Roeder told me that he could get me a job at Montgomery Ward, where he worked, uncrating furniture, setting up toys, and working in the storeroom, for which I would receive twenty-two cents an hour. By today's standards that certainly wasn't much, but it bought food and kept me in school. It is interesting to note that I was paid twenty-two cents an hour because of the National Recovery Act. Later, toward the end of the school year, the NRA was declared unconstitutional, and Montgomery Ward immediately cut the hourly wage to eighteen cents.

Adjusting to college life was not easy for a country boy with practically no money. I hadn't been there a week before fraternities were rushing me. I was told that if I joined a fraternity it would be of great consequence to me after graduation. I protested that I didn't have the money but was told there were other poor boys in the fraternities who were working their way through college, and if they could do it, so could I. It was a great temptation to spend what little money I had left to join, but when I weighed the pluses and minuses, there just wasn't any way I could do it. It wasn't long before I discovered that there were many boys who didn't belong to fraternities and they got along just as well. In fact, I joined an independent group where I met some nice people, and it cost nothing. In retrospect, I don't think a fraternity would have made any difference as far as my future was concerned at that time.

I purposely signed up for a light class load because I knew I would be working. During the first few weeks, I was busy looking for additional work, but it wasn't long before Montgomery Ward gave me the privilege of coming in at any time—nights, Saturdays, even Sundays—to uncrate furniture, set up toys, and work in the stockroom. Later on, I worked in the basement selling tires, batteries, and so on. At times I was asked to work in the service station changing tires, changing oil, and doing light mechanical work. Working so much did cause my school work to suffer, but I was able to maintain a B average, with one A, the first semester. I took all basic college courses even though I had enrolled in premed.

I worked through Thanksgiving vacation rather than try to go home. I worked my whole Christmas vacation in the basement of the old main hall at Illinois Wesleyan, painting pipes and ceilings, in order to make a little more money to stay in school. After all, I really didn't have a home to go to. I could go to Waterman any time to visit my sisters, but they had their own families and I didn't feel I belonged.

I passed all my courses the first semester. When the second semester started, I was able to scrape up enough money to pay my tuition again. I finished the year without too much trouble academically, but financially I was completely broke, and my confidence in my ability to get through two more years of college and four years of medical school was badly shaken. Through Cousin Paul, I was able to get a summer job with some Norwegian carpenters in Shabbona, about five miles from Waterman. I knew I would have to have some means of transportation to get back and forth to work, and after looking around I was able to buy a 1926 Chevy for twenty dollars. It wasn't a very good car; the brakes were poor and the radiator was partially stopped up so it overheated easily. It did get good mileage and allowed me to get to and from work all summer at speeds of thirty to thirty-five miles an hour. The depression was still on, and the pay was only thirty-five cents an hour. I worked nine hours a day, six days a week, a total of fifty-four hours. I felt fortunate to have a job, since many people had none. I saved my money and was able to go back to school in the fall. I sold the car for twenty-five dollars, so I didn't do too badly.

My medical career was almost abandoned before it began because I fell in love with a girl who was a year behind me in high school. Although I didn't see her often during my first year in college, we corresponded regularly. I had a letter from her about three times a week, and at the end of the year when I went back to Waterman for the summer, we saw each other frequently. Being young, in love, and strongly heterosexual can sometimes influence one's decisions for the future. I couldn't imagine waiting five or six years to get married, and I found myself thinking that if I majored in agriculture perhaps I could get through in three more years and then get married and have a family. After all, my second interest was agriculture, and I thought I would make a good Smith-Hughes agriculture teacher. Another factor in my decision to change my college course was the fact that Illinois Wesleyan was an expensive private school. Even though I had a partial scholarship, the tuition was very high, and I was at my wit's end as to how I could continue to pay it and the other college expenses.

[30]

The fall found me registering at Illinois State Normal University in agriculture. I did well scholastically and had almost straight A's throughout the year. I continued to work at Montgomery Ward and at other meal jobs, and because tuition and board were less expensive, I was able to survive. I had the lead in the sophomore class play, which I enjoyed very much. As the year went on, I realized that my relationship with Betty was changing. She started dating other fellows, and I began seeing other girls occasionally. By summer, at the end of my second year of college, our romance was pretty well on the rocks. In retrospect, it was a perfectly natural sequence of events. I was away all the time, and she was a very pretty girl. It was only natural that she would find other company that was more available. She had played an important part in those two years of my life, but my being in love and wanting to get married almost ruined my future as far as being a doctor was concerned.

I worked for the carpenters again in the summer of 1936 and bought a 1927 Chevrolet for transportation. I paid twenty-five dollars for this car and, after running it all summer, sold it for thirty dollars.

When I was sure it was all over between Betty and me, I made the decision to go into premed at the University of Illinois and then go to medical school and become a doctor no matter how long it took. Once this decision was made and the emotional complications were eliminated, there was never any question in my mind but that I would some day realize my ambition to be an M.D.

My application was accepted by the University of Illinois, and my credits were transferred without trouble. In talking to my advisor at the university, I found that I would have enough credits for medical school the next year if I went to summer school and took organic chemistry. I was encouraged by the prospect that I might be able to enter medical school in the fall of 1937.

At Illinois Wesleyan I had roomed with a freshman whose name was also Harry. People called me "Big Harry" and him "Little Harry" because he was considerably smaller than I. I didn't have a roommate during my second year and lost track of him, but I got in touch with him again when I entered the University of Illinois and found that he was going there also. Together, we rented a room at the top of a stairway, and a gas plate on the landing, for eighteen dollars a month, nine dollars apiece. Harry worked at a canning factory and was able to buy dented cans of peas and corn for four cents a can. I contributed tomatoes and vegetables that I had raised during that summer and canned with the help of my sister. We got along fine and were able to survive on about two dollars a week for groceries. We bought skim milk for twelve cents a gallon, hamburger for ten cents a pound, and day-old bread for three cents a loaf.

I went to Montgomery Ward as soon as I arrived in Urbana, and because I had worked for them in Bloomington I had no trouble getting a job. I worked in the basement helping to uncrate furniture, set up toys, and so on for twenty-five cents an hour instead of the eighteen cents I had been paid before. I had no extra money to spend, but I didn't need any. I worked hard on my studies, which included physics, chemistry, biology, and German, all very fascinating subjects, and I did well in all of them. As the year went by, I developed a social life for which I hadn't had time during the other two years when I was working all the time and was in love with the girl back home. That was all history now, and Little Harry and I started going to Wesley Foundation, which is a "home away from home" for Methodist students. We had parties and get-togethers that were inexpensive or cost nothing. For the first time, I really enjoyed college. It was here that I met my future wife, Violet Schoeppel, who was a sophomore at the university and was from southern Illinois. I did not go with her seriously for a long time, but I saw her occasionally and was attracted to her.

I had always been afraid I would be lost in a big school, but I enjoyed it much more than I had either of the other years of college. For the first time in my life I felt that I was in control. I had to do it myself. And that was great!

By working as much as possible, my money held out so that at the end of the year I had a little left over. Something happened then that helped me get that last summer of organic chemistry I needed. Montgomery Ward had a college scholarship plan whereby if one obtained catalogue orders totaling five hundred dollars or more, he could get approximately 10 percent of the amount of each order to use for college. I was able to get enough orders to yield fifty dollars with which to start summer school.

I had a week between the end of the semester and the beginning of summer school, and Violet invited me to her home, about two hundred miles from Champaign, to spend the weekend. I told her that if it was all right with her I would hitchhike, as I didn't have any money. Violet's family was not rich but certainly not poor, and she didn't have to work while she was in college. They were a very proud family and hitchhiking was not in their vocabulary. Although Violet's parents knew I hitchhiked, she tried to keep it from Aunt Clara and other relatives in Ellis Grove who she knew would not approve. I made the trip successfully and had a delightful weekend. I met her mother, father, and two younger brothers, and they made me feel right at home. Mr. Schoeppel was a business man in St. Louis and spent his weekends at home on the farm. After I had gone, he told Violet that she should go with somebody who would be able to support her. Evidently, he didn't have much faith in this thin, scrawny boy with no money. We were not going together seriously at that time, so it was not a problem.

I took organic chemistry in summer school, finishing about the first of August. I enjoyed it very much and made an A without difficulty. As soon as I received my credits, I applied for medical school. I knew there wasn't much time left, that the class roster was almost completed and that there were more applications than openings, but I thought maybe I would be lucky. In recent years I had been unusually fortunate, and I hoped it would continue. I went back to Waterman and worked for the carpenters again, coming home every day and looking anxiously for the mail. About the fifteenth of August there was the letter from the Medical School! I looked at it for a minute, afraid to open it. Trembling, I opened the envelope, unfolded the sheet of paper, and there it was: "Dear Mr. Greeley: I am happy to inform you that you have been accepted in the University of Illinois Medical School, which will start classes September 17. Yours sincerely, George R. Moon, Registrar." Also enclosed was information on the procedures to follow. I read it again and then whooped and hollered, jumping and dancing around. It was one of the great moments of my life! I felt as if I were practically a doctor, and I hadn't really started yet. If I had known what lay ahead for me in study and work, I might not have been so elated.

X/Medical School

Now I had to find a way to finance this education. I had applied earlier in the summer for a congressional scholarship to the University of Illinois Medical School, two of which were given every year by state senators and representatives. Dennis Collins of DeKalb was my sponsor and was able to get this scholarship for me, which paid tuition throughout my four years. The day after I received my letter of acceptance, I went to Chicago to see if I could find a job. There, again, I lucked out. Times were hard and everybody, students and all, was looking for work. I went to the Congress Street YMCA, an eight-story building where some of the medical students lived. It was directly across from the Cook County Hospital and two long blocks from the Medical School. Mr. Hiller, the executive secretary, talked with me for a long time, and I must have made a favorable impression as he gave me a job working evenings, Saturdays, and Sundays at the front desk. I was to start as soon as I entered school. I had never done that kind of work before, but he seemed to think I would have no trouble. Also, I could room at the YMCA at a discount. I held that job throughout my four years of medical school; without it, I would never have made it. I couldn't help feeling that God was watching out for me.

I started medical school in the fall of 1937 and found it much more difficult than undergraduate work. There was so much to learn and memorize and so little time to do it. Medical schools took only the best students, and they were very competitive. There were some very fine instructors, but there were others who were very hard on their students and seemed almost sadistic. We were told when we started that 20 percent of us would not graduate. It seemed to be the policy in that era for medical schools to flunk approximately 20 percent of the students. There were 160 who started in my class and 141 graduated. That, however, included some students who transferred from two-year schools and started with us in their junior year, so the loss of students was just about what was predicted. This certainly put one under the gun, because no one wanted to be one of the lost 20 percent, and yet everyone knew that they were competing with a group of students who were all much above average in scholarship. Thanks to the American Medical Association standards for medical schools, all the Class A schools in the

[34]

United States were excellent. Any of the graduating doctors from those institutions would be well trained.

My getting through medical school was more difficult because it was necessary for me to work thirty to thirty-five hours a week throughout my four years. I washed five hundred glasses a day at the noon hour in the cafeteria of the YMCA for my meals and worked as a desk clerk from 5:00 P.M. to 1:00 A.M. three nights a week. I worked all night every Saturday until eight Sunday morning. On the nights I worked until one o'clock, I frequently studied from one to three, or I went to bed and got up at 4:30 to study until time for class. I used to be envious of the boys who didn't have to work and could apply all their time to their studies; however, in spite of all the work I did, I was able to graduate in the upper 25 percent of my class.

I continued to work for the carpenters in Shabbona during the summer and in 1938 bought a 1928 Chevy for thirty dollars, which I used to go back and forth to work. The price of cars was going up a little every year. This car ran quite well and I hated to part with it, but I needed the money for school. In the fall, I sold it for thirty-five dollars. In 1939, I bought a 1929 Chevy for thirty-five dollars. It seemed that I was always ten years behind. By this time, I was finishing my junior year and did not intend to do carpenter work between my junior and senior years. I might add that these Norwegian carpenters were tough, hard-working, and honest. They liked to tease me—a college boy working to help build barns and houses—but they were always kind, and without that job I never would have made it through college and medical school.

Between my junior and senior years, I worked as a bellboy at the YMCA on Wabash Street on the three-to-eleven shift. I also kept my jobs at the Congress Street YMCA, so I was able to save some money. I spent every morning in the Cook County morgue watching autopsies. I saw approximately fifteen to twenty a day through that summer and learned a great deal.

As I went through medical school, I became very proud of my chosen profession. It seemed to me that most of the discoveries in medicine had already been made and that we could be thankful that we knew so much more than those who preceded us. In 1938 one of our lecturers in pathology spent an hour telling us that nothing could be done for pneumonia because by the time it was diagnosed it was already too late and the damage was done. That very year, sulfa drugs were discovered and found to help pneumonia, and the professor had to retract what he had said and revise his lecture.

When the graduation speaker came to the end of his long address, my mind came back to the present and the ceremonies went on. The chairman started to hand out the diplomas, and as the sequence of names came to mine, he called "Dr. Harry Y. Greeley," and I marched up to receive my diploma. Until then, I had been reviewing the past, but now my mind turned to the future. I now had the key that would allow me to put to use the medical knowledge I had accumulated over four years. In three weeks I would start my internship at Milwaukee County Hospital and enter the field of clinical medicine. I looked forward to this with great anticipation. I would now be in a position where I could learn much more about how the human body reacts in sickness and disease and what can be done for it. From now on I could put the past behind me and work toward my future in medicine, which I knew I would enjoy very much. Graduation was over. I received congratulations from all my friends and relatives, and we went back to Waterman for a special dinner to celebrate the occasion. It had been a great day!

XI/My Introduction to the Dreyer-Denney Clinic

In June 1941 I graduated from medical school, and I started my internship at Milwaukee County Hospital on July 1. It had been a long, hard pull to get through three years of college and four years of medical school without financial help. Now, for the first time, I was in a position where I didn't have to worry about my next meal or where I was going to sleep. I actually was paid $8.37 a month besides my maintenance. The hospital services for interns were excellent, mostly medicine-oriented, although I did take out one appendix in surgery and deliver a few babies on the obstetrics-gynecology service. The instructors and attending physicians were wonderful, and the interns were very compatible.

To top it off, I was in love with Violet Schoeppel and we were married on November 20, 1941. If we had known what was going to happen the next month, we might have postponed our marriage. On December 7, 1941, the Japanese bombed Pearl Harbor and immediately the whole world changed. From that time on, everyone's plans were oriented toward the war effort. I applied for a commission in the army and took my physical in December, only to be turned down because the army said I had diabetes. For some four years I had had a carbohydrate defect that had started as a renal glycosuria and later seemed to be more like a mild diabetes. Nobody seemed able to explain the condition adequately. It was not diabetes as I saw it in the clinics, and I was not disabled. I felt that eventually the army would take me, and I laid my plans accordingly so that I would have no monetary obligations outstanding if I were required to enter the service.

I considered applying for a medical residency at Milwaukee County Hospital, and in retrospect I wish I had done so. However, with everybody going into the service there were many openings for practicing physicians. I had subsisted for so many years on practically nothing that I thought it would be wonderful to get into practice where I would have some income. With this kind of logic, I started looking around for the best opportunity. I had a number of interviews, one of which was with the Dreyer-Denney Clinic, in Aurora, Illinois. Although I had graduated from high school in Waterman, approximately twenty-five miles from

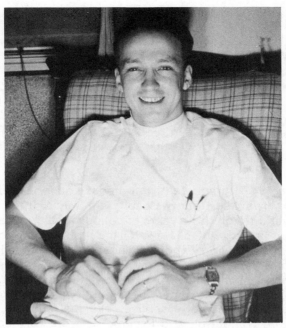

The author as an intern at Milwaukee County Hospital in 1941.

Aurora, I did not know anybody there. I will never forget the day of that interview. Violet and I had driven to Aurora from Milwaukee in the morning, and I was supposed to see Dr. Denney at three in the afternoon. By five o'clock we still had not seen him, although he was in the office and evidently was seeing patients or attending to business. I had almost decided there was not much use waiting any longer when the receptionist suggested that I might see Dr. Gardner. Dr. Gardner was both gracious and informative. I was so impressed with him that I thought the Dreyer-Denney Clinic would be a good place in which to work. The Clinic at that time was made up of Drs. John W. Dreyer, E. S. Denney, Walter H. Milbacher, Clarence L. Gardner, and E. G. Hausmann. Dr. Gardner and Dr. Hausmann both had commissions in the army and would be leaving within a few days, creating quite a gap in the medical staff.

Much later, I did get to see Dr. Denney, and it was agreed that I would come to work for the Clinic, at a salary of $250 a month, as soon as I finished my internship. Today that doesn't sound like much, but right at the end of the depression and the beginning of World War II it was quite a good salary. Commissions as first lieutenant in the army paid about the same. Incidentally, after my long wait to see Dr. Denney, I found him to be a charming person who made me feel right at home. As I learned to

[38]

know him over the years, I realized that always being late was his trademark.

I also had a short visit with Dr. Dreyer, who impressed me very much. Here was a man who had been in practice for many years and could get along with anybody regardless of social position, race, or color. I came to know him as a great person, a competent physician, and a humanitarian.

Two other people I met that day were Alberta Craig, the office manager, and June Evans, the receptionist. Both were young, attractive, and businesslike. Miss Craig later became Mrs. Sickles, assistant administrator. Miss Evans became Mrs. Carew, the Clinic's switchboard operator. Both were still loyally serving the Clinic thirty-eight years later when I retired.

I finished my internship in July 1942 and immediately went to Aurora to look for an apartment. Dr. Denney wasn't very happy when I hunted on the east side of town, but the prices there were much lower than on the west side. I was still very poor and couldn't afford much. We finally settled on a made-over flat, supposedly furnished, on LaSalle Street, a block from Copley Memorial Hospital. The rent was forty-eight dollars a month. The bathroom was divided, with the toilet in a closet in one bedroom and the tub and lavatory off the kitchen where the ceiling slanted so much that standing up straight was possible on only one side of the bathroom. The furniture in the other rooms was very meager and not very clean. We looked forward to the next week when we would move our few belongings into our first apartment.

On July 6, 1942, we drove into Aurora with everything we owned in the back seat of Violet's 1940 Chevrolet. We carried our possessions upstairs and deposited them in the middle of the floor. It was late afternoon when we arrived, and the electricity had not been turned on. When it became too dark to work, there was nothing to do but go to bed. We were just going to sleep when the bed collapsed with a loud crash and we landed on the floor. It was pitch dark, so we felt our way into the other bedroom and lay on the bare bed with no sheets or pillows. We did get some sleep and awoke in the morning to find the next-door neighbors looking in on us through the window.

I was supposed to go to work that day, so I dressed in my only suit, drove downtown, and parked in front of the Graham Building. There were no parking meters in those days and it was safe to leave cars on the street unlocked. I went up to the eighth floor, where the Dreyer-Denney Clinic's complete facilities were housed. The first person I met when I got off the elevator was Alberta Craig. She has reminded me many times that I didn't look very professional with my wire-rimmed glasses and clothes so threadbare that she could almost see through them. On my first day I saw a few industrial patients and one or two others who just happened to come in off the street looking for a doctor. That was my initiation into the practice of medicine.

XII/The Evolution of a Clinic

I started work on July 7, 1942. Dr. Gardner left in a few days for the service, and Dr. Hausmann a few weeks later, leaving Drs. Dreyer, Denney, Milbacher, and me to hold the fort. Not only were the Clinic doctors going off to war, but also practically every other healthy doctor under forty-five years of age. That left a marked shortage of physicians, and it wasn't very long before I was busier than I ever thought possible. I was soon working sixty to seventy hours a week, and within a year, eighty to ninety hours a week.

In October the Clinic employed Dr. William Blackburn, who had also been turned down for the service. He was so sure he would be called soon that he had bought his uniforms. He, too, felt that he would be in the service before the war was over and didn't want to have any long-standing commitments. Dr. Blackburn and I shouldered much of the extra load during the war years, both of us doing mainly general practice with some minor surgery and obstetrics.

The demands of the war brought increased orders to all the factories in the Aurora area and required the building of new plants. As a result, the Clinic's industrial work increased tremendously, especially pre-employment exams, which we did by the hundreds. Every week Dr. Blackburn and I would go to the factories and spend several hours in the morning doing the required exams. Sometimes the companies would have thirty or forty prospective employees ready for us. This was added to our personal office work, our Clinic industrial practice, and our hospital practice.

Because Dr. Blackburn and I thought we probably would not be with the Clinic very long, neither of us made any long-range plans for ourselves or for staying at the Clinic after the war. We assumed that when all the doctors came back we might not have jobs. The medical profession, like all other businesses, was just coming out of a terrible financial depression. Only those who lived through it can visualize the conditions at that time. The profit and loss sheet of the Dreyer-Denney Clinic for 1933 shows the depressed state of medicine. It must be borne in mind that the doctors represented here were some of the busiest doctors in Aurora. If they made $7,500 each, there were many who earned much less.

[40]

PARTNERSHIP RETURN OF INCOME
(TO BE FILED ALSO BY SYNDICATES, POOLS, JOINT VENTURES, ETC.)
For Calendar Year 1933
File This Return With the Collector of Internal Revenue for Your District on or Before March 15, 1934

PRINT PLAINLY NAME AND BUSINESS ADDRESS OF THE ORGANIZATION

DREYER-DENNEY CLINIC
(Name)

33 ISLAND AVENUE
(Street and number)

AURORA ILLINOIS
(Post office and State)

Business or Profession............Physicians

Date of Organization............March 15, 1931.

66a

DUPLICATE

IF YOU NEED
ASSISTANCE IN THE
PREPARATION OF THI
RETURN, GO TO A
DEPUTY COLLECTOR
OR TO THE
COLLECTOR'S OFFICE

GROSS INCOME

Receipts from Business or Profession		31	262 56
ost of Goods Sold:			
) Inventory at beginning of year			
) Merchandise bought for sale			
) Cost of labor, supplies, etc. (From Schedule A)			
) Total of Lines (a), (b), and (c)			
) Less Inventory at end of year			
Profit from Business or Profession (Item 1 minus Item 2)		31	262 56
(or loss) from Other Partnerships, Syndicates, Pools, Joint Ventures, etc. (State name and address)			
t on Bank Deposits, Notes, Corporation Bonds, etc. (except interest on tax-free covenant bonds)			
t on Tax-free Covenant Bonds upon which a Tax was Paid at Source			
Sub Rent Office		670	00
loss			
ofit from Sale of Stocks and Bonds held 2 years or less (From Schedule B, Total (s))			
ofit or loss from Sale of Other Assets held 2 years or less. (From Schedule B, Total (s))			
nds on stock of:			
) Domestic Corporations subject to taxation under Title I of 1932 Act			
) Domestic Corporations not subject to taxation under Title I of 1932 Act			
Foreign Corporations			
ncome: (State nature of income)			
TOTAL INCOME IN ITEMS 3 TO 11		31	932

DEDUCTIONS

of Employees. (Do not include compensation for partners or members)		8	980 83
Business Property		2	920 00
(From Schedule D)			
on Indebtedness			127 87
aid. (From Schedule E)			79 09
by Fire, Storm, etc. (From Schedule F)			
pts. (From Schedule G)			
ation, Obsolescence, and Depletion. (From Schedule H)		1	316 48
ded ctions Authorized by Law (Explain below or on separate sheet):			

t...,1787.54; Gas & L.,184.55; Tel.,345.31; Laundry,91.44;
amps,137.83; X.Ray & Office Supplies,469.37; Insurance
,05; Med. Dues & Mag., 185.59; Express,8.32; Misc.,169.54;
Adj. Serv.,75.69; Credit Bureau,30.00 Paper Towels,9.80;
fund,16.00 = 3704.83.

		3 704 83	
			17 129
			14 803

Name and Address of Each Partner or Member cture of partner or member is filed in another collection district, specify district	2. Percentage of Net Income	3. Dividends (Item 10 (a) Above)	4. Balance of Net Income (Item 21 Minus Amount in Column 3)	5. Capital Net Gain or Loss (Schedule C, Column 9)	6. Income Tax Paid at Source (2% of Item 6)	7. Income Tax Paid Foreign Countries or United States Possessions
t. Dreyer	50		7401 73			
r. Denney	50		74 1 73			

Clinic income in 1933.

[41]

Even before 1942 there was great competition in the medical field. Doctors then did not have the facilities, equipment, or knowledge that were achieved in later years. Physicians often developed individual treatments for diseases, whereas today the handling of most conditions is standardized. This resulted in intense competition and considerable bitterness in the medical community.

It is difficult to know just when the Dreyer-Denney Clinic started because the definition of a clinic is so vague. If it is described as two doctors practicing together, then the Dreyer-Denney Clinic started a long time before the depression. If it is three or four doctors working in a group, then it started about 1928. The partnership was incorporated in 1931. By 1933 there were Drs. Dreyer, Denney, and Milbacher. Dr. Gardner came in 1935, and Dr. Hausmann, in 1940.

The concept of a clinic was considerably different from what it is now. There were no large clinics other than a few like Mayo, Lahey, and Ochsner. The type or organization that the Dreyer Medical Clinic grew into was practically nonexistent at that time. It was fairly common, however, for a dominant doctor in the community to hire two or three young doctors to practice with him and to call this a clinic. He paid them a straight salary, and he reaped the financial benefits from their work as well as his own. Most new doctors stayed long enough to establish personal practices and then left. It was financially advantageous to the older, established physician, because of his good reputation in the community and his drawing power, to continually start new doctors on a salary basis.

As soon as a doctor-owner had several doctors working for him, he could start a laboratory, buy an X-ray machine, and make still more money. This concept was not peculiar to local clinics but was common all over the country. On that basis, Dr. Denney was the doctor-businessman of the Dreyer-Denney Clinic. As the years went by, Dr. Denney gradually relaxed a number of his policies so that the younger men could participate, but these reforms did not occur until many years later. During the war years, the doctors hired were treated as employees.

Doctor Denney had a good business head and a knack for handling people. As the Clinic doctors did more and more work, out of proportion to the amount he was paying them, he knew just how much he could give them as bonuses and still keep them happy. During the war I had no complaints; I was making more money than I had ever earned before. At Christmas of my first year, I was given a fifty dollar war bond, which I thought was quite generous of the Clinic. I also received two raises, so that by the end of the first year I was making $350 a month. To me, that was wonderful; I had never had anything like that kind of money before, and we lived very well on it.

Clinic business arrangements were very simple. Everybody worked hard. Bookings were recorded and the collections, which had been very poor during the depression, were getting better. At the end of the year,

Dr. Denney went over the books and personally decided who was to get how much bonus. The rest went to Dr. Denney. Nobody was privileged to see the books, so nobody knew exactly how much of his billings were collected.

Dr. Dreyer and Dr. Denney were exact opposites in personality and philosophy. Dr. Dreyer did not want to be bothered with the business end of medicine; he was perfectly content to take his salary and his bonus at the end of the year, and he never complained. His whole purpose in life was to care for people. Some of his best friends and patients were men of stature in the community who started some of the big industries of Aurora. He was a friend of Harry Barber, one of the founders of the Barber-Greene Company. When the company was new and short of capital, Dr. Dreyer lent it money to keep going, for which he was given some Barber-Greene stock. In later years, this stock had grown and split so many times that Dr. Dreyer was almost able to retire on his dividends.

The true multispecialty clinic had not yet appeared. It evolved later as a result of the drastic change of life-styles that was brought about by World War II. During the war, the fee structure of medicine was still very low. In 1942, when I joined the Clinic, office calls were $1.50 to $2.00; house calls were $3.00; hospital calls were $1.50 to $2.00. As these made up the bulk of my charges, it took many house calls, office calls, and hospital work to make any kind of bookings at all. There was a wage and price freeze during World War II, and it wasn't until afterward that prices began to break and inflation started.

XIII/The Senior Clinic Doctors, 1942

I would like to describe the doctors who were the backbone of the Clinic during the war. Dr. John Dreyer was always a special person to me. Although he was one of the busiest doctors in Aurora, he always had time to talk and give me advice, which helped me get adjusted to a fast-growing practice. As I said earlier, it didn't matter to him whether a patient was poor, rich, black, white, or Spanish; the treatment was always the same. He was treating the patient and the disease, and he did not care about race or social status. Dr. Dreyer came to Aurora in 1905 and for a while practiced by himself. He came in the days when doctors actually did surgery on the kitchen table, since there were no hospital operating rooms. He made his house calls all over town on a bicycle. I recall a story told by an early Aurora barber, Will Marion, who remembered giving Dr. Dreyer first aid in the barbershop after his bicycle wheels caught in a streetcar track and he was thrown in the mud. The doctor received some superficial cuts and bruises but no serious injuries.

Dr. Dreyer was one of the most progressive men of his generation. When a woman of the 1940's had a baby, the usual procedure was to keep her in bed for five to seven days, then gradually allow her to become ambulatory and send her home about the eighth day. Dr. Dreyer said this was not right; he got his patients up the same day as their delivery and urged them to walk immediately. He said, "They do not get weak that way. When patients are kept in bed for seven days they lose all their strength, and it takes them several weeks to get back to normal." His surgical patients were out of bed on the second day. Whereas other physicians would keep appendectomy patients down for a week to ten days, Dr. Dreyer had them up and out of the hospital in three to four days. He was criticized by the medical profession for this practice. His critics predicted that his patients would suffer some dire calamity, that the obstetrical patients would have fallen uteri and that hernias would break down and have to be repaired again. They further predicted that incisions would break open and that there would be severe complications. Of course none of this ever happened, but it was a long time before early ambulation was accepted. Dr. Dreyer was the first in Aurora to do it, and his patients always did well.

He was the first surgeon to do thyroidectomies and to pin fractured hips in elderly people. He always felt that a hip operation was an emergency, that elderly people who had fractures should not be kept in bed lest they develop complications. If possible, he would operate on them within twenty-four hours. That he was right in his thinking has been proven over the years.

Dr. Dreyer was instrumental in starting the blood bank. He was always ready to accept new procedures and to establish them in his practice. Sometimes he was a little too eager and adopted medications or procedures that had not been entirely proven; however, he could admit his mistakes and see his own shortcomings, and he was not ashamed to backtrack.

He was a great outdoorsman and loved to fish. Every time he got a chance he went up to Wisconsin or Minnesota with friends for a fishing vacation. There in the north woods he was in his glory and completely relaxed from the tensions of medicine.

There was much sadness in Dr. Dreyer's personal life. His first wife died of cancer at an early age in the 1920's. His second wife helped him raise his two children, her two children, and their own baby, Sarah. She later became an invalid after a stroke and for many years required complete care. He loved her and cared for her at home, even getting her out for rides in the car long after she had lost all her mental processes. She was hospitalized for several years before she died in 1959.

No doctor was more deserving of having the Clinic named after him than Dr. Dreyer. I regarded it as a great day when the Board of the Clinic voted in 1963 to change the name to the Dreyer Medical Clinic in his honor.

To Doctor Dreyer

Near fifty years you've cured our ills—
With surgery, comfort and little pink pills;
You've travelled all over this town of ours—
There are not enough numbers to count the hours;
You used a car but first a bike—
And prior to that you had many a hike;
You called East or West and on Pigeon Hill—
Any place at all if we were ill;
You were kind and generous to all of us—
You took us on without a fuss;
You cared not whether we were good or bad—
We each received that skill you had;
Be we white or black, big or small—
We always knew you'd make the call;
You were on the job in sun or rain—
You seemed to consider—a pain a pain;
About bedside manners young doctors stew—
You never thought of it—it was born in you;
Aurorans had much to be thankful for—
And we hope and pray that we'll still have more;
Hear Ye! Hear Ye! says our Town Crier—
Thank you, Dear Lord, for Doctor Dreyer.

L. M. O.
One of your 1910 babies

A tribute to Dr. Dreyer, written by Lambert Ochsenschlager, an Aurora attorney.

[45]

Dr. Walter Milbacher was a general surgeon with whom I enjoyed working for many years. He had a young family when I first moved here, and lived at Mooseheart. His father had also been a doctor in Aurora before him. Dr. Milbacher was well known and had the most faithful patients of any of the Clinic doctors. They loved him. He was hard-working and talked little, although he was very friendly and cooperative. If I had a patient who needed to be seen in surgical consultation, he was always there no matter whether night, day, Sunday, or holiday. If he was in town, he was available. Like the rest of us, he worked many hours, day and night, during World War II. I am sure he shortened his life by the long, arduous days that he put in. He continued practice with the Clinic until his death in 1970.

I have commented on Dr. Elliott Denney to some extent before, but I would like to say further that there wasn't a better-trained surgeon for the era in which he lived. The surgery done in those days was limited to hysterectomies, appendectomies, cystoceles, rectoceles, hemmorrhid-ectomies, and cholecystectomies. Even though most of the surgery was performed by general practitioners, it was skillfully done. The complex surgical procedures that are common today were not known. Dr. Denney's training was taken at Harvard Medical School, and his internship and residency were also in Boston. Dr. Denney had an intense interest in business, investments, and other matters outside of medicine that often interfered with his practice. He was always on the board of one of the larger banks in town, and he had financial interests in several downtown business buildings. His outside activities frequently made him late for office hours so that his patients often waited two or three hours to see him. They rarely complained, because when they did get into his office, he put them at ease and was able to help them mentally, physically, and emotionally. He had a very loyal group of patients from the upper social echelons of Aurora, and the only charity medical work he did was when other doctors referred indigent patients needing surgery. Throughout that early period, he ran the Clinic completely from a business standpoint.

Dr. Denney was very civic-minded. He was generous in contributions to various charities and was highly respected in the Aurora community. One of his pet projects was Mooseheart, which is a children's city operated by the Moose Lodge near North Aurora. Although he was medical director at Mooseheart, he did very little of the work himself, except perhaps some referred surgery from time to time. Mooseheart had its own small hospital, and various doctors in the Clinic were given charge of it, lived at Mooseheart, and did most of the work. Dr. Milbacher and his family lived there for a number of years during World War II, followed by Dr. Blackburn, and later, Dr. Landes. It was an excellent place to raise a family. The surroundings were good, the housing was excellent, and the work not too difficult.

[46]

XIV/The Polio Epidemic

In August 1942, a month after I started practice, Aurora was hit with a polio epidemic that created panic, heartaches, and crippling tragedies. We had approximately seventy cases of polio in Aurora alone, many of which were paralytic. There were so many cases that the Medical Society, with the help of the township, activated a separate building in Montgomery as a polio isolation hospital. It was improvised rather quickly, but I do believe it was helpful in confining the epidemic. The community felt safer when the polio cases were isolated. I treated three people who became permanently paralyzed, and I followed these patients for many years. They were typical of the tragedies that resulted from poliomyelitis. One young woman, who had not been married more than a year, developed polio when she was eight months pregnant. Nobody knew how it would affect the baby, but Dr. Denney was able to deliver a healthy baby with no complications. The mother, however, developed complete paralysis of her lower extremities and has been in a wheelchair ever since. She raised two wonderful children quite successfully in spite of her handicap and almost complete isolation from society. She always smiled and never gave up hope, despite such a cross to bear.

A man in his thirties, who was my patient, developed polio with complete paralysis of both legs and partial paralysis of the arms. Previously an active man who did heavy physical work, from then on he was in a wheelchair. Again, I was amazed at how this man was able to accept his tremendous handicap. He operated a successful shoe repair shop and enjoyed fishing, ballgames, and other sports events.

A third case was a lawyer who at the age of forty developed paralytic polio. Later he had extensive physical therapy in Chicago and at home. He improved to the point where he could walk with the aid of a cane or crutch, but he never was able to be physically active. In spite of this, he carried on a busy law practice and did not let his handicap interfere with his enjoyment of life.

I might say a word about the early medical treatment of polio. At that time doctors felt it was best to immobilize the affected legs or arms of the patient for several months and then gradually, after the disease was completely gone, institute physical therapy to try to restore the muscles. In retrospect, we see that this was the wrong approach. Sister Kenny, a nurse from Australia, was the pioneer in treating those muscles with hot packs and mobilizing them early in order to achieve all the recovery possible. That was the mainstay of therapy until, after many years of research funded by the March of Dimes and the Polio Foundation, the Salk and Sabin vaccines were discovered and first used in 1954. I regard that as one of the greatest discoveries of the twentieth century. I have not treated a case of polio since, and many younger doctors have never even seen a case.

XV/My Medical Practice
During the War Years

My medical practice rapidly developed a pattern: (1) house calls, (2) office calls, (3) hospital work, and (4) industrial exams and first-aid work. At that time house calls were an integral part of the practice of medicine, and all doctors made them. The patient had only to request it. Day calls were $3.00, and night calls were $2.00 more. It was sometimes hard to distinguish between a day call and a night call: at what hour of the evening was it logical to charge another $2.00—eight o'clock, nine o'clock, ten o'clock? I finally worked out my own criterion. The day schedule continued as long as I was dressed. If I had to put on my pants, it was $2.00 more, pure and simple.

In the early days of my practice, house calls were abused by the public, and frequently one was called for conditions that could easily have been taken care of in the office. Night calls, especially, were very annoying. As the doctors remaining in Aurora during the war became busier and busier, I found that I would be out after midnight on house calls or hospital work at least four or five nights a week. Sometimes for a whole week running, I would be out one to two hours in the middle of the night and still have to go to the office and to the hospital the next day. Often I wondered if I could keep up with it. I would be so tired that when calls came in the night it took several minutes to wake up enough to talk sensibly.

During one particularly bad time, I remember that the phone rang and it was the hospital asking what to do for a student nurse who had severe diarrhea. Without even waking up enough to know what I was saying, I advised giving her some paregoric. When the nurse asked how much, I said, "Oh, about a quart." Luckily, the nurse realized that I was still asleep, and she kept talking until I finally got the dosage straightened out. The next night I told Violet that I was going to be sure that if the phone rang I would be awake enough to know what I was saying before I gave any orders. Then I put the phone far under the bed, knowing that by the time I got up and retieved it I would be awake enough to talk. Sure enough, at 3 A.M. the phone rang. I crawled sleepily out of bed, got down on my stomach, and reached for the phone to answer it, only to find it was the wrong number. I never did that again.

Answering the phone in the middle of the night, one never knows what is going to be on the other end. There might not seem sufficient reason for a patient to wake a doctor, but most of the time the caller is in trouble or he would not have made the call. I will give you several examples of calls that I felt were not necessary. I had a very good patient, a woman, who had a dog to which she was very attached. About three o'clock one morning she called and said, "Dr. Greeley, my dog has been in a fight and he has a laceration on his abdomen. I wonder if you would come out and sew it up." I said, "No, I do not take care of dogs; why don't you call your veterinarian?" Her response was, "Why, I wouldn't want to wake him up at this time of night." Sometimes it is hard to be nice to people under those conditions.

I remember another call at three o'clock in the morning from a perfectly healthy woman. When I asked her what she wanted, she said, "Dr. Greeley, I can't sleep, and I just wondered what I could do about it." I said, "I can't sleep either because the phone keeps ringing. Why don't you come to the office in a day or two and we will go over your problems and see if we can help you." I didn't think that phone call was necessary.

Another time the phone rang at one A.M. and the person on the other end, obviously calling from a tavern as I could hear the tinkle of glasses and bottles, said, "Dr. Greeley, my wife is two and a half months pregnant, and I wondered if it is all right for her to drink sloe gin." I said, "You mean you called me up at this time of night to ask me a question like that? Is it so important that it couldn't wait until tomorrow?" The man answered, "Of course it's important. She is afraid to drink it and we are having a party, and I want her to be happy." I didn't think that phone call was necessary either.

During my first thirty years of practice I made many house calls, but in the 1970's I saw the pendulum swing completely the other way so that doctors refused to make any house calls. Their reasoning was that there is nothing to be done for patients at home anyway, and they should go either to the hospital or to the office. I feel that is oversimplifying it. There is no better way to get to know one's patients than on house visits. One learns a lot about the family and their habits and cleanliness, so that when the patient is seen later in the office, the doctor has a pretty good ideas of the human relationships involved.

I have never regretted making house calls, even though sometimes they were tiring and not necessary. Many times I have made fifteen to twenty calls in a day, each taking ten to fifteen minutes. My record number was twenty-two calls, made on an Easter Sunday when there was an epidemic. I think that the pendulum is beginning to swing back now so that doctors, especially the family practitioners, again go to homes when it is needed. Already, groups in the cities are setting up home call services in which the doctors go out to see people who are unable to come to the office. It is especially difficult for an elderly person to leave his home and get to the office alone. I think a house call in this setting is not only very rewarding, but essential. Older people need occasional checkups and reassurance; they need someone to talk to them for a few minutes, to check their blood pressure and listen to their heart. If anything serious is found, the patient can always be referred to a hospital or an emergency room. This is the type of house call I continued to make in the later years of my practice.

In the 1940's we did not have the vast array of medicines and equipment that we had in later years, but we did do good physical examinations and we did have effective medications for many conditions. We figured that an office call should take fifteen to twenty minutes and scheduled them three or four per hour. Physical examinations took from forty-five minutes to an hour, depending on whether the patient was there for the first time or was a repeat. The biggest problems were the extras who came in, and they were often the sickest people. With the shortage of doctors, it was very difficult to see everybody who wanted to be seen. Dr. Blackburn and I were in the office every night of the week. I covered Tuesday, Thursday, and Saturday nights, and Dr. Blackburn covered Monday, Wednesday, and Friday. Some of the doctors outside the Clinic even opened their offices on Sunday morning, but we never did that. Most people were engaged in war work, and they preferred to come to the office nights and Saturdays, so we made ourselves available for them. I would often be in the office until ten or eleven o'clock at night. My receptionist would go home at nine, and there might be six or eight patients still waiting. I would see them all by myself and go home tired but satisfied that I had done all I could for that day.

At the Clinic we had a small laboratory in which we did blood counts, urinalyses, and blood sugars. We also had an X-ray unit with which we could take X-rays of bones, stomachs, and colons and also do fluoroscopies. Dr. Gardner had done stomach and colon X-rays in the office, and Dr. Denney thought I should also learn to do this type of examination. I took a short course in X-ray fluoroscopy at Cook County Hospital, and for many years I did my own gastrointestinal work at the Clinic. I think that basically I did a good job, but I did not have the training necessary if there were any serious complications. I felt very relieved when, in 1964, we hired a full-time radiologist and I did not have to do that type of work anymore.

Our employees in the office consisted of one receptionist, two nurses in X-ray and laboratory, and one person in the business office. In those days, before plastic gloves and disposable syringes, the nurses spent a lot of time washing and sterilizing the syringes and needles that we used again and again and again. After all, they were expensive. They were glass and not easily replaced, especially during wartime. Another unpleasant job the girls had to do was wash and sterilize the rubber gloves that we used for pelvic and rectal examinations. When the disposables became available, the practice of medicine was much easier.

Sometimes when I was extra tired I would wonder why I had ever become a doctor and think there must be easier ways to make a living. But when I got a little rest, I realized that there were satisfactions in the practice of medicine that I could not get in any other profession. I never was really sorry that I went into medicine. At times I recalled the factors that influenced my teenage decision to become a doctor. My father had a dental education, and his twin brother was a medical doctor. I had three cousins who were doctors, so an interest in medicine seemed to run in the family. Other events in my early life also influenced me. The school superintendent of my high school had tuberculosis; the school board felt sorry for him and let him keep on teaching. My brother George developed the same disease in his teens; it made him an invalid for a great part of his life, and he died at an early age. When I saw how he suffered, it made me want to go into a profession where I might be able to help people like him.

One night when I was sixteen years old George developed a pulmonary hemmorhage. I can still see him spitting up blood and scared to death. All of the family were frightened because they didn't know if the bleeding would ever stop. We didn't have a telephone, didn't have a car—only horses and buggies—and my father said to me, "Harry, we need a doctor. Why don't you ride down to Arenzville and ask Dr. Streuter if there is anything he can do for George." I went out to the pasture, caught Fanny, the riding horse, and put a bridle on her. I didn't have a saddle but rode bareback at a gallop to Arenzville, five miles away. The fact that it was raining hard made the trip even more arduous. The horse was breathing hard and was very sweaty by the time we arrived. I went to Dr. Streuter's house, which was dark, and pounded on the door. After a few minutes he came to the door in his nightshirt, looking very, very tired. He asked me to come in and sit down in his parlor, and he talked to me for a long time. He explained all about George's illness and the complications that are apt to occur, including some bleeding, and that there was really no known way to get in and stop the bleeding. He said that if it kept up much longer, George should be taken to Jacksonville or Beardstown to a hospital, but that there was very little he could do for him at home. I could see that what he said was true and did not insist that he go out to our house. As I rode home I wondered to myself if I could ever be a doctor like that. When I arrived, George had quit bleeding and felt considerably better. However, that night was indelibly impressed on my memory and was one of the incidents that influenced me to become a doctor. The memories of that night also inspired me to try to be as nice to my patients as Dr. Streuter was to me.

As I became more experienced, I found that the best way to be a successful and knowledgeable doctor was to get to know my patients, always keeping on the alert and trying not to make errors in judgment or diagnosis. My diagnostic acumen increased considerably over the first few years as I adjusted to practice. There is no other profession in which there are so many ups and downs. After a doctor has saved somebody's life or has had a successful outcome for a bad disease, he feels as if he is on cloud nine and the whole world looks rosy. However, he cannot stay on the cloud very long before something bad happens—a patient dies who wasn't supposed to die, or a case doesn't respond to treatment— and he goes from the heights to the depths. That is true of all doctors— something that the public does not understand. There isn't a doctor in practice who has not had cases in which he would give anything to have had a second chance. No matter how hard he tries, or how careful he is, occasionally a case doesn't work out. He realizes, when it is too late, that if things had been handled differently it might have changed the out-come. It is very sobering and keeps one from being on a pedestal for very long at a time. A doctor's judgment is not infallible, as I found out very quickly.

The day before Christmas of my first year of practice, a very sick patient came in and was seen in consultation with a surgeon. We felt that she should have surgery immediately, but the patient wanted to go home for Christmas with her family first. She came back the day after Christmas in much worse condition and died in spite of surgery. I learned something from this case that I never forgot: one should never let his judgment be overruled by his emotions. The woman wanted to go home, and we sympathized with her wish to enjoy Christmas with her family; however, our judgment as doctors indicated that she should have had surgery right away. Ever after that, I always made my decisions strictly on a professional basis.

About 25 percent of our work was industrial medicine during World War II. The factories were all busy and hiring, and they wanted preem-ployment physicals on all their new men. As the work load of the facto-ries increased, there were more industrial accidents. The victims were brought to the Clinic if they were not too bad, and we took care of them there. If the accidents were serious, the victims were taken to the hospi-tal. There were many fractures and lacerations and some serious crush-ing injuries that required surgery and hospitalization. Industrial medicine was an integral part of our whole Clinic operation, and it grew rapidly. We hired a male nurse named Raymond Cantrall, who was inval-uable to us. He has since spent approximately thirty-eight years with the Clinic. He was capable of all first-aid work and interpreting X-rays and was a tremendous help to us.

XVI/The Aurora Community During the War Years

Aurora, a city of approximately forty-five thousand in 1942, had varied industry. The Burlington Railroad was one of the pillars of the community. All its trains came to the railroad workshops in Aurora for repairs. The Burlington established a major hub here and employed many local people. There were other stable and productive industries, such as Barber-Greene, All-Steel Equipment, Lyon Metal, Durabilt, Stephens-Adamson, Austin-Western, and many smaller factories. The variety of industry provided more stable employment through the depression than that of other communities of like size in the suburban area. It was generally felt that Aurora had not been hit quite as hard by the depression as other cities. Most of the industries were home-owned, and the people who founded them were civic-minded mainstays of the community. With the beginning of World War II, other industries began to locate here. United Wallpaper in Montgomery, although founded as a nonwar industry, turned its entire production over to war contracts and was one of the main employers.

Aurora streets were very haphazardly named and laid out. The Fox River flowed directly through the middle of the city, and streets changed their names as they crossed the river. Upon arriving here, we bought a map of the city, which projected many streets that did not yet go through, especially in the southeast section of town. When I tried to get from one place to another to make calls, I often found that what looked like a street on the map was not there. Violet was a big help to me then by going out on her bicycle in the daytime and mapping out the streets that went through and those that didn't. When she finished, I had a very accurate map.

The business section of Aurora was situated between East Aurora and West Aurora on the banks of the river. Stolp Island, in the middle of the river, was the site of some of the biggest business and office buildings. The Dreyer-Denney Clinic was situated on Stolp Island in an eight-story office building called the Graham Building. The Clinic occupied part of the eighth floor. Downtown Aurora then had some excellent department stores, such as Sencenbaugh's, Block and Kuhl, Lietz and Grometer, and a number of others, all locally owned. The only department stores not home-owned were Sears, Roebuck and Montgomery Ward. There were no surrounding shopping centers. The nearest place offering more extensive shopping was downtown Chicago, which was not very convenient. It seemed as if Aurora's downtown business area would be a permanent business community. I remember well when Dr. Denney said, "If you ever want to make investments, buy downtown Aurora property." That shows the fallacy of such predictions, as is evidenced by the present deterioration of the downtown area and complete takeover by the suburban shopping centers.

The population of Aurora included a number of nationalities, some of them first-generation Rumanians and Hungarians, who lived in the northeast section of town. They were honest, hard-working people, many of whom kept pigeons. The area in which they lived became known as "Pigeon Hill," a name that stuck for many years and is still used even in 1982. About 5 percent of the total population was black. There were a black physician, a black dentist, and some very respected black businessmen. Although there was some prejudice against them, I did not feel that it was nearly as great in Aurora as in other communities in the Chicago area. I took care of a number of black families through the war. There were a few Spanish-speaking residents then, but the marked growth of the Spanish communities was a later development.

The government of Aurora during the war was aldermanic in form, and some of the more prominent leaders were represented. It stayed aldermanic until 1953, when the commission form was adopted. However, as I remember, during the war years the board of alderman was extremely efficient, not controversial, and did an excellent job.

Aurora had many respected service clubs: Kiwanis, Lions, Rotary, Phoenix, Exchange, and Elks, all very active and community-oriented. I had been in Aurora only three months when I was approached by the Kiwanis Club and asked to join. They customarily admitted two members from each profession, and I would be the second physician, replacing Dr. Gardner, who was now in the service. A former country boy, I didn't know what a Kiwanis Club was. I went to Dr. Denney and said, "Kiwanis Club has asked me to join them; should I?" Dr. Denney was very civic-minded and I remember well his reply, "Harry, Kiwanis Club is an excellent social and service club in which you will meet many nice people. They carry on many projects of civic importance. You make your living in this city, and this is one way for you to become part of the community. Every doctor should do something besides medicine for the town in which he lives." I joined the Kiwanis Club, and it has been one of my most pleasant associations. Kiwanis always had interesting and successful projects going, especially to help underprivileged children.

Commuting from Aurora to Chicago was excellent. The Burlington Railroad commuter service started in Aurora and ended at the Union Station in Chicago. Several thousand people traveled daily to Chicago to work. As time went on, I became acquainted with many people who had spent as much as thirty to forty years riding the Burlington trains back and forth. The railroad made this possible by issuing monthly tickets that were purchased at a discount. Passengers could read newspapers or relax on the way and have a pleasant, safe journey.

In addition to the Burlington Railroad, the Chicago, Aurora, and Elgin also provided service to Chicago. This electric line was often called the "Third Rail," as the electricity to run the trains ran along a rail inside the regular tracks. This was a very popular way to commute to downtown Chicago, as it went all the way to the Loop, and the travel time was almost the same as the Burlington. There was daily bus service to Chicago, but that was not as popular as the trains. The expressways were not completed, and the drive took one and one-half to two hours because of the many stop signs and traffic lights and the heavy traffic.

For people who were going to Chicago for shopping, there were at least twenty trains a day each way. Most people made several trips a year to downtown Chicago for shopping, going to theaters or plays, or eating in fine restaurants. The newer movies did not get out to the suburbs for months, until after they had finished their downtown run, so those who wanted to see the latest films went to the Loop in Chicago. Aurora was also situated on the main line of the Burlington for travel to the West and Northeast. Since all trains stopped in Aurora, connections were easy.

Because the city had grown up with an East Aurora and a West Aurora, there were two separate school systems. This made for great rivalry between the high schools, especially in athletic contests. Actually, both school systems were excellent. The athletic contests between the two sides of town were greatly anticipated, especially the East-West football game, which was played on Thanksgiving Day.

I was surprised to find out how many churches there were in Aurora. About 40 percent of the people were Catholic, and they had a number of fine Catholic churches and parochial schools. About 55 percent of the people were Protestant of various denominations, the most numerous being Methodist, Presbyterian, Christian, Congregational, and Baptist. Violet and I joined the Fourth Street Methodist Church and were members until we built a home on the west side in 1948. I have always valued my church connections as being important to me and my family socially as well as spiritually.

When we moved to Aurora there were three hospitals: Copley, St. Charles, and St. Joseph Mercy hospitals. Copley Hospital, in the southeast section, was the largest. It had started as a city hospital many years earlier. In the 1930's it received a large donation from Ira Copley, an Aurora native who started in the gas and electric business and later went into newspaper publishing. Copley became owner of the Aurora *Beacon-News* and the newspapers in Elgin, Joliet, and Springfield. He also developed six to eight newspapers on the West Coast, all of which were quite successful. He was one of Aurora's great citizens, and over the next twenty years he gave more than $2 million to Copley Hospital. New sections were added, so that when I came to Aurora it was a 110-

bed hospital. Later it grew to be a modern, fully equipped, 325-bed hospital.

St. Charles Hospital was also on the east side of Aurora. It had 110 beds and offered similar services but was not as well equipped. St. Joseph Mercy Hospital, also a 110-bed hospital, was on the west side of the river. In the late 1960's it was replaced by a 250-bed facility farther north and was converted into a nursing home.

When I came to Aurora, all three hospitals had three-year nursing schools and provided the nurses for the entire Aurora area and a large part of the Fox River Valley. Nursing was a popular choice of profession for young high school graduates, since they could become R.N.s in three years. Each hospital had its own residence for nursing students. The schools employed some instructors but relied on local doctors to help in teaching. Doctors donated their knowledge in lectures to all of the hospitals.

There was always competition among the three hospitals. If one hospital acquired a new X-ray machine or special equipment of any kind, it was not long before the other two followed suit. The medical staffs were almost identical at all three hospitals. Any new doctor in town applied for membership on all three staffs, which usually was approved without much trouble. Although most doctors belonged to all three hospital staffs, they did most of their work at one hospital. I made it a policy to take patients to whichever hospital they chose. Most of my patients wanted Copley Hospital, and so I became oriented primarily to Copley. However, I always had patients at the other two hospitals, and I maintained excellent relations with all three. Each hospital had points in which it excelled over the others, which made for healthy competition but at times also caused some bitterness.

The Aurora community was progressive, and during World War II Aurora probably did as much for the war effort as any other city of its size in the Midwest. People who were born after 1940 cannot understand the sacrifices demanded by the war. The people of Aurora were inconvenienced by shortages of food and gasoline. We had a limited number of food stamps for many of the necessities, and other things were not available at all. People always thought doctors were fortunate because they could get more gasoline stamps than the average person; however, this was not really an advantage because it was strictly geared to the doctor's practice. If he were found using gasoline from gas stamps for pleasure, he could be prosecuted.

The public was well aware of the tremendous shortage of doctors and did everything they could to help. For example, if one went into a barbershop where six or eight people were waiting for haircuts, the barber would say, "We have a doctor here, is it all right if we let him go first, as he is so busy?" The customers were always willing because they knew he was working day and night. Never did I hear any complaints because I was put first.

[57]

XVII/The Emotional Effects of the War

The practice of medicine in the Clinic continued in a pretty routine manner for Dr. Blackburn and me throughout the war. The Clinic, as well as the community of Aurora, was caught up in the spirit of the times and contributed with great fervor to the war effort. There was hardly anybody in Aurora who didn't have a husband, a son, a father, or somebody in uniform. The United States was not prepared for this war, and the first two to three years were primarily a holding operation while the factories converted to building airplanes, guns, and tanks by the thousands. Within a few months after the war started, the Philippines fell and we had one military reverse after another.

One of my best friends in medical school, with whom I roomed for a while, was taken into the Marines and found himself on the beaches of Guadalcanal. It was a very brutal and dangerous place to be, and Dr. Steinberg came back a changed man. That was my first contact with doctors returning from combat areas. Our friendship continued, but I found him completely altered in his philosophy and thinking. I realized that he had been through experiences that were hard for me as a civilian doctor to understand. I later found this universally true of my friends who had been in the service. I felt considerable remorse at times that I had not been in the service; at other times I felt relieved that I could work hard at home, as I was needed here also.

Aurora was emotionally very much involved in World War II. Bond sales programs featuring movie stars and entertainers were held on the courthouse steps here as well as in other suburbs. When Aurora had its first combat death, the body of the soldier was brought back and the coffin paraded through the streets. Full military honors were given this young person who had given his life for his country. Many of Aurora's sons and husbands were serving in the army and other branches of the military. As time went on, the reverses in the Pacific were stopped and the United States began slowly winning against the Japanese. In England, a big buildup was started for D-Day. Africa was invaded. Italy was invaded, and everyone knew that there was going to be a D-Day in France and looked forward to it, not only with apprehension but also hope that this would be the way to end this awful war. D-Day found the Aurora community, our Clinic, the doctors, the nurses, and everybody in a state of great concern and emotional upheaval, wondering what the results would be. As the invasion of Europe became successful, there was a universal feeling of relief. However, victory also carried with it many deaths, and a number of homes in Aurora were touched by sorrow.

Of course VE-Day was not the end of the war, and as the summer went on preparations were made to take an invading army to Japan. That was never necessary, however, as VJ-Day came in August after the dropping of atomic bombs on Hiroshima and Nagasaki. When VJ-Day finally arrived, all the pent-up emotions of four long years erupted in a celebration such as the United States has never known before. I remember the hour that the news came over the radio. I was on my way from St. Charles Hospital and was driving across the New York Street bridge. Everyone seemed to get the news at the same time, and there was a complete traffic jam. Everyone just stopped his car, got out, and yelled and danced in the streets. It took me a half hour to get across the bridge, but I didn't care. With the termination of World War II, there came a new era of economic freedom and prosperity.

One thing that marred the ending of the war was a serious accident that occurred at the United States Wallpaper Company in Montgomery a few days after the Japanese had surrendered and the country had begun to disarm and cancel army contracts. The company was preparing to return to domestic business and was cleaning up the plant on the last day. Two men were working with drums of explosives on the banks of the Fox River. The drums accidentally blew up, and one man was thrown into the middle of the river and the other about thirty feet on the bank. I received a call from the Clinic to come immediately. I made as fast a trip as I could and found one man beyond help and the other in very serious condition. He was taken by ambulance to Copley Hospital, where Dr. Denney and I worked on him for five hours. We were able to save his life, but he was crippled and walked with a limp. It seemed ironic that the accident happened on the last day and the last hour of the cleanup job; certainly such cases were also casualties of World War II.

Just a few weeks before the war ended in 1945, President Franklin D. Roosevelt had a stroke and died within twenty-four hours at Warm Springs, Georgia. He had been sick for some time, but his illness had been kept secret so well that the United States public, as a whole, did not realize that he was near death. Although many people did not agree with his policies, he still was a great leader and war president. He had immense popularity among the majority of voters and was our president from 1932 until his death in 1945, the first president ever to be elected for four terms. Certainly many programs that he initiated have stood the test of time. It was on his decision alone that the go-ahead was given to develop the atomic bomb. This was one of the great gambles of World War II as it cost several billion dollars and its success was not certain. Roosevelt's leadership through the war was superb, and his rapport with our allies was also excellent. In retrospect, one can see that he was a very sick man during the last few years of his presidency and probably was not capable of making good decisions. When his death was announced to the public, there was mourning such as had never been seen in the United States. Radios played funeral music with no advertising for three days until his funeral. Whether one agreed with his policies or not, there was the feeling that a great man had left the scene.

XVIII/Personal Notes

I soon found that medical practice during the war did not leave much time for anything else. I could get to church only occasionally and had little time for any other activities. After being at the Clinic a year, Violet and I did find time for a week's vacation in Colorado Springs. We did our sightseeing there in a four-horse stagecoach because there was no gas for recreation during the war. It was a delightful train trip and was a good rest for me because I had had a very hard year and was completely worn out.

At the end of my first year in Aurora, the army called me up for another physical, as they did every year during the war. Every year I thought this time they will take me, but every time they sent me back to Aurora, saying that I had diabetes and was not physically qualified for service.

During this busy time for me, Violet was trying to find outlets for her energies. She had been a schoolteacher when we married, so it wasn't long before she was teaching Red Cross nutrition classes to wives of Burlington Railroad employees. Even to this day, I occasionally hear people talk about the classes she taught back in 1942. We found the community delightful, and we were happy that we had come to Aurora.

When we had been in Aurora about six months, Violet became pregnant. Since our landlord did not allow children, we had to look for another place to live. By then we had a few dollars saved, and we looked for a house instead of an apartment. We found a nice brick house on a corner lot in the southeast section of town; it was owned by a man who had planned to live in it himself but was called into the service. He agreed to rent it to us, for sixty dollars a month. We had room for a garden in the back and raised many of our own vegetables to supplement the shortages in the stores. We had to fire a coal furnace, take out the clinkers, and have coal delivered frequently through the winter. There was no stoker, and no gas heat was available. I didn't mind the work because I had never lived in such a comfortable house. We also had wonderful neighbors in Art Miller and his wife, who lived next door. Art noted how hard I worked and how many nights a week I was out, and he helped me in many ways, such as shoveling my walks and keeping the driveway clear of snow so that I would have no trouble getting out at night. When I offered to pay him, he would say, "No, we have to keep the doctor going.

His work is more important than pay." Art Miller and his wife and family became my patients, and Art came to me until his death at the age of 93.

During those years, we had two sons: Richard, who was born on September 9, 1943, and Donald, on September 9, 1945. The boys added a lot of joy to the Greeley household as well as a lot of work. Violet was left with most of their care since I had so little time at home. I have often regretted this as I grow older, but I guess it is the price I had to pay for being a doctor at that time. Richard and Donald were both delivered by Dr. Denney, who found it very difficult to get there on time—I almost had to deliver them myself before he arrived on the scene. They were both strong, healthy boys and did well, for which we were grateful. To have two boys born on the same day, even though two years apart, took some special planning, but in our case it worked out very well. The thing that we hadn't thought about at the time was that we would always have to have two birthday cakes and two sets of presents on the same day.

XIX/New Medical Discoveries

During the early 1940s penicillin was developed, one of the great medical discoveries of all time. When I studied bacteriology in college, our teacher mentioned that certain molds inhibited the growth of some types of bacteria. This fact had been noted, but no way was known to make clinical use of it. It seemed impossible to extract the active ingredient in these molds to use against pathogenic bacteria. I forgot about it until the development of penicillin during the early years of World War II. At first it was very expensive and was used only in the armed services. It was only in the last part of the war that we began to get small amounts for use in civilian practice. It was so expensive to produce that we used what might now be called "minute doses." In a case of pneumonia or infection, we used a small dose of twenty thousand to twenty-five thousand units intramuscularly and gave it every six hours. The drug was so scarce that we couldn't always get it even for our most severe cases. Later, we didn't know how to use it most effectively, so we ended up using it on anything infectious. On most infections, the results were miraculous; we couldn't believe what we saw and wondered how we ever got along without it.

One case in particular comes to mind. I made a house call on a patient and found him unconscious with high fever, stiff neck, and obvious meningitis. Upon hospitalization, a spinal tap was performed, and the spinal fluid was purulent and greenish in color. Bacteriologically, examination showed that the patient had pneumococcic meningitis, a disease that I had been taught in medical school was 100 percent fatal. Nobody knew whether penicillin would be effective in a case like this, or how much to use, and whether or not to give it in the spinal canal. I decided that if this man were going to die anyway I had nothing to lose by trying everything I knew, even if it was experimental. After consultation with his wife, I did a spinal tap on him every six hours for several days, each time injecting twenty-five thousand units of regular penicillin into the spinal canal. I also gave him an equivalent amount intramuscularly. After twenty-four hours of this treatment, to my amazement, he began to wake up, his fever came down, and there was no question that he was much improved. I kept on with the treatment for several more days, then stopped the intrathecal injection but gave him more penicillin intramuscularly. The patient, except for a few residual effects from the infection, continued to improve. He made a good physical and mental recovery and was able to enjoy life for many years. It was emotionally traumatic for all concerned to follow the dramatic course of this man's recovery from an illness that up to that time had been fatal.

When I thought about the great discoveries that were being made, I began to appreciate more and more the medical era in which I was living. The use of simple liver extract now completely controlled pernicious anemia, a disease that had always been fatal with many bizarre symptoms and progressive paralysis. Great strides were made in the dietary care of diabetes; then came the discovery of insulin. If a person developed diabetes before 1922, he knew he would be dead within five years. Thanks to the experimental work of Frederick G. Banting and Charles H. Best, insulin was discovered in 1922, and the whole life outlook changed for the millions of people who had diabetes or would contract it in the future. A means of controlling the disease was available so that diabetics could live an almost normal life span.

The medical schools and the big research clinics began spending more and more money and time on research, and many more students became interested in this phase of medicine. The discoveries came thick and fast, not only in medicine but in surgery and every other specialty. It soon became apparent that no one man could learn all there was to know about all areas of medicine. It was necessary to narrow one's field and attempt to keep up with a limited phase of it. The general practitioner began to disappear, and medicine was taken over by specialists. As will be brought out later, this probably was overdone; the pendulum is swinging back and there is a very definite place for the family practitioner again.

Although I had been doing general practice throughout World War II, I realized that there was no way in the future that I could do my best work by trying to cover all fields. It just wasn't possible. I decided that as soon as the doctors came back I would try to limit my practice to internal medicine. Even that was a large field, which a few years later began to be divided into subspecialties such as allergy, gastroenterology, and hematology. The field of surgery also advanced rapidly and became extremely complex. These events made me realize that if doctors were to practice medicine most effectively, the ideal way would be to have multispecialty clinics. Doctors trained in all the specialties would work together as a unit for the common goal of good patient care. To put together such an organization would require a lot of understanding and skill, diplomacy, tact, and good public relations. There would be many problems, but when one is young it seems as if all things are possible and all problems solvable. It was this type of thinking that advanced the development of multispecialty clinics throughout the United States.

XX/Development of Aurora After World War II

The city of Aurora experienced a large increase in population and in industrial development following World War II. Caterpillar started to build a plant that would employ four thousand people; it grew to such an extent that by 1970 it was hiring almost twice that many. Western Electric took over United Wallpaper and started building telephones and telephone parts for AT & T and furnished employment for many people. Thousands more worked in Chicago. The Chicago, Aurora, and Elgin (the Third Rail) went bankrupt, and after that the only alternatives for commuting to Chicago were the Burlington Railroad and driving one's own car. The Tri-State Tollway was still on the planning boards, so most people used the train. It was too much of a struggle to drive to Chicago through all the stoplights and heavy traffic. With the increase in population from people moving to Aurora and from the baby boom after the servicemen came back, many new schools were built on both the east and west sides of Aurora. As the devastation of World War II sank into memory, people enjoyed a prosperity that they had not known for a long time. After all, the depression had lasted some twelve years.

The creeping inflation that developed through World War II is still in existence today. A good example of that is the hospital bed charges. When I first came to Aurora, it cost $7.50 a day for a private room and $4.50 for a ward bed, and people thought that was too high. There were few additional charges, as many of the current laboratory tests and X-rays had not been discovered. During the war, sometimes there was only one laboratory technician in the whole hospital to run all the tests. Following World War II that changed rapidly, and now there are probably forty-five lab technicians at each of the two hospitals. Of course, all this adds to the cost of medicine, but it also has saved many lives.

In 1948 Copley Hospital added a wing to provide fifty more rooms, modern and mostly private. This addition cost around $750,000, most of which was donated by Colonel Copley. The same structure today would cost several million dollars.

Our clinic was very busy, the doctors outside the clinic were busy, and the community was growing. The practice of medicine had come a long way since I started, and I thought: We have learned about as much as we can learn. When I look back on it now, I see we really hadn't scratched the surface. I wonder if twenty-five years from now people will say the same thing.

In 1950 I was elected president of the Aurora Kiwanis Club. I had been on the board for several years and had advanced from board member to vice president. It was a fantastic year for me, and I felt that I was able to be of some benefit to our club. We had many successful projects that raised funds for underprivileged children. Socially, we had good attendance through that year, and we worked well together. We chartered a DC-3 plane and flew twenty-one of our club members to Cincinnati to attend a Kiwanis meeting there. This was a continuation of a project that was started the previous year by flying to Detroit to visit a club there. The year after I was president, we took a similar trip to Toronto. The plane was flown by one of our club members who was a United Airlines pilot. An Aurora *Beacon-News* reporter attended all our meetings and went on our trips with us. She gave us excellent publicity, probably more than we deserved, but it did a lot of good for our whole club. I felt that my year as president was very successful.

XXI/Growth of Our Clinic
During the Years 1945 to 1950

Following the end of hostilities, there was a fairly rapid demobilization of troops, which included, of course, the Medical Corps. We looked forward to the time when Dr. Gardner and Dr. Hausmann would be back in our group. For me, there was some apprehension as to whether there would be a place for me when they returned. I had always felt that I was taking care of their practices until the end of the war. If there were no room for me at the Clinic anymore, I would start out in practice by myself somewhere, probably in a small town. I had even gone to the point of investigating towns around Aurora and sizing up their medical needs. However, Dr. Blackburn and I had been very busy in the past years, and as the time came for doctors in service to return, Dr. Denney, Dr. Milbacher, and Dr. Dreyer met with us and said, "You have worked hard during the war and have brought many new patients to the Clinic. We feel that there is plenty of room for you to stay with us." I was glad, because I had become settled in the community and knew many people, had established church connections, had started my family, and was happy living in Aurora.

Not only did they ask Dr. Blackburn and me to stay on at the Dreyer-Denney Clinic, but they offered to sell each of us a 5 percent interest. On December 7, 1945, this stock became available because Dr. Dreyer was sixty-five years of age and was selling out his shares in the Clinic. His interest was to be divided among the partners. We were happy to buy into the Clinic. We were both making more money than ever before, and it looked as if we might have a good future.

In September 1945, after getting out of the service, Dr. Oliver Kobisk joined the Clinic. Although he had had considerable training in urology, he had been in general practice in Batavia before World War II. He did not want to go back into general practice and was accepted by the Clinic as a urologist. He took special courses and over the years developed into a fine specialist and a valuable addition to the clinic.

It was also at the end of World War II that the Clinic's name was changed to the Clinic of Dreyer, Denney, Milbacher, and Gardner in deference to the senior partners of the group. This name was retained until 1964, when it was again changed to the Dreyer Medical Clinic, as it is today. The ownership stayed the same until 1949, when Dr. Hausmann and Dr. Kobisk each bought 5 percent from Dr. Denney. During the war the cost of 5 percent of stock was $2,000. By the time Dr. Blackburn and I bought in, the price was $3,000 and this price was maintained until 1952.

The postwar Clinic grew rapidly, not only in private patients but in industrial work. Factories returned to peace-time production, and many more of them sent their industrial work to the Clinic, since we always had doctors available. The chief roadblock to our further growth in patient load and industrial work was the absence of parking space close to our building. We were in an eight-story business building in the middle of downtown Aurora, and the city would not give us any restricted parking spaces in front of the building to accommodate patients. Thus cars had to double-park on a narrow street to let out sick or injured people, and the nearest parking lot was a block away. Parking meters were later installed but, again, the city did not make satisfactory parking arrangements for the Clinic.

With Dr. Kobisk added and Dr. Hausmann and Dr. Gardner returning from the service, there was not enough room on the eighth floor, so we rented the seventh floor also. This floor was used primarily for industrial work and some private patients. Ray Cantrall, the male nurse who joined us in 1943, had charge of a great deal of the industrial work, always with doctor backup for all procedures. The Clinic bought a dental X-ray unit capable of taking X-rays of small bones and joints, which was to be used for industrial cases. More serious accidents were sent to the hospital. We also did hundreds of preemployment exams for the factories. Industrial work was a definite addition to our income.

It was a great pleasure having Dr. Gardner and Dr. Hausmann back with us. I had always been fond of Dr. Gardner ever since our original meeting, at the time of my interview with Dr. Denney. Dr. Gardner had taken his Boards in internal medicine and was a certified internist, and I considered it a privilege to work under him. Over the years, I was always impressed with his kindness to his patients, and I learned a great deal about public relations and patient care from him.

Dr. Hausmann's interests were in other fields. Although he did general practice, he was an excellent general surgeon and outstanding at orthopedics. He and Dr. Dreyer worked together extensively on hip fractures. Dr. Hausmann became known as one of the best surgeons in Aurora for fractured hips. To me, he was always a respected colleague, good friend, and close neighbor.

All in all, things seemed rosy for my continued practice of medicine in Aurora, Illinois. I was enjoying the community, the doctors, and the hospitals. The Clinic was developing and growing.

XXII/Settling In

The war was over, and the economy was going through some reverberations as it settled down into peacetime. All war contracts were canceled. People feared that we would fall right back into a serious depression, as in the 1930's. The national debt was $240 billion, a sum so huge that nobody could even imagine it, but that was the cost of winning the war. Fortunately, the country suffered only a brief lull in business. The factories were way behind in peacetime goods, and as soon as they started operating there were jobs for everyone. There had been considerable inflation during World War II and, whether by plan or chance, the country went into a pattern of creeping inflation that some economists thought would help with jobs and avoid another depression. We have had continual inflation ever since, sometimes out of control, as in the late 1970's and early 1980's. Planning for the future was difficult, since one did not know how much money would be required to maintain a family in a changing economy.

Dr. Blackburn and I had been apprehensive that after the war the patients would go back to their former doctors, not only in the Clinic but outside, and there might not be enough work for everybody. This was true to some extent, but not as much as we had anticipated. One factor that counteracted it was the many new people who had moved into the Aurora area. There was a slight lull in my practice immediately after the war, but not for long. Whereas I had been working ninety hours a week through 1943, 1944, and 1945, I was now able to cut my hours to about seventy a week. My habit patterns were becoming pretty well established by this time. I was always an early riser, a habit formed in early life when I got up at 5:00 A.M. to get the chores done before school. I continued to get up about 5:45 and was at the hospital by 6:30. The hospitals came to expect me to be the first doctor to arrive. It may have been somewhat inconvenient for them because of shift changes at 7 A.M., but they were always cooperative and adjusted to my pattern of practice.

I had fewer patients at St. Joseph Mercy Hospital (now Mercy Center for Health Care Services) and usually went there first. I generally arrived about the same time as Father Millen, who was making communion rounds. Sometimes I had to do some scheming in order not to interfere with him. I then went to St. Charles Hospital and to Copley and tried to get my rounds done by 9:00 or 9:15, after which I went to the office to see patients until noon. Sometimes I had time for two or three house calls between hospital rounds and office hours. I usually had about two hours at noon, during which I made four to six house calls and sometimes went back to the hospital for rounds if I hadn't finished them in the morning. Between 2:00 and 2:30 P.M., I returned to the office for the afternoon and usually was about the last one to leave at 6:30. I ate a quick dinner and then made two or three more house calls and perhaps did more hospital work at night. Finally getting home between 9:30 and 10 o'clock, I read the paper quickly and went to bed. If I wasn't called out, which I was several times a week, I was up again at 5:30 to do the same thing over again. Sundays were a little easier in that I had only hospital rounds and house calls, and I could spend several hours with my family.

Many doctors, especially the younger ones, were critical of my habits and felt that I did not leave enough time for my family. In some respects they were right; however, I totally enjoyed the practice of medicine, even though I was often so tired that I didn't know how I could go on. It was a new challenge from day to day, and I always looked forward to it. I never seemed to lack patients, and I was devoted to them. On the wall in my office I put up a framed quotation from Maimonides that I thought typified what a doctor should be, and I have tried to live up to it.

> "When wise men teach me
> Let me be humble to learn
> For the mind of man is so puny
> And the art of healing so vast.
> Let me be intent upon one thing
> Oh Father of Mercy
> To be always merciful to thy suffering children."

After the war, there was an explosion of medical discoveries, including antibiotics that were effective against types of bacteria over which penicillin had no control. These became known as broad-spectrum antibiotics. They did not displace penicillin, but they did add to our medical armamentarium. In the late 1940s the surgical side of medicine progressed rapidly also. Surgeons began performing open-heart surgery, which in my medical school days was not even considered. Pulmonary surgeons, in taking out lungs, had always been afraid to touch the heart for fear it might stop beating. After World War II, with new surgical skills and heart-lung machines, a pneumonectomy was no longer a highly fatal operation. Many elaborate cardiac procedures became possible and successful.

After I decided to specialize in internal medicine, I continually studied medical papers, read dozens of professional magazines, and attended scientific meetings in order to improve my skills. The five years following

World War II were very stimulating and satisfying to me because I was maturing and developing along with the life-saving medical discoveries.

Many things, both good and bad, happened to me through the five years after the war. The following case study describes a real tragedy that left me wondering if I had done the right thing to go into medicine. I was called one day to see a twelve-year-old girl with a sore throat. I found her to be exceptionally ill, with large plaques in her throat. She was so sick that I admitted her to the hospital and ordered cultures of her throat and blood counts. I hadn't been home long before the hospital called and reported that the girl had diphtheria. I had never seen the disease in medical school or in my internship. It was fast disappearing because of the advent of prophylactic shots for children. This girl had never had shots for any of the childhood diseases. The hospital asked me to take her out immediately lest she give diphtheria to the other patients. They were upset with me for admitting her in the first place. Diphtheria is a very serious disease and highly contagious. I sent her back home, set up a hospitallike situation there, and gave her diphtheria antitoxin. I stopped to see her twice a day and started intravenous fluids. The next day she was worse, and by the second day, in spite of treatment, her throat was beginning to close and she couldn't breathe, one of the complications of diphtheria. I called an ear, nose, and throat specialist, Dr. Clifton Boon, who had just returned from the army. I had never met him, but when I explained my problem he was very gracious and said, "Of course I will help you." He arrived in about fifteen minutes and did a tracheotomy on the girl immediately. I continued seeing her two to three times a day, and he checked her at least once daily and kept the trachea open. At first she seemed to get better, but after a few days she began to get more toxic. Her heart rate became faster, she became very restless, listless, and delirious and finally died. It was a sad day for the family and for Dr. Boon and me, but we felt we had done the best we could. Dr. Boon and I practiced in the same medical community all our lives, and often we have looked back and wondered if there was anything more we could have done.

XXIII/Happenings Along the Way

I was called one night to see a seventy-six-year-old woman who was comatose. She was a new patient and I didn't know much about her, but on hospitalization I found that she was in what we called a myxedema coma, which is caused by a complete lack of thyroid. After administration of thyroid, she made a miraculous recovery and was discharged in good shape for her age. When she left the hospital, I jokingly told her, "You will live another ten years." Then I forgot I ever said it. I continued caring for her, and ten years to the day from the time she left the hospital, she called me and said, "Dr. Greeley, ten years ago today you told me I would live for ten more years. The ten years are up. What do I do?" I laughed and said, "Well, Mrs. Hunter, I will give you another ten years." You know, that lady lived until she was just a few weeks short of being ninety-six years old, but she kept a clear mind right up to the last and remembered that I had said she would live until ninety-six. Aren't people wonderful!

Too often, doctors and the general public feel that when a person gets old, that's the end of sex—they should forget about it. It has been brought out recently in magazines and in the press that that is not necessarily true. This was brought home to me very forcefully by a man who had been a patient of mine for years and had been very healthy. He came in at the age of eighty-four with a marked epididymitis, a swollen testicle, and it was necessary for the organ to be removed by a urologist. The patient got along fine, but four or five months later he came in angry as could be at the urologist and me.

I asked, "What is the matter? You're better than you have been for years."

He said, "Dr. Greeley, I am going to sue that surgeon for malpractice. I haven't been able to have intercourse since he did the operation." He added, "I have a girlfriend and we have always been able to have sex together until my operation, but we haven't been able to have it since. She's upset, and I'm upset."

"How old is your girlfriend?" I asked.

"She's 76."

At first I thought the man was joking but he was dead serious. The operation had spoiled his sex life, and he was furious about it. I guess we lose track of what things mean to different people.

So many wonderful people were part of my medical practice. I can't help but mention Nellie, who ran a nursing home for many years. I took care of most of her patients, and after she grew too old to run the home, I took care of her until I retired. By that time, she was in her 90's and mentally very sharp. She always said, "Dr. Greeley, you look so good in blue. I don't think you should ever wear anything else." I said, "Nellie, I like blue, and if you will just let me know every time you are coming, I will always wear a blue suit." Sure enough, the day before each appointment, Nellie would call my receptionist and say, "Tell Dr. Greeley to wear his blue suit tomorrow." I would wear my blue suit and Nellie would be happy.

Sometimes things happen in the hospital which, in retrospect, are humorous but at the time are quite serious. One noon I happened to be at the hospital when one of the student nurses came running into the nurses' station, all upset, with tears in her eyes, and told the head nurse that she was taking a rectal temperature on one of my patients when she lost the thermometer. She wailed, "It's up Aggie's rectum, and I can't get it out." The nurse turned to me and asked, "Well, what do we do about it?" I went into Aggie's room and examined her, and sure enough, way up at the tip of my examining finger in the rectum I could feel the end of the thermometer, but I couldn't get hold of it. I explained the situation to Aggie and told her we would have to put her up on a proctoscopic table and use an instrument to look down her rectum and see if we could retrieve the thermometer. Aggie was very good about it and said it would be OK. Without too much difficulty, we were able to extricate the thermometer. You never saw a more relieved look than on the student nurse's face. She was so sure she had done something fatal to the patient.

One part of my practice that began to build up after the war was the treatment of diabetics. Dr. Denney knew about my carbohydrate defect, which had never been definitely evaluated as true diabetes, but he told everybody that I was a diabetic and for that reason was going to specialize in the care of diabetes. For the rest of my practicing life, I continually had patients ask how I took care of my own diabetes. Because I thought that I probably would develop the disease some day, I studied it extensively, and patients came to look upon me as a specialist in the field. Diabetes is a disease that requires constant adjusting of insulin, diet, and activities. Every patient is a special case. The only way a patient can take good care of himself is to learn as much about his disease as his doctor knows. There are always a few brittle diabetics whose blood sugar goes up and down unpredictably. Even on the same daily dose of insulin, they sometimes have an insulin reaction, which occurs when the blood sugar falls too low. It can be caused by the patient's getting too much insulin or perhaps going without meals while taking the usual amount of insulin. Exercise may also lower the blood sugar and cause an insulin reaction. In an insulin reaction, the patient becomes mentally upset, delirious, has hallucinations and, as the blood sugar goes lower, becomes comatose. If the blood sugar falls low enough, the patient may go into convulsions and die. Patients are instructed in all this and know when the symptoms start. When they feel restless and sweaty they take sweet things, a candy bar or orange juice with a little extra sugar in it, which will counteract the low blood sugar. Sometimes this condition occurs in the middle of the night when the patient is asleep and does not wake up to do anything about it. Over my years of practice, I always carried a vial of 50 percent glucose and a syringe in my bag in case I should ever get a call for that type of emergency. In those days, we didn't have full-time doctors to cover the hospital emergency room, and it was up to the private physician to take the patient to the hospital to administer glucose, or to carry a supply of glucose and give it at home. There is nothing more miraculous in medicine than to see a patient who is comatose from an insulin reaction respond to 20 cc of 50 percent glucose intravenously and immediately sit up and say, "What is the matter; why are you here?"

I always had one or two patients who would get in trouble two or three times a year in spite of my best efforts to keep them stabilized. A woman called me one morning about two o'clock to tell me that her husband was having an insulin reaction and was unconscious. In the early stages of his hypoglycemia, he had become delirious and had crawled under the bed and passed out. She knew what was wrong and called me to come immediately. When I arrived, I loaded my syringe and crawled under the bed, found his arm, and was able to insert the needle into his vein. I gave the glucose as rapidly as I could, and when I had finished he woke up, recognized me as his doctor, and asked, "What are you doing under the bed?" I said, "Well, I had to catch you somehow." He felt quite sheepish about it, but we both knew that he couldn't help it. The patient lived for years, and we joked about it many times.

I had another patient who slept very soundly and often had insulin reactions around two or three A.M. His wife was used to them and knew what to do. She tried to give him glucose and sweet things by mouth, but sometimes he was so far out he wouldn't cooperate and would need intravenous glucose. By the time I got there, the man would be almost comatose but still somewhat violent and combative. His wife, who was a good-sized woman, would sit on him and hold his arm while I put the glucose in his vein. He always snapped right out of it and woke up wondering what was going on. For these night house calls I charged ten to twenty-five dollars. Once when I was out of town, her husband went into an insulin reaction and she called a doctor who did not know him. The doctor immediately called an ambulance and took him to the hospital, where he was kept overnight and given intravenous feedings. In order to get out of that insulin reaction, it cost the patient about two hundred dollars. It really pays for a doctor to know his patient and his disease.

There are always lighter happenings that make a doctor feel more relaxed. I had a patient who was confined to her home with a heart condition. She lived alone, and her friends came in daily to help her clean and to prepare her meals. She had the smartest parakeet I have ever seen. I had always read stories about parakeets' being able to talk, but our own never learned a word. When I made house calls there, her parakeet, who had a vocabulary of about 120 words, would talk for me. He could say quite plainly, "Twinkle, twinkle, little star; how I wonder what you are." He knew his address and would repeat it again and again, "709 East New York Street." I was somewhat surprised one day to hear him say very clearly, "You're a jackass, Dr. Greeley." I made house calls there frequently over a period of about two years, and the parakeet always greeted me with the same irreverent comment. Unfortunately, he met a bad end. Someone left the door open, and he flew out of the house and never returned. My patient was heartbroken. She said it made her feel as bad as when her husband died. I can understand what she meant. She certainly had lost a good friend and one that had given her a lot of pleasure.

I cannot leave this subject without relating a tragic case that occurred in a farm family that lived about fifteen miles from Aurora. It was about 10 A.M. one winter day when I received a call from the frantic parents, saying that their ten-year-old son was buried in the corn crib and they feared he was suffocating; they were trying to get him out but wanted me to come at once. A corncrib is an overhead granary filled with shelled corn, with an opening below through which corn can be drawn out and loaded into a wagon or container. When the opening below is closed and there is no commotion up above, children can play in the crib without any danger, but once that slot is opened the shelled corn acts as a sort of quicksand or whirlpool and sucks anyone in it down to that opening. It will pull a child or even an adult down to where he is completely covered with corn and cannot breathe. The family discovered that their son was in the corncrib when they found the slot open and saw the child's foot sticking through it. They got everybody available to help, and by the time I arrived, after making the trip at ninety miles an hour, they had lifted him out and had him up on a platform, high in the corncrib. I climbed the ladder to where he was, but he was beyond help. I injected adrenalin into his heart, breathed into his lungs, tried to start his heart again, and did everything I knew, but to no avail. I helped the family get him down from the corncrib and shared their sorrow with them. At a time like that, there is nothing to say. I drove back to Aurora at a safe speed, but with a sad heart. To this day, if I go into that area, memories come back to me of that cold day up in the corncrib.

In the practice of medicine, there are many ups and downs but they tend to balance out. I do think that the cases that involve tragedy leave their mark on a doctor more than those that turn out successfully. Sharing the tragedy makes the doctor an integral part of the family. After years of sharing their sorrows and their joys, their successes and their failures, a strong bond develops between doctor and family that makes the practice of medicine worthwhile.

XXIV/Aurora Homes

After it was decided that I would stay in Aurora to practice with the Clinic of Dreyer, Denney, Milbacher, and Gardner, the next major decision was finding a new place to live. The owner of our house at 802 Hinman returned from service and wanted to move into it. By that time we had two sons, and it was not easy to find a place to rent. I was now earning more money than I ever had, $7,500 a year. We finally bought an older two-story house at 366 Marion, about one and a half blocks from Copley Hospital. It lacked a number of conveniences; for example, it didn't have a bathroom or powder room on the first floor or in the basement. The house, which had been remodeled many times, was very well built and rather attractive. It had hot water heat with radiators. The unattached garage opened onto an alley, which proved to be a bad setup in the winter. With snow, the alley became impassable, and the city did not come through with snowplows until all other streets were open. Even though I put on car chains, I was sometimes stuck for a day or two before I could get out of my own garage.

Our neighbors were very friendly, and eventually most of them came to me as patients. We were only half a block from the Fourth Street Methodist Church, where we had established our membership. We moved into the house in early 1946 when Donald was only a few months old and soon found out the disadvantages of a two-story house. Donald was a heavy baby and by the time he was a year old weighed about thirty pounds. One day when he was sick with diarrhea, Violet counted thirty-four trips up and down stairs. It was then that we decided our next home was going to be on one floor.

Although the house was very livable in many ways, some things needed changing. For instance, we had to put in a new hot water heater and a new boiler in the furnace. These things were expensive, but necessary. By the time we moved out, the house was in much better condition than when we bought it.

It was while we were still living at 366 Marion that our daughter, Barbara Jean, was born on September 1, 1947. We now had two boys and one girl, which made a lovely family. When we married, we told all our friends that we were going to have four children, two boys and then two girls—that they would all be two years apart and all born in September. It was amazing how nearly this worked out. Richard was born on September 9, 1943; Donald was born September 9, 1945; and Barbara Jean was born on September 1, 1947. When Violet was pregnant with Barbara Jean, we reconsidered our ambition of having four children. She had a rather difficult pregnancy and developed a lot of chest pain on exertion—typical angina, and her electrocardiogram was abnormal. Going up and down stairs brought on considerable chest pain and some dyspnea. Then when Barbara Jean was born, Violet had a postdelivery hemorrhage, requiring a number of transfusions. It was at that point that we decided that if we raised three children well, it would be enough.

Not long after Barbara Jean was born, we began planning to build a house that would be on one floor to make less work for Violet, who still was having pain on exertion. This condition has been nonprogressive, and because Violet is very efficient in everything she does, nobody would ever know she had a problem unless she told them. She is able to carry on a normal life as long as she goes at a slower pace.

During the first years after the war, few houses were being built; the building boom started a little later. It was so unusual to see houses under construction that on Sunday afternoons people enjoyed walking through them, even though they had no right to. After all, few houses had been built since the depression started. We also looked at a number of unfinished houses and some older homes. The older homes were all two-story or bungalows that were too small for our family. Violet, being a good artist and architect, drew up a plan of the house she would like, a one-story ranch house. She not only drew all the plans for the house but also made a working model of it. She then made actual blueprints from which our present home was built.

We began looking for a site and purchased a corner lot with sewer and water one block from Freeman Elementary School on the far west side of town. We thought three thousand dollars was expensive, but we now realize it was a bargain. We built our ranch-style house in 1948. Violet preferred to have it entirely on one floor with no basement, but I wanted a basement for storage and for the furnace and water heater. We compromised and put the basement under half the house; later we wished that we had a full basement. However, it is very dry and we have space for a rumpus room with a Ping-Pong table and pool table.

The house was built during the summer and fall of 1948. As was the custom, every Sunday people would tramp through it, looking and trying to guess what kind of home we were building. Fortunately, we were able to sell our house on Marion Avenue at a profit, and that helped in financing the new house. When I looked for a long-term loan, I was surprised to find that, even though I had about 30 percent of the money as a down payment, it was difficult to get credit. Several places turned me down flat, saying that I would need at least half the money available for a house of this type. The Home Savings and Loan in Aurora acted favorably on my application and lent me $17,000 on what was anticipated to be a total cost of $30,000, at 5¼ percent interest. It looked like a lot of money in those days, and I wondered if I would ever get it paid off, but by that time I was making $15,000 a year and thought I could probably handle the payments without trouble.

The house was finished in early January 1949, and the Greeleys moved to 179 South Evanslawn, where we have been ever since. It was a beautiful house in which to raise a family. We had two complete baths on the first floor, and a shower, toilet, and lavatory in the basement. If we had it to do over again we would have enlarged the family room at the time the house was built instead of later. Other than that, the house was convenient and perfect for our family. We landscaped it in the spring. There were four large elm trees on the lot. Dutch elm disease killed every one of those trees in the early 1960s, and we had to start over again with maples. It is interesting to note that when we built the house we could see the sunset out our kitchen window. Our house was at the farthest edge of Aurora. As this book is written, houses extend a mile or two west of us, which shows how Aurora has grown.

Moving from the east side of Aurora to the west side entailed considerable reorientation. We were no longer close to the hospital, which necessitated a much longer trip across town to make my hospital rounds. We were also farther from my office in downtown Aurora. Freeman School was very handy for the children, as it was only a block away. I had a lot more lawn to mow, and that was in the days before power mowers.

As our children started to school, we realized how important good teachers are. When Richard entered first grade, he had an uncaring teacher who had been there for only a year and had little experience. For some reason, their personalities clashed and he did not do well. At the end of the year, she told us that our son was below average and might even be mentally handicapped. Of course we were depressed but decided to make the best of the situation. The next year, his teacher was entirely different and was very successful in developing each child's potential. Before the year was over, this teacher told us our son was brilliant, was doing well in school, and she predicted that he would have a good future. That was the difference between two teachers. Richard did well all the rest of grade school and high school and graduated fourth in his class of four hundred students. He graduated with honors from the University of Illinois and went on to get a Ph.D. in organic chemistry at Stanford University. He did valuable research throughout his graduate work. All this came from someone who was supposed to be mentally retarded.

XXV/Family Vacations

About 1951 Violet and I started taking the children on automobile trips with us. I would work hard the whole year and then take three weeks off in the summer to go somewhere in the United States. It was quite a chore to take children as young as ours; however, our experiences together as a family were good for all of us. For the children's convenience, we carried a small commode in the back seat of the car: one of them would invariably have to use it while we were going through a fair-sized town. There were certain hazards in taking children along on such trips, but except for two incidents we always did quite well. Our trip in 1952 took us to Colorado, to Shadow Mountain Ranch, where we spent a week riding horses, which the children thoroughly enjoyed. We then drove southwest to Durango, Colorado.

Donald, seven years old, had been sick all afternoon, and we assumed that his vague abdominal pains were car sickness. At the motel, I examined him and found that he had acute appendicitis. I knew there were no outstanding hospitals in Durango, and I didn't know any of the doctors. I thought we should get him to Denver to a modern hospital to have his appendix removed. At the local airport I found that the last plane for the day had gone. I told the ticket agent about our problem and asked her if she knew any good surgeons in Durango. She straightened up and said, "Dr. Greeley, I am the wife of the local undertaker, and I know who kills them and who cures them." And with that, she told me about a young surgeon who had had four years of surgical training in Michigan and who she thought was the best in Durango. I went back to the motel and examined Donald again. I thought he seemed a little better so, wishfully thinking, we battled it out through the night, gave him large doses of penicillin, and watched his progress.

Unfortunately, by morning he was worse, and there was no question that we had to do something. I called the young surgeon, and he met us at the hospital. The hospital was an old frame house with an operating room in the attic. We took Donald's blood count and it was very high; it was obvious that he had to have surgery immediately. The surgeon inspired confidence right away, and I could see that we were not dealing with a novice. I asked him about the equipment they had in this old hospital. He assured me that if we would forget about the surroundings, the boy would have good care, the nurses were excellent, and he felt perfectly adequate to handle it. He had a good surgical assistant and a good anesthesiologist. I went out to the car and told Violet that our son was going to have an appendectomy. With a look of disbelief on her face, she said, "You mean he is going to have it done here?" I assured her that I had confidence in the setup and the doctors and that we had to go ahead—we had no choice. We put Donald to bed and got things ready in the operating room. When it was time, he had to walk up the stairs under his own power and get up on the operating table. The anesthesiologist used open drop ether. Donald had a gangrenous appendix that couldn't have waited much longer. I watched the whole operation and was satisfied that we had had good surgeons, good anesthesia, and good care. Donald did well and was up the next day. Since he was doing well, we decided to take some short sight-seeing trips in the mornings and visit with him in the afternoons and evenings. The next morning we toured Mesa Verde. When we returned to the hospital to see Donald, there was no Donald. We were really concerned until we found him hiding under the bed—feeling good enough to play tricks on us. He was in the hospital for four days; then we took him home by car, and he got along fine.

One other time, in upper Michigan, Donald fell on a boat and cut his lip, and I had to use my first aid kit to put in stitches. I guess we can only conclude that it could have been much worse. Those are the hazards of traveling with a family, but there are many benefits and joys in the things a family does together. We took many more trips until the children were in high school and wanted to take trips on their own, and we enjoyed every one of them. We covered a good part of the United States and Canada. We traveled to the Northwest—Washington and Oregon, Yellowstone, Yosemite, California; to the East Coast—Washington, D.C., New York, Maine, up into Quebec, Toronto, and so on. One of our trips could have ended in tragedy, but again, I guess the Lord was with us. Violet had never liked to fly, especially with the children. I had spent the winter of 1956 trying to convince her that the following summer we should take the Zephyr out through the mountains, Salt Lake City, and Feather River Canyon, California, and then fly back. She finally consented, and I made reservations for the train and also for the plane to come back from Los Angeles on Monday after the Fourth of July weekend. I had originally considered making the plane reservation for Saturday of that weekend, but I decided on Monday so that we could get the family plan, which was much cheaper. We had a beautiful trip on the Zephyr through Feather River Canyon and the mountains, then rented a car in San Francisco and visited many places in California, including Disney Land, ending up in Los Angeles. On the Saturday morning before the Fourth, as we were driving in Los Angeles, over the radio came a special news bulletin that two passenger airplanes had collided over the Grand Canyon. They had crashed into the Canyon, and over one hundred and twenty people had been killed. One was a United Airlines plane with the same flight number as the one we were booked on two days later. When we heard the news, Violet looked at me and said, "That's our flight number!" I said, "Yes, I know, but we aren't going until Monday." The plane that crashed was the one on which I had almost made reservations. That's how close we came to not having any family left in this world.

XXVI/Clinic Changes in the 1950s

By the time the 1950s came around, I was working very hard and had built up a large practice, but I became increasingly dissatisfied with the way Clinic business was handled. Dr. Blackburn and I never knew where we stood. The books were kept secret, and so was the distribution of profits. Also I felt that I was due for more ownership of Clinic stock; it had been seven years since I had bought my 5 percent.

Other things happened to cause discontent among the young doctors. Dr. Denney was taking more and more time off and still held 25 percent of the partnership, which they felt was unfair. Finally, in June 1953, I made plans to leave the Clinic if I couldn't get a better agreement. I had arranged matters so that I could be practicing alone within three days if I decided to leave. One day I went in to see Dr. Denney and laid my cards on the table. I told him I was unhappy and did not think things were handled fairly for the lesser stockholders. No one had ever challenged Dr. Denney like that before. He said that I didn't appreciate all he had done for me, that nobody else could run the Clinic successfully, and that if I wasn't happy perhaps I would like to leave the Clinic. I told him that I had been very happy working with the group, but I was prepared to leave if that was the way he felt about it, and that I could open up my own office within three days. I then looked him squarely in the eye and said, "Dr. Denney, if you think I am the only one who feels this way, you are mistaken. Everyone in the Clinic feels the same. If I leave I am sure there are others who will do the same." I got up and walked out, not knowing if I had a job or not.

An interesting thing occurred the next day. I did not tell anyone of my talk with Dr. Denney. However, Dr. Kobisk, who was also very unhappy, saw him the following day and told him exactly the same thing. The next day Dr. Denney announced to the group that he was going to sell all of his stock and retire from the practice of medicine. The partnership was reorganized, and there was a steady democratic growth of the Clinic until it reached what it is today. The Clinic as we know it today started when Dr. Kobisk and I challenged Dr. Denney.

I was able to buy 10 percent more stock at that time, although it cost $18,000, which was three times what I had paid for the first 5 percent. When Dr. Denney sold his stock, he asked to stay on as Clinic manager, and we decided to try it. Three years later, however, Dr. Denney retired.

An executive committee was appointed consisting of Dr. Gardner, Dr. Milbacher, me, and a short time later Dr. Hausmann. Dr. Gardner and Dr. Milbacher were put in charge of the business office, with Mrs. Sickles working under them. I was given charge of personnel, and Dr. Hausmann was to manage the industrial work. At our first meeting, we pledged to each other that there would be no secrets from the stockholders or the owners of the partnership. Income was to be divided on a mathematical formula of 52½ percent of a doctor's collections and the rest divided by the percentage of ownership. The system has stood the test of time and is used by the Clinic today—twenty-five years later—with basically no change. We also resolved that operation of the clinic would be democratic. The Board was empowered to make many decisions, but none involving more than one thousand dollars without having the whole partnership vote on it. We have abided by that principle ever since.

A policy had been adopted in 1952 that we would accept only doctors who were Board Certified or Board Eligible. By sticking to this policy, we were able to get doctors of the highest caliber, well trained, the best in Aurora. Dr. John Abell, pediatrician, and Dr. John Landes, surgeon, joined the Clinic in the early 1950's, and a few years later we were joined by Dr. Glenn Richmond and Dr. William Donovan. Dr. Richmond was a very conscientious and capable internist; if anything, he worked too hard for his own good. Dr. Donovan had many new ideas in the Obstetrical Department and was a great help to Dr. Blackburn, who had now confined his work entirely to obstetrics. A couple of years later, Dr. Thomas O'Shea joined our group, another fine internist. With this group we entered the 1960s with a much stronger clinic financially and professionally than we had ever had before. We worked very harmoniously together.

XXVII/Armistice Day 1953

This is a chapter that I did not really want to write, but I felt that I must include it to make my book complete. It concerns one of the worst events of my life and one that had profound effects on me.

Wayne was one of my best friends and was originally a farm boy from the Waterman area. We often played pool with two local lawyers, and afterwards the losers took the winners and their wives to dinner. It seemed that Wayne and I had always won. He was superintendent of schools in Aurora and was well liked. He was a pillar of the community with a beautiful family, a wife and two daughters, ten and fourteen years old.

On November 11, 1953, I made my hospital rounds and was just leaving to go to Maywood to look at an automobile I was thinking of buying. The phone rang, and it was Wayne asking for me. He said he had a severe sore throat and thought he might have some fever. He had planned to go pheasant hunting but didn't feel too good. Wayne had had previous penicillin shots for infection in his foot. I thought it would be indicated to give penicillin for his throat and told him so. I called my nurse, Helen, at the Clinic and ordered a penicillin shot for Wayne and then went on to Maywood. When I returned to Aurora two hours later, I stopped at the Clinic to check on my mail and phone calls. The minute I walked off the elevator, I knew something was wrong. The receptionist said, "Dr. Greeley, Dr. Gardner would like to see you at once. We have been looking for you." I went into Dr. Gardner's office and he gave me the sad news. Wayne had come to the Clinic and Helen gave him the penicillin shot. Before he could even get to the elevator, he collapsed. In another few minutes he was dead. The nurses did everything they knew, but to no avail. He was dead from an anaphylactic reaction to penicillin. They had already moved him to the funeral parlor, and an autopsy was to be performed. I was stunned, unable to grasp the enormity of the situation.

I went to the lab to talk with Helen, and she told me again what had happened. She was crying. There were others around, and we wanted to be alone. We went into the dark room where X-rays were developed and closed the door. We held each other and cried. I don't know how long we were there, but the release of grief was necessary. When we both had regained our composure, we came out to face the world.

I went to see the autopsy findings, which confirmed the cause of death. The next few days were difficult, but after the initial shock I was outwardly in control. I attended the funeral and the coroner's inquest, at which I had to testify. Although outwardly composed, inwardly I hurt, and hurt, and hurt. It was the hardest thing in the world to go to my friend's funeral knowing that I had given the order that was responsible for it. The hardest thing as time went on was to face Wayne's family, which I frequently had to do. They were wonderful about it and didn't blame me, but that didn't keep the hurt from coming back whenever I saw any of them. Every November eleventh, memories return, and I try to keep busy to forget. As a rule, I am quite stoic in nature, but this tragedy was almost more than I could master. The passage of time has dimmed the memories, but they are still there to constantly remind me that many medicines that we doctors use today can kill as well as cure. Perhaps the shock made me a better practitioner and more careful in handling drugs of all types.

I have seen anaphylactic shock several times since then but never had another death from it. One was due to penicillin, and again the patient went into coma and could not breathe, but prompt intravenous injection of adrenalin saved the day. On another occasion the reaction was brought on by a bee sting. It happened that I had seen this patient in the office a day or two before. She had told me then that she was allergic to bee stings and had been warned that if she was stung again she might have an anaphylaxis from it. We discussed giving her immunization shots to build up an immunity to bee stings, but we had not had time for further workup. The next day her family called to say that she had just been stung by a bee and asked what they should do. I said to take her immediately to the emergency room at Copley Hospital, and I would meet her there. I rushed to the hospital and had a syringe full of adrenalin ready. When she arrived, she indeed was in anaphylactic shock. She was lying comatose on the floor of the car and could not breathe. She was sweating and was very acutely and critically ill. I gave her adrenalin immediately, and we were able to save her life.

Anaphylactic shock is one of those things that all doctors hope they never see, but if they do, they hope they are prepared, because it is one of medicine's true emergencies. If something isn't done immediately, death can result in a few minutes. Allergists now understand anaphylactic shock better than they used to, but it is still difficult to explain why the immune mechanisms of the body break down and how such a violent reaction can occur in such a short time.

XXVIII/Paying my Debts

The year was 1954, and I found myself driving two hundred miles to Arenzville, where my mother and two brothers still lived. I was going on a mission that I had always wanted to carry out. In order to explain it, I shall have to go back in time. I have described our poverty when I was of high school age, the deteriorating family structure, and the deepening depression, during which time my family ended up on relief. During those years, my mother tried to buy groceries on credit to feed her family. A few stores gave her credit although knowing that they might never get their money. The groceries that fed me through the last two or three years I was at home were never paid for.

After I was established in practice and had paid my own debts, I started paying the grocery bills for my mother and two brothers, who were still desperately poor. I asked the store to send me the bills and I paid them directly. If I had sent the money to my mother, she would have spent it on furniture or books. When she became ill a few months later, I paid to have a practical nurse stop two or three times a week to clean the house, give her a bath, and take care of her needs. It was at this time my mother began to think that maybe I wasn't quite as black a sheep as she had always made out, and she began to appreciate the things I did for her. All this went through my mind as I drove to Arenzville that day. There was a lot of nostalgia connected with the farm, which I really loved, my school, Arenzville, and the people I knew there. I was going there today for one purpose: I was going to find all the people to whom my folks owed money and pay them.

When I arrived, I went from one business to another. They were very surprised when I told them that I wanted to pay my family's debts, which were then twenty years old. One grocery store, Onken Brothers and Meyer, I remembered especially because they were so good to us when we were almost starving. Their unpaid bill was about a thousand dollars. They had to look deep in their old files to find the bill. I gave them a check for the whole thing, as I did to business after business. One old farmer near Arenzville had sold corn to my folks to feed their hogs. My mother had given him notes, which, of course, were of no value. He went to the bank and got those twenty-year-old notes from his lock box, and I paid them all. There must have been at least fifteen people that I found that day and paid all the money that was owed them. Several would not take money, saying that my family had been good, religious people and that the debts were forgotten.

After I had paid all the debts, I put the receipts in an envelope, sealed it, and put my mother's name on it. I then drove out to the old farm to see her. As I left, I handed her the envelope and told her to open it after I was gone. It was a great satisfaction to me to know that these debts were all paid. My father had died in 1950 of a coronary thrombosis, but I know he would have been proud of me. He was the finest man I have ever known. Though he was helpless to assist me financially, he had more influence on my life than any other person in the world. After I left the farm I drove to the local cemetery, which had not been kept up and was pretty much grown up in weeds. I stood by my father's grave for a few minutes and rededicated myself to the principles that he had laid out in his letter on the day I graduated from medical school:

". . . I hope that you will make the right turns as you continue to advance—that you will be a blessing to the people you meet and that you will always be an honor to your profession."

It was with a great feeling of satisfaction that I drove back to Aurora. It had been a long day, but I had accomplished something that I had wanted to do for a long time. I felt sad that my mother and brothers still had to live under such bad conditions, but there was little I could do about it other than help them financially. My mother absolutely refused to leave the farm, although I had offered several times to buy a small house for her near Aurora or Waterman, where she and George and Wilcox could live out their years. I still felt frustration that I could not do more.

XXIX/Further Growth of the Dreyer Medical Clinic

In 1955 I was approached by the Edison Dictating Company about the possibility of installing a dictation system for our clinic. Each doctor would have a unit in his office, which would be wired to a central unit on another floor, where the dictation would be transcribed. All my life I have hated to write, so I thought this sounded like a pretty good idea. It would cost about two thousand dollars. I proposed it to the group, pointing out that it would save us a lot of time and money. It would give us time to see more patients and also would result in better records. Doctors always dictate more and better than they write. This idea was not very well received by the group, with the exception of Dr. Denney, who insisted that we install the system. After some searching, I found a secretary, Helen Wullbrandt, who was working at the Old Age Pension office and who knew some medical terminology. For me, the system was a great help. I dictated everything right from the start, and I know I made much better records. The other doctors were slow to adapt to the innovation, but they gradually found that by dictating they could also save time, especially on letters. Within a year it became a valuable asset to the office. This system expanded as the Clinic grew, and we had to buy more equipment and hire more secretaries. By the time I retired in 1980, we employed twelve full-time girls, and doctors dictated all their letters and records. The original secretary was with us for the next twenty-five years, until she retired in May 1981.

The Clinic developed in other ways also. We added to the industrial and physical therapy departments. Dr. Richard Foth, an internist, joined us in 1961. It was at this time that, at the insistence of the younger doctors, it was decided that a clinic administrator was needed to run the business for the practicing physicians and to be a contact for outside businesses. We also anticipated that eventually he would be needed to oversee a building project and a move from the downtown area. In 1961 we employed Ronald Frazer, who had been a clinic administrator at the Straub Clinic in Honolulu for a number of years and wanted to move back to the mainland, to the Chicago area. He was a great addition to our group and helped us tremendously over the next nine years.

We realized more and more that the only way we could grow as a multispecialty clinic was to move away from downtown Aurora to some place where we would have ample parking. We were seeing three hundred to four hundred patients a day in this downtown business building. Many of them had to be let out in front of the door. We approached the city fathers about setting aside parking spaces where injured or sick people could be let out. They turned us down on the ground that they could not make exceptions. I think that turn-down was what stimulated us to try much harder to find a place to go. When we did start to build, the city came to us and said, "You can have all the space you want. We don't want you to move out of downtown." We told them that we were sorry but they were too late.

Over the next two years we considered many pieces of property. We would have liked to build near Copley Hospital, but the only way would have been to buy ten houses, get zoning, and then tear them down; the price was prohibitive. We finally bought three and one-third acres of land on the far west side of Aurora, in a developing area. Across the street a small shopping center was under construction. We hired Ellerbe and Company, an architectural firm in Minneapolis that specialized in clinic planning, to design the building.

Dr. Dreyer breaking ground for the new clinic building. Also shown are (left to right) Dr. John Landes, Dr. C. L. Gardner, Dr. Glenn Richmond, and Ronald Frazer, clinic administrator.

In early 1963 we took bids for the building. Abens and Company, a local firm, was selected as contractor, and work was started in June. That was one of the most exciting years in the development of the Dreyer Medical Clinic. I will never forget the ground-breaking ceremonies. Dr. Dreyer was in his late eighties and had had a partial stroke, but he was able to participate in the event. All the doctors, their wives, and a number of business people attended. The area at the time was an open alfalfa field, and we all stood in the hot sun as Dr. Dreyer turned over the first spade of dirt. That was followed by a prayer by Dr. Jacobs, pastor of the New England Congregational Church, and so the project was started.

Physicians in the clinic in 1963: (left to right) Thomas O'Shea, Richard Foth, John Abell, Harry Greeley, William Donovan, Edwin Hausmann, Walter Milbacher, C. L. Gardner, Glenn Richmond, Oliver Kobisk, John Landes, and William Blackburn. Seated is Dr. John Dreyer.

Everyone went out almost daily to check the progress of the building. Construction was somewhat slow, but basically we felt that Abens was doing an excellent job and that Ellerbe's plans were good. We watched the building develop day by day, week by week, and month by month. The original plans had called for an eight-foot wall around the sunken garden on both sides of the front entrance, so that children would not climb over and fall into the depressed area. After the wall was constructed, it looked terrible, but it seemed that the die was cast. As it happened, however, we had a severe winter storm with the hardest north winds in history. The eighty- to ninety-mile-an-hour wind blew the whole wall down into the sunken garden. When we saw what had happened, everybody called it an act of God. We were insured for wind damage, so the insurance company paid for putting up a very nice decorative wall, only four feet high, that served the purpose well over the years and added to the attractiveness of the building.

The new Clinic building was pretty well closed in by cold winter, and the men worked inside through the winter months putting in the partitions, plumbing, and wiring. By May it was clear that we would get in sometime in July. We had new X-ray machines, new laboratory equipment, and new furniture. Each doctor had two offices, and there was plenty of room for the business office. The laboratory had about eight times as much space as before, and we thought it was more than we would ever need. At the time we were building, Dr. Otto Siewert, an ophthalmologist, joined us, and space had been planned for an Eye Department. Finally, moving day was set for August 1, 1964. It was a great day in the history of the Dreyer Medical Clinic when we threw off the chains of renting space downtown and moved to a beautiful new building with plenty of parking space.

In the midst of moving and organizing the clutter in my new office, I received a phone call from a former nurse-employee who was quite sick with nausea and abdominal pain. She came in and was examined on my dusty, new examining table and was found to have acute appendicitis. She was the first patient cared for in the new Dreyer Medical Clinic building.

The new building of the Dreyer Medical Clinic in 1964.

There had been some apprehension by the doctors that patients would not follow us from downtown. That did not happen. People heard about the new building, and before long we had to think about hiring more doctors to take care of them all. On the business side of the Clinic, everything was better organized than it had been for years. Ron Frazer had many new ideas, which we instituted. We wrote a new partnership agreement in 1963 in which we spelled out the principles of operation even more clearly than before. Later, with Ron Frazer's help and the advice of a Chicago law firm, we made arrangements to incorporate our business. When we moved, we employed a radiologist to read all of our films and do our gastrointestinal work. It was a great help for all of us to have Dr. Harry Slobodin, a very talented man, who was always there when we needed him for X-ray interpretation.

XXX/Recruiting

It was about this time that we realized we had more room than we needed for the current staff of doctors. We also realized that as a multispecialty clinic we needed to add other specialties and perhaps add more doctors in some of the specialties we already had. We needed more internists and another pediatrician, and if we grew much we would need another surgeon. I don't know how I got the job—whether I was appointed or just started doing it—but I became recruiter for the Clinic. I had no previous experience and didn't know quite how to go about it at first. There was a serious doctor shortage all over the United States. Several years would go by without one new doctor being added to the staff at either hospital. At the same time, we were losing doctors in the community through attrition. The shortage was so great that a doctor finishing his residency would get hundreds of offers from a single ad in the AMA *Journal*.

I set up some recruiting guidelines. I had a number of sources from which I got the names of potential staff members, for instance, the AMA Placement Service and the ads in medical journals. In Chicago, I obtained the names of all the senior residents in the specialies in which we were interested and tried to get interviews with them. I worked every night on the phone, calling doctors all over the United States and even in Canada. If they seemed interested, I sent them complete information about the Clinic, the type of medical community, and the financial future they could anticipate if they joined the Dreyer Medical Clinic. The group gave me free rein to negotiate within a certain range, so that I didn't have to go to the Board every time I wanted to offer a prospective doctor another thousand dollars a year. I began to enjoy the work, but it was sometimes very disappointing. We first offered to pay the way of a doctor and his wife to visit Aurora for a weekend. We met them at the airport or had them rent a car and drive to Aurora. We furnished them with a motel room, entertained them, introduced them to the group, and showed them the Clinic and the Aurora area. A brochure from the Aurora Chamber of Commerce was given to each doctor. Because a qualified recruit had many offers from which to choose, he did not always choose Aurora. As a result of all this work, over the next fifteen years I personally recruited twenty-five doctors for the Dreyer Medical Clinic.

With successful recruitment, it was not too long before we needed more room and had to add another sixteen thousand square feet of space. This we did by adding a two-story wing to the south of the original building. That was in 1967, only three years after the building was completed. The original building was financed by a loan from the local Home Savings and Loan with an interest rate of 5¼ percent. By the time of the addition in 1966-67, interest rates had gone up to 7½ percent, but we still thought it was within reason. When the addition was completed, all the internists were put in the new wing. Otolaryngology, orthopedics, and ancillary services such as physical therapy were installed in the lower level of the new wing.

During this time, I made many trips to Chicago to the AMA Building and the Physicians' Placement Service and studied their files to find the names of doctors to contact. I also visited the Chicago hospitals that had residencies in the specialties we needed and talked with senior residents in efforts to get them to consider Aurora as a place in which to practice. It seemed that doctors trained in the Midwest all wanted to go to California or Colorado where they could swim and ski or enjoy the mountains. I found it almost impossible to get doctors trained in other areas to come to the Midwest, so I concentrated mostly on the Midwest graduates. During this time, about 60 percent of Chicago graduates were leaving Illinois. For instance, in 1968 there were eleven senior urology residents in Chicago. I interviewed every one of them, and of the eleven, seven went to California, two stayed in academic medicine in Chicago, and two went out to practice in the Midwest. Of those two, one came to the Dreyer Medical Clinic. That was Dr. Daniel Susmano, who was an excellent addition to our group and a great help to Dr. Kobisk, who was getting ready to retire. The hospitals in Aurora were so happy that we were acquiring new doctors when no others were coming to the community that both Copley and Mercy Center expressed their appreciation for my recruiting work.

XXXI/Professional Responsibilities

By the 1950s I had a very large practice. I had expected work to ease up after the war, but I found that I was working just as long hours, but with more responsibilities. As time went on, I developed more skills in diagnosis and practice than I had ever thought possible. Every year I attended medical meetings for one or two weeks. As we added more internists and specialists to the clinic, I found that every one of them brought new ideas from their residencies. I learned that one of the most important objectives in the Clinic operation was to take in young doctors on a planned, continuing basis. These doctors have had the best of training in the most modern technology, and they bring us new ideas that help us to practice better medicine. During this time, I thoroughly enjoyed my practice; even though I worked hard and didn't have as much time for my family as I would have liked, I was quite happy and contented.

In the 1950s, I was involved in a lot of medically related committee work, especially at Mercy Hospital, where I was on the Board for a number of years and then became president of the staff for two years, 1958 and 1959. This took a great deal of time, but it was valuable experience for me. I served on other committees also and was chairman of the By-laws Committee for fifteen years at Mercy Hospital. In the early 1960s I became secretary of the staff at Copley hospital which meant climbing up the ladder to presidency, in which I served for two years, 1964 and 1965. When I retired from the Copley Board at the age of sixty, I had served in various capacities for twenty years.

In 1963 all of the Aurora hospitals were filled to capacity, and it was obvious that we needed more beds in the city. A study was made by outside consultants, who recommended that we have a combined building drive for funds for Mercy Center and Copley Hospital and that St. Charles Hospital, which was the smallest of the three, should be discontinued as a general hospital and made into a nursing home. Dr. William Blackburn of the Clinic was made chairman of this drive. It was a community effort to raise $6,000,000, which would be divided equally between the two hospitals and would be the basis for a building fund. Dr. Robert Harriage and I were made chairmen of the doctors' division of the building drive, and we worked hard canvassing all the staff. For the most part, our doctors responded magnificently. We raised, altogether, between $450,000 and $500,000 from the doctors alone. Some of the doctors gave as much as $17,000, but the average was approximately $4,000 per doctor. Three or four doctors refused to give anything, saying they did not feel it was their responsibility. I could never understand their reasoning, on this, but it is a free country and one has a right to do as he wants with what he earns. I do remember telling one of the non-contributing doctors, "Mercy Center is going to build a brand new hospital. When it opens and you are admitting patients, I am going to say to you, 'Dr. Blank, isn't this a nice hospital that you didn't help build?'" Two years later, when the hospital was finished, I did just that. It didn't really do any good, but it made me feel better.

Copley Hospital was to have a $10 million addition, and Mercy Center was to build a new hospital from the ground up on land that they owned in the north part of Aurora. The fund drive headed by Dr. Blackburn was oversubscribed by about a million dollars. It was so successful that hospitals all over the country wanted to know how he was so successful when two competing hospitals were involved.

Copley Hospital broke ground immediately, and the addition included all new X-ray facilities, laboratory facilities, emergency rooms, and approximately 120 new beds. Mercy Center was a little slower getting started, but in the early 1970s a 250-bed facility replaced the old 120-bed hospital. When both were opened Aurora had the most modern hospitals of any community of its size in the area.

XXXII/King of the Gypsies

Sometimes things happen that stand out as unusual and remarkable. One morning in the early 1950s, a man came into my office suffering
from chest pains. On examining him and taking an electrocardiogram, I
found that he was critically ill with an acute myocardial infarction and
needed to be hospitalized. Then I became aware that this man was the
King of the Gypsies. There was a large gypsy encampment at Lake
Plano, about twenty miles from Aurora, where they had been through
the fall and winter. I had never before treated a gypsy, and Copley Hospital had never had one as a patient. I did not realize the closeness of the
gypsy family to their king and to each other. The King of the Gypsies
was put in a private room on the third floor of the hospital and was a very
sick man for several weeks. We had a "No Visitors" sign on his door and
told his friends and relatives that not more than one person should visit
him at a time and then for only a few minutes. This did not fit into their
scheme of thinking, and they refused to abide by the order. They came
in three, four, six at a time, sometimes up to ten and crowded into his
room. I am sure it did him no good. They sneaked in the back door,
through the windows, and every other way in order to see the King. At
that time, the administrator of the hospital lived in a house next door and
on the same side of the hospital as the King's room. A number of the
gypsies camped out in the backyard of the administrator's house. That
way, they could run up the fire escape, through the windows or the front
door, or any way they could get in, but they were constantly in the King's
room, and it was very difficult for us to take care of him.

The gypsies kept everyone on edge—the employees, the cleaning
women, doctors, and other patients. The storage cabinets had to be
locked to stop the loss of linens, towels, and other supplies. The King
did gradually improve, and at the end of three weeks they spirited him
away one night and took him back to Plano without the doctor's or the
hospital's permission. They evidently moved the whole tribe to Michigan, as a few months later I read in the paper that the King of the
Gypsies had died in a hospital in Michigan. I don't know much about
gypsies and their life pattern, but I know that neither Copley Hospital nor
I ever got a dime for our care of the King. This experience made such an

impression on Mr. Peterson, the administrator of the hospital, and me that we never forgot it. Twenty-five years later, at his retirement party, he made a speech about things that had happened at Copley while he was there, and one that he stressed was "the time Dr. Greeley admitted the King of the Gypsies as a patient at Copley Hospital."

XXXIII/Experiences with the Schiffer Family

About 1960 I became doctor for a family whose experiences I shared for fifteen years. The Schiffers lived about two miles from Aurora on a twenty-seven-acre farm. The farmhouse was old, run-down, and filthy and looked as if it might fall down any minute. There were two brothers and two sisters—Charlie, Fred, Emma, and Louise. Charlie, Fred, and Emma lived in the big house, and Louise lived in a made-over chicken house about one hundred yards from the house. These buildings and a barn stood in a grove of old trees. The Schiffers raised pigs, had a cow and a horse, and farmed in a small way. The only one who had been married was Louise, and her husband had died years earlier. Fred was a stable person and farmed the land. The other three were quite eccentric. Charlie was mentally handicapped but strong physically. Part of his trouble resulted from his restricted environment, but how much was environment and how much was hereditary no one could tell.

My first contact with the Schiffers was on a Sunday, when I was called off the golf course. I was told that these people needed a doctor right away, that a man was deathly ill and had to be moved to the hospital. I didn't like leaving my game, but I did go. They had called a number of doctors, all of whom had turned them down. When I arrived, I found that Charlie had gone beserk and was threatening to kill everybody with a shotgun. He was being held down by Fred and a neighbor, and all he could say was, "You S.O.B.s, if you let me up I will get my gun and I will kill all of you." Emma was standing around wringing her hands, not knowing what to do.

I gave Charlie a hypo to quiet him down, but it was obvious that he had to be admitted to a mental institution. Mercyville was only a few miles away, but Charlie was very strong and we didn't know how to move him. Since this happened in DuPage County, I called the sheriff's office and asked him if he could help us. He refused me flatly, saying that he didn't want anything to do with it. I tried to explain that Charlie was threatening to kill us if he got loose and that we needed help badly. Again, the sheriff said there was nothing his office could do about it. Finally, I said, "Sheriff, we are dealing with a violent individual. He is threatening to kill all of us with a shotgun if he can get loose. If anything happens here and somebody gets hurt, I will be sure that every newspaper in the county is told how we were turned down by your department." This seemed to shake him up a bit, and he did send a couple of deputies out to help. We were able then to get Charlie to the mental hospital, where he was confined for some time. Over the next ten years, he was confined there on several occasions when he went into one of his bad cycles.

Following this incident, Fred came to my office once in a while to have his blood pressure checked, but for the most part everything was calm. About two years later I received a call about 9:30 at night saying that Charlie was "real sick" and asking me to come right away. I remembered my first experience at the Schiffers' and was somewhat hesitant, but I felt duty bound to go. When I arrived I found one of the most miserable messes I have ever experienced in the practice of medicine. The house was filthy, with dirt everywhere, papers, flies, and cockroaches, and Charlie, black with dirt, was lying on the davenport with dirty blankets over him. He was moaning and groaning and obviously very sick. On examining him, I found that he had a distended abdomen and a bowel obstruction from an incarcerated hernia. I tried to explain to the family that Charlie would have to be hospitalized and would need surgery to correct this condition. Fred could understand this, as he was very stable and sane, but Emma and Charlie could not see why I couldn't just give him a hypo to relieve his pain and then he would be all right by the next morning. Charlie kept begging me for a hypo. I explained what would have to be done, and he had just reached the point where he was ready to go willingly when Emma said, "I know of somebody who went to the hospital and got operated on once and he died." That did it! Charlie balked, "I won't go. I won't go." Finally at my wit's end, I got up, put my stethoscope in my bag, closed it, and said, "Charlie, I will not give you a hypo. You need to go to the hospital, but I can't talk to you any longer. I am going to leave here now, and you will be dead by morning." Hoping my bluff would work, I picked up my bag and started toward the door. I walked slowly, giving him time to think. I was just going out the door when he yelled, "Come back, Dr. Greeley, I'll go." I don't know what I would have done if it hadn't worked. From then on he did not fight the situation further.

In those days, the funeral homes provided ambulance service for Aurora. I called Terry Dieterle, undertaker, and asked him to come and take Charlie to the hospital. This was the first contact Terry had had with the Schiffers, and he was appalled at what he saw. He took Charlie to Copley Hospital, where he was seen at once by one of our surgeons, Dr. Landes. Charlie had had this incarcerated hernia for several days and was in critical condition. He was also so dirty that it took the nurses a long time to get the abdomen cleansed so that they could do any kind of sterile surgery. Dr. Landes operated that night for about five hours. It was very difficult surgery; a piece of gangrenous bowel had to be removed. Finally, at four o'clock in the morning, the repair was done and the patient was taken back to his room in critical condition. It took the nurses four days of giving him baths two or three times a day to get his feet, fingers, and head clean. The long and short of it was that Charlie made a good recovery and was able to go back to the farm in about two weeks.

An interesting sidelight was that when Terry took Charlie to the hospital, Fred rode along in the ambulance. Later he took Fred back to the farm, and Fred asked Terry how much he owed him. Terry felt really sorry for him, thinking he was penniless, and said, "Five dollars." Fred pulled out a roll of bills big enough to choke a cow and gave him a twenty dollar bill, saying, "Keep the change." That was the beginning of a lasting friendship between Terry and the Schiffers.

The Schiffer family was an interesting study in sociology. Louise had a small pension from her deceased husband, but basically she was dependent on Fred, who owned the property and also had saved some money over the years. Her life was spent cleaning her little house, doing garden work, and sometimes helping with the field work. Occasionally Fred took her downtown to do a little shopping. Emma lived in the big house with Fred and Charlie and almost never left the place. Her whole life revolved around taking care of her brothers, doing their cooking and helping with the garden work. She was a very poor housekeeper and also a poor cook, but she was all the Schiffers had. Fred was the stable one of the four, and without him the family would not have survived. As it was, all four of them lived in this small world and had no social contacts, with the exception of a few by Fred. They lacked most modern conveniences. Their house was heated by coal and wood stoves, and water came from an outside well with a pump. They did have electricity, but the house was not well lighted. Fred had acquired the farm during World War II for a very low price. About half of it was tillable, and he raised some corn and other crops. He had an old tractor with which he was able to do some of the farming. He also had a twenty-year-old Cadillac and a forty-year-old Model-T Ford. During World War II he worked in a factory and saved his money. Over the years he had accumulated enough of a bank account that he could get along quite well. Fred felt his responsibility to the family very strongly and never complained. He knew that they could not survive without him. Because they were never on relief and never became wards of the county or the state, the social workers never knew about them. All four of them were suspicious of strangers and wanted to be left alone. So their isolated little world existed on this farm for a great many years.

About two years after my experience with Charlie, I was called to see Louise. She was in far-advanced cardiac failure and almost moribund. I got her into the hospital, and we did everything we could for her, but after about a week she died. Charlie's and Fred's faith in me was severely shaken, and in their narrow thinking, they felt her death was my fault.

They could not accept the fact that this was an elderly woman who had been failing for some time and had not had medical help until she was almost dead. They thought I should have been able to cure her as I did Charlie.

For some time they held this against me and did not come to see me. They were in contact with Terry at times. He conducted Louise's funeral, and she was buried in the cemetery near their childhood home. About two years later I was called one Sunday morning to come out to the Schiffers'. I guess they didn't know whom else to call. When I got to the house, I found Emma lying on the floor, dead, at the foot of the stairs. She had been dead for perhaps two days. She had many bruises over her body and arms, and Fred said that she had fallen down the stairs. I went over her the best I could and thought the bruises could possibly have come from falling down the stairs, but I couldn't help wondering in the back of my mind if Charlie, in one of his violent episodes, had hurt her in some way. It was necessary to call the police and coroner, and after an investigation they concluded that death was accidental. I don't think she weighed over seventy-five or eighty pounds. She had been malnourished and weak for a long time. She had had no medical care and, as Charlie and Fred said, they "just trusted to God that He would make her well again." Terry took over the funeral arrangements, and she was buried beside her sister. Terry was exceedingly good to this family, and they appreciated him.

From that time on, Fred and Charlie began seeing me more often. Fred would come in for a blood pressure checkup occasionally, and he sometimes brought Charlie along. Where there had been four, there were now only two. They still had their own little world in the old farmhouse. If the house was dirty and rundown before Emma died, it was much worse afterwards. I don't think Charlie or Fred ever cleaned the house in any way. The windows were black with dirt and there were no shades. Their food was insanitary and of poor quality. They had disposed of all their livestock and now they had only a dog. During the summer of 1968 the dog died, and they were brokenhearted. Terry provided a small infant casket and dug a grave in the front yard. Neither Fred nor Charlie could do it. Night after night, Charlie would sit in his rocking chair by the dog's grave and cry because he had lost one of his best friends.

During the fall of 1968 Charlie was sick for a while but seemed to recover well. Then during the winter Fred became ill. It was necessary for him to go to the hospital about the last of November, when it was beginning to get cold. The problem was what to do with Charlie while Fred was gone. Terry and I tried to find a place for him, but he refused to go anywhere. He said, in his childish way, that he was going to stay right there on the farm and that he could take care of himself. He wasn't eating. He was crying all the time. He was upset. He had lost his two sisters, and now his only brother was in the hospital. Charlie didn't seem to become violent any more, but he did become quite agitated and upset. He could not be trusted to do anything for himself. I did not leave medication for him because he did not know how to take it. His little world was caving in around him. Since he refused to leave the farm, and we did not want to make him go forcibly, Terry and I alternated in taking him one good meal a day. My wife and I cooked a hot meal and took it out to Charlie for two or three days, and then Terry and his wife did the same. In his simple way, Charlie was very appreciative. We continued providing his meals until Fred died, in early 1969, without ever going home from the hospital.

We knew that Charlie would be upset, and we tried to break the news gently to him and to help him through the trying times ahead. Terry made all of the funeral arrangements. Charlie had no clothes to wear to the funeral except dirty overalls and shirt and work shoes. He was a big man, and so was Fred, about my size. Terry asked me if I didn't have a suit that Charlie might wear to the funeral. I looked through my clothes and found a dark suit that I thought would look well on Charlie. When Violet and I went to the funeral home for visitation, lo and behold! Terry had used my suit for Fred and had gotten Charlie a suit somewhere else. At first we were quite surprised, but as I thought of all my experiences with Fred and of all the things he had gone through for his family and how he had tried to make a home for them against insurmountable odds, it seemed quite all right that Fred should be buried in my suit. I felt good about being able to furnish it for him. Terry arranged for a preacher and a service. The only ones who attended the visitation and the funeral were Terry and his wife, my wife and I, and two distant cousins. In a way, it was too bad that Charlie could not have died first, as he was completely lost after Fred was gone.

When Fred had first become ill, he asked for a lawyer and drew up a will creating a trust that would take care of Charlie as long as there was money left. The trust was to be controlled by the lawyer, Terry, and me. If, when Charlie died, there was any money left after expenses were paid, it would be divided between Terry and me. We agreed, when we talked with Fred, that we would see that Charlie never suffered and that he had good care. Most of the money was tied up in the farm, which was directed to be sold and the money invested. That was done, and the money was kept in trust and paid out as needed for Charlie's expenses.

Following the funeral, it was obvious that Charlie could not stay on the farm any longer. He was put first in a retirement apartment home, but that did not work out because he couldn't get along with the rest of the residents. He was then put into a small nursing home, but there he caused so much trouble that they refused to keep him. He had a short stay at Mercyville, following which he was put in the best nursing home in Aurora. This home was well run, and the nursing staff had years of experience and knew how to handle people like Charlie. It wasn't long before he learned to trust and love all his nurses, and they returned that love. His wants were few. He was somewhat irrational at times, but they

[103]

knew how to handle him, and he followed them around like a puppy. His medication was balanced so that he did not have wild spells any more, and he got along beautifully. He lived about six years after Fred's death. Terry and I visited him occasionally, and he was always glad to see us. Over the years, he gradually deteriorated. In the spring of 1975, he became much worse, and one morning he was found dead in bed. Again, Terry did everything to provide as nice a funeral as possible. He had a beautiful casket, put his obituary in the paper, and arranged for a minister to preach a short service. The only ones at the funeral were Terry and his wife, James Jepson, our clinic administrator, and Violet and I. Charlie was a forgotten man. He was buried with his brother and sisters. It was a sad moment for all of us when Charlie was laid to rest and we realized that the saga of the Schiffer family was over.

One might ask why Terry and I became so involved with the Schiffer family over this fifteen-year period. It certainly wasn't money, although some might accuse us of that. By the time he died, he had used up practically all the money in the estate. Terry and I said many times that we didn't care if we got a dime from the Schiffer estate, that our first obligation was to take care of Charlie as long as he lived. There was only a small amount of money left after all the bills were paid. If Charlie had lived another year, there would have been none left.

Over the years, we had learned to love these simple people in their own little world on Molitor Road. Nobody was ever able to crack that shell except Terry and me. Even though there was a world of difference in our social status, we both enjoyed sitting down in the old house with Fred and Charlie, having a cup of coffee with them, and listening to them talk about their lives. It was a humbling experience for both of us. Maybe the way they lived brought back memories of my childhood, of when I lived in a house that was not much better than the one in which they lived.

XXXIV/Growth of the Clinic 1963 to 1980

After we moved into our new building in 1964, the next ten to fifteen years were probably the most exciting in the development of the Dreyer Medical Clinic. Its growth was steady and controlled. I had recruited about twenty-five doctors since 1963, and very few of our doctors left us. I attribute this low loss of doctors to our policies and to the fact that the doctors were treated fairly. At American Group Practice meetings every year, we became aware of the fact that many clinics had as much as 30 percent loss of medical staff. Comparing our turnover to those clinics, we had an outstanding record.

In 1969 a sad thing happened. Ron Frazer, who had been such a help to us during the planning and building of the new clinic and the addition, developed cerebral symptoms. On diagnostic workup at Northwestern Medical School and Wesley Hospital in Chicago, he was found to have a metastatic melanoma in the brain. In spite of chemotherapy, he became progressively worse. Late in the year it was apparent that we would have to look for another Clinic administrator. We found James Jepson, who came from Austin, Texas, where he had managed a group of internists. He joined our group in early 1970. Shortly afterward Ron Frazer passed away. It was a sad occasion for all of us. He had been a special person, and the Dreyer Medical Clinic missed him very much.

As our clinic staff grew, our services also increased and expanded. We put in further expensive laboratory equipment, added a physical therapy department, and built an excellent orthopedic department. It was a happy time for the doctors in the Clinic, and everybody got along harmoniously. In 1973 we were bursting at the seams again and needed more room. We decided to add an entire third floor to the Clinic building. When that was completed, it gave us room to enlarge existing departments and to add new departments. We added neurology, dermatology, hematology, allergy, orthopedics, and otolaryngology. Whereas our original mortgage had been 5¼ percent and our second mortgage 7½ percent, the interest rate by 1973 was 9 percent. That seemed like a big jump at that time, but it was cheap compared with the current rates of 16 to 18 percent. We now had a multispecialty clinic with most specialties

The Dreyer Medical Clinic after expansion in 1973.

represented, all in one building, all using the same equipment. It was a remarkable institution.

During this time, both of the Aurora hospitals completed expansions, which insured their place among the fine hospitals in the suburban Chicago area. We could not do open-heart surgery and coronary bypass operations, but we conceded that some things were just not feasible in Aurora. The hospitals in Chicago were only about forty-five minutes away, and it worked out very well to refer such cases to them. The doctor shortage continued into the mid-1970s, and it was still hard to get the best doctors. During this time, foreign medical graduates became available, and many of them set up practices in Aurora. Both hospitals started twenty-four-hour emergency room services in which doctors were present at all times.

The number of full-time Clinic employees grew from twenty-seven, when we moved into our own building, to approximately 175 full-time lay employees by 1980. James Jepson was instrumental in getting computer services for our accounts receivable. At first I opposed the move as just extra expense, but I was proved wrong. The Board out-voted me, and it proved to be a very wise move. It enabled us to keep efficient records of the day-to-day operation of the Clinic's increased business. At any time, one could get instant reports on exactly what the Clinic was doing financially and what every doctor and department were billing and collecting—quite remarkable information.

XXXV/Our Travels

On our twenty-fifth wedding anniversary we were invited to dinner by close friends in a nearby town. When we arrived we realized that something unusual was happening. We had just greeted our friends when out of a neighboring room came our three children. We were greatly surprised since they were supposed to be in school—Richard was in California in graduate school at Stanford, Donald was at the University of Illinois at Champaign, and Barbara was at Illinois State University at Normal. Then we found that a number of our other friends were there, also, and that this was a party in honor of our anniversary.

The children presented us with a first-class ticket to England on the Queen Mary, to be used in July of the following year. They said they couldn't afford a round-trip ticket, but they would give us the return ticket on our fiftieth anniversary. We next asked, "Where did you get enough money to buy the one-way ticket?" This was explained as follows: All three children had worked in 4-H Clubs when they were in grade school and high school, and the money they had earned from projects they had invested in E-Bonds. To get us a present they had cashed in all their bonds. It was a very touching experience for us. We had never traveled outside the United States, and our children thought this would be a good chance to give us a little push to see the world.

As it turned out, we combined the voyage to England with a trip to Norway, Sweden, and Denmark, a tour that started after we got to London. It was a wonderful experience, and my wife and I decided that we should do more globetrotting.

Our travels followed a pattern. I worked hard all year, and then we took three to four weeks off in the summer for a trip. Over the next twelve years we visited forty-four countries. We went to the British Isles, Scandinavia, the Russian bloc countries, and central Europe. We visited southern and central Africa, western South America, Mexico and Canada, the South Pacific Islands and Australia, Japan and Southeast Asia. We had many exciting experiences and learned a lot about how people in other countries live. We came to realize how big our world is and how insignificant is the little corner of the earth in which we live and die. I am sure we both have a much greater tolerance for other people's ideas and activities than we ever had before. When we returned from some of the

The Greeley family: (standing) sons Donald and Richard, (seated) Harry and Violet Greeley and daughter Barbara.

poor areas, such as Africa, it was with increased appreciation for what we have at home. After our trip to Russia and the eastern European countries, we were thankful for what the United States has developed and the freedom that we enjoy. I don't suppose seeing all those countries made a better doctor of me, but it did give me a better appreciation of other peoples and nations.

XXXVI/The Miracle of the Pacemaker

"Doc, am I going to die?" Charles Smith asked nervously.

"Charlie, you are a very sick man. You are eighty-two years old, and your heart is not working as it should. The problem is in the conduction system of the heart—that is the system by which the impulses are carried down from the top of the heart to the lower portion and make it beat at a certain speed. Recently, they have discovered a new way of making the heart beat at a normal rate again. It is what they call a 'pacemaker.'"

Charlie listened intently as I continued. "It has been used with considerable success in cases like yours. We would like to have your permission to try the pacemaker on you."

"I am eighty-two years old. Do you think it will work on a man that old?"

"We don't know for sure. We do know, though, that your heart is at the end of its rope if left as it is. Over the past twelve hours your heart rate has dropped to about twenty-five to thirty beats a minute. In spells its rate is only ten times a minute, and it goes ten to fifteen seconds without beating at all."

Charlie nodded. He knew the feeling very well.

"To install a pacemaker, we put what we call an 'electrode' down the jugular vein of the neck, clear down to the right ventricle of the heart. The electrode is then attached to a battery mechanism that we implant under the skin just below the clavicle. The battery gives off impulses that make the heart beat at about seventy-five times a minute, and the battery will last about eighteen months."

"Well I sure would like to try it. I'm not feeling very good this way. When can it be done?"

"The Medtronics Company makes these pacemakers, and they can have one out here in about two hours. In the meantime, we could be getting you ready for the operation. It will be done under local anesthesia, so you will know what is being done at all times."

"Well, let's get going. I'm so short of breath, I don't know what to do."

That was the conversation between Charlie and me before we implanted the first pacemaker that had ever been put in place in Aurora. A few Aurora people had received pacemakers in Chicago, but we didn't think that we could move Charlie safely. Charlie had a very active mind for eighty-two years of age and a terrific sense of humor. He was not afraid of death if it happened, but of course he wanted to live if he could.

After a few telephone calls, the Medtronics pacemaker arrived at St. Joseph Hospital and we prepared for the operation. We had to work fast, as Charlie's condition was quite precarious. In spite of drugs, his heart did not respond and seemed to be going slower and slower. We knew that death was impending. It was only a matter of time until his heart failed.

Dr. James Sandrolini had catheterized many hearts, so it was not hard for him to insert the electrode through the jugular vein into the right atrium and through the tricuspid valve into the right ventricle. The procedure was painless after the local anesthesia took effect. Since this was a first for everyone in the operating room, there was a good deal of tension in the air, even though everyone acted very calm. As the electrode passed through from the atrium to the ventricle, it caused some irritation that resulted in a few seconds of arrhythmia, and the ventricle went into ventricular tachycardia. This lasted only a few seconds and then it settled down to a slow, almost stopped rhythm. The electrode was now in place, and the heart rate was approximately ten a minute. Charlie was getting oxygen, but he was still cyanotic and very pale. We attached the other end of the electrode wires to the pacemaker. The time had come to turn on this new instrument to see if it would work. Everybody was tense, and an air of expectation and excitement filled the room. The pacemaker was turned on and promptly took over. Charlie's heart almost immediately began to beat at the rate of seventy-five times a minute. His blood pressure, which had been low, came up to normal. Almost at once, Charlie started to talk and exclaimed, "Boy, do I feel better! I feel alive again."

I said, "Charlie, we were able to brush St. Peter off your shoulder, and if this instrument works as it is supposed to, you may live for a long time yet."

It was a simple surgical procedure for Dr. Sandrolini to implant the battery under the skin, in the soft tissues just below the right clavicle, and Charlie was brought back from the operating room feeling much better. He was kept quiet for a few days, but it wasn't very long before he went home. His heart continued to beat well. The first battery of the pacemaker lasted about eighteen months, at which time it was not difficult to operate and put in another one.

Charlie, who was almost dead when we put in the first pacemaker, lived for another six years, and most of that time he had a good quality of life. His mind was good, he enjoyed being with people, and he enjoyed the bonus of the extra years that we were able to give him. Charlie was very independent, and when we put in the last battery he told us, "This is it. I am eighty-eight years old, and when this battery runs down, I am ready to quit." We kidded him and said, "When the time comes, you will want another battery." That was not the case. When his battery ran down, Charlie refused to have another put in, and he died peacefully six years after the first pacemaker was inserted.

Since that time, many pacemakers have been implanted, and they have been improved so greatly that they now last eight to ten years without a battery change. The first pacemaker was about as big as a pack of cigarettes, but now they are less than half that size and make little bulge under the skin. Pacemakers can be implanted in people of all ages, although most of them are in older people. I titled this chapter "The Miracle of the Pacemaker," and a miracle it is. It has resulted in many more years of life for many people.

XXXVII/Other Miracles in Medicine

To describe all the advances that have been made in medicine in my lifetime would take volumes. I shall mention only a few and tell how they affected my practice and what they have meant to mankind.

As I grew up, there were three diseases that I feared most—poliomyelitis, tuberculosis, and stroke. I feared polio all through college, medical school, and up until 1954. In that year, the Salk and Sabin vaccines for polio immunization were discovered, and I have not seen a case since.

The second disease, tuberculosis, struck my brother George as a young man. I saw how he suffered and hemorrhaged from it. I realized that it was contagious and that in taking care of a large number of patients I might be exposed to it frequently. I could visualize myself with a lung half gone, coughing up blood, and almost at death's door. When I started practice, the treatment for tuberculosis was primarily rest. Most counties had sanitariums or had access to them. All TB cases were isolated, which was a good thing for the general public. The poor patient who had tuberculosis looked forward to two or three years of confinement, and even then he might become chronically ill or suffer further progression of his disease and die. It was a miserable existence at best. Then research doctors discovered Isoniazid and Rifampin, which revolutionized the treatment of tuberculosis. Tuberculosis could now be treated and arrested. The need for sanitariums was over, and within a few years practically all of them were closed. Now the tuberculosis patient is treated in a general hospital with the new drugs and usually is back at work in a month or two. The incidence of tuberculosis declined sharply in countries where these drugs are available, but the disease is certainly not eradicated. In countries where the drugs are not used or are not available, and where sanitation is poor and many people live in crowded conditions, tuberculosis is still a killer. However, we have found the key. If we can get the knowledge and the drugs dispersed around the world to the needy areas, millions of lives can be saved.

The third illness that concerned me was a stroke that might paralyze but not kill. It might even cause complete mental and personality changes. A person could be partially or completely paralyzed, be a complete invalid, and still live for years. That is still a possibility, but the incidence of stroke has gone down considerably in the past fifteen years. When I first started practicing medicine, little could be done for high blood pressure besides mild sedation and low-sodium diets, but in the last few years many drugs have been developed for hypertension, or high blood pressure. The types of hypertension have been classified, and treatment for each has been perfected. We are slowly but surely unlocking the mysteries of disease and are able to do more for the sick than we have ever done before. We can't rest on our laurels, however, because many challenges still lie ahead.

There have been other great discoveries. When I started practice, antibiotics were just coming into use. Sulfa drugs had been discovered, and at the end of World War II penicillin became available. Since then, many antibiotics have been developed that are effective against different types of bacteria. Nowadays when we see a severe infection, our first act is to get a culture and grow the bacteria that are causing the trouble. Then we test the organism against a series of antibiotics that are likely to be effective and use the antibiotic that proves to be the best.

The research on cancer deserves high praise. Many scientists all over the civilized world are working on this problem, and I am sure that in the next generation it will be solved. When we see friends and relatives dying of cancer, some at an early age, we become depressed and think that we haven't come very far. There are, however, many cancers that we can help. We have come a long way in the treatment of leukemias, and certain types of leukemia can be completely cured. Hodgkin's disease, if diagnosed at an early stage, can be cured. Cancer of the testicles has an 80 to 90 percent cure rate with modern chemotherapy drugs. One can name cancer after cancer that has been at least partially controlled by the new array of drugs that are available. Treatment has become so complex that we now need specialists, called oncologists, who do nothing but treat cancer. There still is a long way to go, as there are some cancers for which we can do very little. Some of those are of our own making. It is a sad commentary on human nature that one of the most prevalent cancers, cancer of the lung, which takes 100,000 lives a year, could be practically abolished if people would quit smoking. Nicotine is one of the worst and most dangerous addictions that we have. Anything that causes 100,000 deaths a year from lung cancer, and possibly 200,000 more from cardiovascular disease, certainly should be banned for human use.

The key to the most effective treatment of cancer is early discovery. It always made me sad when a patient came into my office for a Pap smear, not having had one for five years, or ever, and I found that she had an incurable cancer of the cervix. That shouldn't happen in this day and age, but it does. Early cancer of the cervix is curable, but after it has spread outside the cervix into other organs and through the lymphatic vessels, it is very difficult to treat successfully. Breast cancer, if it is found early, is about 70 percent curable, but if neglected it is 100 percent fatal. It is very important that women be educated in the value of self-examination of the breasts and periodic checkups of the breasts and cervix by a doctor.

Another cancer that can be cured if found early is a colorectal cancer. Generally, this type is being found much earlier by the use of proctoscope and X-rays. Here, again, it is very important that we educate the public to the dangers of this cancer and how to recognize the symptoms.

One of the greatest achievements of this country is the eradication of smallpox (I have never seen a case in my lifetime). Few people are aware of the human devastation this disease has caused in the past. Millions of people have been scarred, blinded, or have died of smallpox. It has been worse in countries where sanitation was poor, but before the use of smallpox vaccine it was seen worldwide. It was a killer disease. As late as 1975 there was a smallpox epidemic in Bangladesh in which 130,000 people contracted the disease and over 30,000 of them died. Through the efforts of many agencies, spearheaded by the World Health Organization, doctors and nurses went into those areas and vaccinated and educated people. They were so successful in their efforts that in late 1979 they announced that there had not been an active case of smallpox reported for two years. Now, some four years later, as far as I know there still is no active smallpox in the whole world. That is truly one of the great achievements of this century.

Aside from the new medicines, of which I have mentioned only a few, there have been many surgical advances. When I started practice, surgeons were trained to take out gallbladders and appendices and perform colostomies, but extensive surgery was not known. Over the years, our great research institutions developed the finest surgeons the world has ever known, and surgical techniques advanced to a point never before attained. One of the most dramatic areas is in cardiovascular surgery. When I was an intern and scrubbed with surgeons, the nearest we came to the heart was to take out a lung, and I was warned that one had to be careful not to traumatize the heart or it might go into a fatal arrhythmia and the patient would die. As time went on and surgeons became bolder, they found that the heart is really a very rugged piece of machinery that can be taken apart and put back together again. Any valve can be replaced one or more times.

During my early practice, patients with rheumatic heart disease usually had a mitral stenosis or mitral insufficiency, which is a damaged heart valve, and little could be done for them except give them digitalis and diuretics. It was generally known that they would not live to be over thirty-five or forty years of age. All that changed when some brilliant surgeon found that he could enter the heart and dilate the mitral valves in what we call a commissurotomy. Later, scientists made valves to replace the damaged ones, and now these people can live almost a normal life span with artificial heart valves. That was only the beginning of the heart surgery that has been done in the last generation. Surgeons have been able to take out aortic aneurysms, which they would not have thought of touching a generation ago. They have been able to completely replace diseased hearts with other hearts. Although this is not a common operation, it has been relatively successful. More research and further evaluation are required before it can become commonplace.

Orthopedic surgery has made advances that were not thought possible twenty-five years ago. Specialists replace hips, knees, and many other joints. Surgery on intervertebral discs has become common. There is no field of surgery that hasn't made such advances that it is difficult to keep up with the new information.

XXXVIII/Resistance to Scientific Medicine

I hadn't been in practice long before I realized that many people do not trust scientific medicine but elect to believe in miracles and faith cures instead. Among them are some of the best-educated people. Shortly after I began practice, a college graduate came to see me and told me about the miracle cure she had had for pain in her back and legs. She had been in Chicago to see some type of healer, not an M.D., who told her that her ills came from the groin and that by manipulation and massage of the flank and groin areas he could cure all disease. He proceeded to massage the inguinal area on both sides and she felt instant relief of her pain. She came to see me to urge me to send other patients to this "miracle man." As so often happens, her pain returned shortly afterward and did not respond to his miracle treatments the next time.

Another example of quackery is the use of copper bracelets for arthritis. There is no scientific basis for belief that these have ever helped arthritis. Yet people from all walks of life believe in them and come into my office wearing copper bracelets on legs or arms. It is futile to explain that this could have no value in the treatment of the disease because they wouldn't believe me. A doctor finally gives up and goes ahead with his own treatment, ignoring the bracelet.

Over the years I have seen a number of patients who felt that if they had enough faith, it would cure all diseases and no medication would be needed. Their religion teaches that faith can be reinforced through hearing Bible passages. The official readers of this religion make a living by accepting fees for this method of treatment. I had a near neighbor who had serious asthma and cardiovascular disease but refused all treatment and finally died from the disease. I am sure that if he had had cardiac medications he would have lived much longer and more comfortably.

I knew a lawyer's wife who did not believe in doctors until she became ill with acute appendicitis. When that developed, she lost no time in having her appendix removed, which was done successfully.

Another case involved a man of about fifty years of age who developed severe pneumonia. His wife urged him repeatedly to go to a doctor, but he refused. I had seen him before for lacerations that required minor surgery, and that was not against his religion. This time, he developed double pneumonia and died. With the antibiotics now available, we almost never lose a case of pneumonia in a man that age. I am sure that he would be alive today if we could have used antibiotics.

The human trait of wanting to believe in something miraculous makes it easy for charlatans to prescribe unproven medications and cancer "cures" of various kinds. They know that desperate people will come to them. Over the years of my practice, I have seen many cancer "cures" come and go. The two that received the most publicity were krebiozen and laetrile. Krebiozen was developed by an eastern European and introduced into this country with a lot of fanfare and the help of the media so that practically every terminal cancer patient was asking for it. Even some prominent scientists thought there might be something promising in krebiozen. I never believed that it had a scientific basis or that it would help cancer, but if a patient brought the drug to me I obliged him by administering it. That happened only a few times. Eventually krebiozen was analyzed and found to contain only inert material. Today it is only history.

Laetrile is of more recent origin and is still used in some states for terminal cancers. I have had patients who, knowing that they had fatal cancer, went to Mexico to take the drug. Without exception, they died within a few months, sooner than they would have if they had taken chemotherapy as prescribed by our oncologists. Although laetrile is still being used, it has been found to be toxic because of the cyanide in the peach pits from which it is made. It is fast fading from the scene of medicine.

There is something about human nature that makes people want to believe in miracles. For this reason, the witch doctors of Africa and Samoa have large followings. The field of nonscientific medicine is so vast that I can do no more than touch on the ways that it affected my practice. I certainly can sympathize with people who have an incurable disease and are willing to spend thousands of dollars in hope of finding a miracle cure. Charlatans take advantage of their desperation and become rich.

XXXIX/Changes in Drug Use During My Lifetime

I will never cease to be amazed at the human race, which has made fantastic advances in complex sciences and can be so efficient and inventive and yet so irresponsible about things that are damaging. People will take care of their cars—grease them, put air in the tires, put gas in the tank, and keep them spotlessly clean—but when it comes to their own bodies, the same concern does not hold true. One would expect health to be the first priority, but nothing is more neglected than the human body. People put so many things into it that don't belong there. Harmful drugs gain social acceptance. It is difficult to explain these aberrations.

The human being is always searching for new experiences, but often he cannot see how much harm those experiences can do him. I will start with the growth of habit patterns in the legally and socially accepted drugs, that is, alcohol and tobacco, concentrating principally on what has happened during my lifetime. I will then comment on other abused drugs with which we have to contend today.

Alcohol

Although socially accepted, alcohol does more harm than all other drugs put together. It has been used at least as far back as biblical times. In the early part of this century, there was a movement to outlaw alcohol because of the harm it was doing to individuals and to the family structure. This resulted in 1918 in the passage of the Eighteenth Amendment to the U.S. Constitution, which prohibited the sale of alcoholic beverages. The amendment was repealed in 1933. Undoubtedly considerable bootleg liquor was sold in the 1920s and early 1930s, and the alcohol interests used this information to convince the American public that there was much more drinking under Prohibition than before. That was not true. Studies have shown that consumption was down and that alcohol-related deaths were greatly reduced during Prohibition. Until 1933 I had never encountered drinking in the two high schools I attended nor among the young people with whom I associated. Since

Prohibition was repealed, statistics show that alcohol usage has increased manyfold per person. Prohibition never had a chance because the liquor interests did everything they could to convince the public that the amendment should be repealed.

Following repeal, the consumption of alcohol grew by leaps and bounds. I was influenced by the propaganda as well as everyone else, and I came to a point in my life where I had to decide whether to be a social drinker or not. I had already left home, and it wasn't long before I was presented with opportunities to drink. I gave it a lot of thought, realizing that my grandfather had been an alcoholic and that there was some question that the tendency might be hereditary. I tried to analyze how I would be better off physically or mentally if I drank. Peer pressure was great, but I decided it was dangerous for me and I would not be a part of it. I have not been sorry for this decision. Once I had made up my mind, there was never a problem. During my whole lifetime I have been a "teetotaler."

I have seen the awful effects of alcohol on people and families. It damages the body and changes the personality when taken in excess. The effects are horrendous. In a day when we all drive fast vehicles, there are thirty thousand auto accident deaths a year that can be directly attributed to the effects of alcohol. It is also mind-boggling to think that one out of every fifteen people who drink will become an alcoholic. That is a high percentage: as you walk down the street, one out of every fifteen people you meet will have a drinking problem in his lifetime. The liquor industry has so brainwashed the public through advertising that most people do drink.

Alcohol abuse is a progressive disease. The progression from one stage to another is usually not recognized until there are lost jobs, personality changes, broken homes, or suicide attempts. In addition to the mental changes brought on by alcohol, continued heavy drinking causes cirrhosis, brain atrophy, alcoholic gastritis, and innumerable other problems. In the practice of medicine, alcoholism has been one of the most difficult diseases to treat. When a person becomes addicted to alcohol, he cannot comprehend the fact that he is sick, and without treatment he will go downhill until he dies from cirrhosis or from an accident. In the mid-1950s medical science recognized alcoholism as a disease. Up to that time, people who became alcoholics were treated as if they had done it on purpose and could control it if they tried. Nothing could be further from the truth. When an alcoholic reaches a certain point, he can no longer control his mind or body, and he becomes a slave to the drug.

The fellowship of Alcoholics Anonymous was formed in 1935 and helped many drinkers; in fact, it was the best treatment that had been devised up to that point. In the '60s and '70s alcoholic treatment centers began to appear all over the country. Most of them were serious institutions researching the best way to tackle the alcohol problem. I have seen these treatment centers develop and feel that many of them do an outstanding job. They completely isolate the alcoholic for a period of three to four weeks, or until they feel he is ready to return to the pressures of society. Sometimes that takes many months. First, the alcoholic is completely detoxified, and then he participates in educational lectures, counseling, and discussions to "get his head on straight." After discharge he is advised to go to Alcoholics Anonymous two to three times a week. Some treatment centers maintain half-way houses where they follow the patients' progress.

An alcoholic can never let down his guard; he is an alcoholic for life. Further drinking will result in a return of the disease, and it may be harder to break away the next time. A certain number of alcoholics relapse after they leave the treatment centers, but the number of arrested cases ranges as high as 80 to 85 percent. When I started practice, it was common to think of the alcoholic as being a skid-row bum. Today, we realize that alcoholism is no respecter of sex, age, or affluence. It is seen in the best of families and in women just as often as men. There is no question that we have more alcoholics today than ever before. Every newspaper, every magazine, practically every television show and radio program in some way advertises to the public that they must drink, that it should be a part of everybody's life. The hazards are, of course, minimized or ignored. The liquor industry has done a great job of transforming our society from one where only about 40 percent of the people drank to one where 80 to 85 percent do. It is a sad commentary on human intelligence.

I feel that the treatment of alcoholism offers a great challenge to a doctor who is concerned about his patients. Moderate use of alcohol can be a pleasurable experience and can seem to enhance social affability; still one cannot overlook the tremendous damage that has been done by its use. The human race learns slowly, and I feel that it will be a long time before the problem can be controlled adequately. Nothing in medicine is less understood by physicians than the treatment of alcoholism. Most doctors receive little instruction on this in medical school, and they fall into the trap of thinking it is a disease that can be controlled by willpower. It is customary to send alcoholic patients to psychiatrists, but that has not proved to be successful. Most psychiatrists are poorly trained in the treatment of alcoholism and invariably try to find psychological causes. They blame the parents or the spouse of the alcoholic and so turn the patient against the very ones who love him and want to help him. Treatment of alcoholism is complex and requires the cooperation of many people. The backing of family members is all-important, as they have to participate in treatment. A good alcoholic program, lasting from three to six weeks, followed by AA or a half-way house, has proven to be the best therapy so far.

Tobacco

What can I say about tobacco and nicotine addiction? Volumes have been written about it, so I will confine my comments to the changes in the use of tobacco during my lifetime.

The pleasures of using tobacco have been known for several hundred years. Until World War I, however, tobacco use was limited to cigars, pipes, or chewing tobacco. After the war, cigarettes became popular, at first among men, but later among women also. The nicotine in tobacco, regardless of form, is the substance that gives the pleasure, the high, and the mental stimulation. The tars and carbon monoxide are undoubtedly the cause of a lot of the lung cancers that have developed after many years of smoking. As I look back, I am thankful that I did not become addicted to nicotine. It would have been easy to do. Most of the boys in my neighborhood and at high school learned to smoke at an early age. I tried smoking cornsilks a few times, but that only gave me a bad taste in my mouth. I am sure that if it hadn't been for my father's counsel, I probably would have smoked like everyone else. He told me in such a rational way about the effects that I didn't want to become addicted. I can remember so well his saying, "Harry, there are certain drugs and substances that when taken by human beings cause addiction. These drugs cause changes in the body metabolism so that the cells become completely dependent on their being present in small amounts at all times. Anybody will become addicted to nicotine if exposed to it long enough. It may take just a few cigarettes, several packs, or maybe several months of smoking, but you can count on it that it will cause an addiction that is very hard to break. All people start experimenting, thinking that they can quit anytime they want to. They do not realize until too late that they have to have that cigarette." Because what he said seemed so rational, I decided then that I would never take up smoking, and I did not even try a cigarette until after medical school. I not only didn't want to become addicted; I couldn't afford the cost. Since then, I have smoked fewer than eight or ten cigarettes altogether in my lifetime.

In the 1930s, primarily because of advertising pressure from the tobacco companies, more and more women began smoking. At first only the bolder women smoked, but during and after World War II the habit was adopted by as many women as men. When I was in medical school, research had not yet proven all the harm that tobacco tars and carbon monoxide could do. When I was a senior, I helped a pulmonary surgeon in Chicago take out a cancerous lung. He told me then that practically every lung cancer he removed was in a cigarette smoker and that the mortality rate was approximately 100 percent.

As time went on and more research was done, it became clear that lung cancer cases were increasing steadily every year, especially in men. I attended the medical meeting in Atlantic City in the early 1950s when the original Hammond and Horn work was brought out showing irrefutable evidence that there is a definite connection between cigarette smoking and lung cancer. The tobacco companies screamed to high heaven and insisted that it wasn't so. Since that time, there have been over 30,000 papers reporting on research done on the effects of tobacco in lung cancer and cardiovascular disease, and almost 100 percent of them show a definite causal relationship. In spite of this overwhelming evidence, the Tobacco Institute, which represents the major tobacco companies, says it isn't so. One wonders how the men who run those companies can sleep at night knowing the statistics and realizing that there are 100,000 lung cancers a year, 95 percent of which are going to be fatal, and another 300,000 cardiovascular deaths that have been caused or precipitated by smoking. The expensive advertising campaigns to get people to smoke continue to grow. The tobacco companies know full well that all they have to do is get a young person to smoke a few packages of cigarettes and he is hooked for life. It is so inconsistent that the government brings out all kinds of literature about the harmful effects of tobacco to get people to quit smoking, and on the other hand subsidizes the tobacco planters to raise more tobacco so that people can smoke more. We have all seen the advertisement showing a beautiful, liberated young woman with a cigarette and captioned, "You've come a long way baby." Women certainly have come a long way from the day when there were almost no lung cancers in women to the present day when, because of smoking, there are 40,000 cases a year. It is recognized that women have a harder time breaking the nicotine habit than men do, and still they are taking up smoking in greater numbers all the time. The terrific peer pressure and advertising make it hard for them to escape.

Other Addictive Drugs

During the 1960s and 1970s there was steady growth in the use of marijuana, heroin, LSD, amphetamines, tranquilizers, and other drugs. All of these drugs have bad side effects, and some are addicting. Marijuana, especially, has gained a great foothold in the United States. The effects are not all known, but research results so far sound ominous. My wife taught high school at Naperville, Illinois, from 1967 to 1977. During that time it began to be popular to smoke marijuana. She observed early that the boys and girls who smoked marijuana daily became apathetic and indifferent and lost all ambition even if they had been good students before. She could see a definite mental deterioration in them. At first, published studies said that marijuana didn't hurt anybody and wasn't as harmful as tobacco. In the past few years, however, research has shown quite clearly what my wife observed ten years ago—that it has definite and long-lasting mental effects. In addition, the smoke is very irritating to the lungs, and no one knows what the long-range effects will be. It also has lasting effects on other organs of the body, mainly the liver, but the extent of these effects is not yet proven.

Here, again, one wonders about the future of the human race when people deliberately addict themselves to drugs that are capable of so much harm. I only hope and pray that we will all wake up before it is too late. There seems to be more awareness now of the hazards of tobacco in lung cancer, and more and more people are quitting smoking, especially men. Perhaps it is a sign that our civilization is beginning to recognize the hazards and will do something to lessen the use of these drugs.

XL/The Tragedy of Wilcox

On September 8, 1925, my youngest brother, Wilcox, was born the day before my mother's forty-sixth birthday. I am sure that my parents had not planned this pregnancy, as my younger brother, Clarence, was then eight years old and my mother was almost past childbearing age. Nevertheless, Wilcox was loved by all the family and soon took his own place in our lives. He seemed normal, both mentally and physically, and was a bright, amiable boy. Unfortunately, when he was about four years old the depression came on full force and the family began to disintegrate. It was more and more difficult for my mother to cope. My father was working hard on the farm but was unable to make a decent living when the price of corn went down to ten cents a bushel, oats to four cents a bushel, and hogs brought only four to five dollars a hundred pounds at market.

Wilcox started to school at the age of six in the same country schoolhouse that his brothers and sisters had attended. He learned rapidly and got along well with his teacher and apparently with the other boys and girls. When he was seven, something happened that was the turning point in his whole life. That was the year I left home.

After I had gone, my mother was so upset to think that she had lost a boy who could have done the farm work for nothing that she stated publicly and to the rest of the family that she was going to be sure Wilcox never grew up to be like his brother Harry. She clamped down on him completely. She did not let him associate with other boys or participate in any school activities. He was to go to school and come home immediately afterwards. At no time was he permitted to play with the neighbor children, nor did she allow them to come to our house. This completely thwarted his social development, and his little world was confined to home on the farm with his mother, father, and his older brothers George and Clarence. George's many illnesses had hampered his own social adjustment to a great extent.

As soon as Wilcox was old enough, he was put to work in the fields and was expected to help with the chores. He was a good worker, although he lacked initiative and had to be told everything to do. He did well in his studies through the eighth grade and graduated first in his class, but he was completely antisocial. He could not relate to other boys and girls his age. By the time he entered high school, busing had been instituted, and the Virginia school bus picked him up every day. He still was not allowed to participate in any school activities. He never had any friends his own age, and there was no way he could grow up to be a normal, socially well-adjusted boy. When the depression became worse, Wilcox had practically no clothes to wear to school other than a shirt and overalls, which were conspicuously unlike the clothes the other boys wore. He was looked upon as "different" by his peers. Whereas he had been an excellent student in the lower grades, in high school he lost interest, and his work and grades deteriorated to the point that he barely graduated at the age of eighteen.

As time went on, Wilcox developed many antisocial tendencies. When he and George went into a neighboring town, Wilcox tried to find small children with whom he could play. He did not know how to adjust to anybody in his own age group, and his abnormal social tendencies increased. Although our neighbors were nice to him, they regarded him as very queer and were afraid to have him play with their children for fear he might harm them physically or sexually. During all this time, my mother refused to face the fact that he was abnormal and that probably a lot of his strangeness was due to the way he was raised.

After Wilcox graduated from high school, he and George settled down to working on the farm and did not try to do anything else. Neither of them was ever given a penny for the work they did, and they lacked all the modern conveniences that were becoming available in that day. During World War II, Wilcox received his draft notice, but when he took his physical he was rejected as mentally and physically unfit for service. Wilcox could not have survived outside an institution if he had not lived on a farm that was fairly well isolated from other people. There he was able to keep busy with the farm work under supervision.

By the late 1940s, my folks did have an old car, which George drove occasionally to Jacksonville or Arenzville and took Wilcox with him. On one trip to Jacksonville, Wilcox slipped away from George and for some reason put a piece of iron on the railroad tracks. I don't believe he did it with the idea of wrecking the train, but rather of seeing how flat the iron would be mashed by the train's wheels. I do not think he realized the consequences. He was caught before a train came along and was arrested. At his trial, it was obvious that he was not responsible for his acts, and he was sent to a mental institution in Jacksonville. He stayed there for some time, but the psychiatrists felt that they could do nothing for him and that he would be safe on the farm, so he was released. He went back to his old life, helping on the farm and living in his own world, occasionally getting down to Arenzville, always with George so that he could not get into trouble again. He lost further stable influences when our father died in 1950. His thwarted life continued until 1962, when the home finally broke up because of the illness of my mother. Mother finally consented to leave the farm and live with my sister Cynthia in

Waterman, where she would receive the care she needed. She failed steadily and died in 1963.

There was no way that I or any of my sisters or brothers could have Wilcox live with us; he was so maladjusted that he required constant supervision. He was first taken to Mercyville, where he was evaluated, then committed to a mental hospital in Elgin. Members of his family were able to visit him occasionally, and sometimes he was allowed to go home with us for short trips.

In the early 1970s the State of Illinois instituted a program to decentralize its mental patients, feeling that many of them could be cared for in half-way houses and in nursing home-type situations. Wilcox was sent to a home in Chicago, where he lived for about a year, but he did not do well. In 1972 he developed an acute illness and died within forty-eight hours, at the age of forty-seven.

Wilcox was buried at Waterman in a part of the cemetery where many of his relatives were buried. It was a sad day for the brothers and sisters who were left. I am sure that all of us had some pangs of conscience and wondered if anything we could have done would have made a difference in Wilcox's life. I, especially, wondered if Wilcox would have developed normally if I had stayed on the farm instead of leaving home. However, had I stayed there much longer, I probably would have developed some abnormal tendencies of my own, and that wouldn't have helped Wilcox very much.

In trying to analyze it, one has to feel that Wilcox was born into a situation over which he had no control but which had a profound influence on his social development. There is no question that he had a tragic and unhappy life from the time he was a little boy. The stubborn insistence of my mother that he not be allowed to socialize was undoubtedly a large factor in his abnormal development. My mother, herself, developed many abnormalities because of her unhappy situation caused by the depression and lack of money. Her inability to cope with adversity caused disaster in the development of her family. One can only speculate how the lives of her husband and children might have been different had the depression never occurred.

XLI/Interesting People

An Aurora Lawyer

When one practices medicine for thirty-eight years, patients become close friends and the doctor becomes an integral part of many families. I had been in practice only four months when Dr. Denney sent me to see an Aurora lawyer, aged sixty-five, who had complained of chest pain. I found him in his office in severe pain and obviously having a myocardial infarction. He was rushed to the hospital, and for a number of days it was not known whether he would live or die. On the second day, I went to the hospital to see him only to find that he had no blood pressure and was deteriorating rapidly. The house doctor had informed his wife that he probably would not live more than a few minutes or hours. In those days we did not have sophisticated medications for this type of illness, but as a last measure I gave him adrenalin, to which his heart responded and brought his pressure back to a livable level. I continued to give him adrenalin every four hours for the next three or four days. This man of sixty-five made a good recovery and lived for another twenty-six years. He was very grateful for the care I had given him, and we became fast friends until his death. I came to recognize him as an unusual person with a strong personality and mental alertness that did not fail him even when he was over ninety years of age.

Shortly after recovering from his heart attack, he called me at the office and asked if I would come to the Leland Hotel, as he wanted me to meet some people. I found him in the midst of a serious business meeting with a number of well-known lawyers and newspaper publishers. He introduced me to all of them and said, "This is the doctor who saved my life." For a young doctor who had been in practice only a few months, that certainly made me feel good.

This man had other physical problems besides coronary heart disease, the main one being severe rheumatoid- and osteo-arthritis, progressive in character. It wasn't long after I first saw him that he began using a cane continually. Later he needed crutches, and by 1950 he was so disabled that he could not get back and forth to his law office. He lived in a large, stone, two-story family home in which he had an elevator and a stairlift installed so that he could get from the lower floor to the upper-level study and bedroom. His arthritis then became so bad that he was confined almost completely to his study, which he set up as an office for his legal business, and his bedroom next to it. That, for the next seventeen years, was his world. I saw him at least once a month throughout this time and found that his world was not as small as it seemed. His mind was exceedingly sharp, and he read extensively. He had many political and business friends who came to see him frequently. He kept up his outside interests and had an excellent grasp of what was going on in the world, even though he could not be an active part of it.

Aurora was developing rapidly and needed land for housing. This lawyer owned a farm on the west edge of Aurora; he subdivided it into good-sized lots and then directed its development. He would not sell a lot to anyone unless he interviewed them and saw their house plans. He wanted only ranch-style houses. From his room he was able to supervise this development so that it became one of the finest subdivisions in Aurora—all this from a man who could scarcely get from his bed to his chair.

I saw him professionally frequently and several times had him back in the hospital. His wife, who had been much the healthier of the two, developed a fatal illness and died in 1956, eleven years before her husband. After her death, he continued his activities with the housing development, some legal work, much reading, television and radio; his mind was never lazy. On his ninetieth birthday, his family held a party to which about 150 people came to pay their respects and enjoy his company. My wife and I felt especially honored that we were asked to come and to sit at his table. Shortly after the party, he began to fail steadily, and he died quietly a year later. In spite of seventeen years of invalidism, he made the most of it and led a productive and interesting life. I am glad I was privileged to have his friendship and to be able to take care of him during those hard years.

Betty

During my life as a doctor I have known some wonderful and unusual nurses. Betty was a nurse whose life was difficult in many ways but who never complained. She worked as a night nurse at St. Joseph Mercy Hospital for many years, until she became disabled because of a far-advanced cancer that caused her death at the age of forty-six. All my life I made my hospital rounds early, and I usually got to St. Joseph Hospital around 6:15 A.M. Unless she was tied up with other work, she made rounds with me before the change of shifts at 7 o'clock. She was extremely conscientious and took good care of her patients in every way. I thoroughly enjoyed working with her. As time went on, I got to know a good deal about Betty's background. Her husband had dropped out of her life completely, leaving her with three small children to raise, aged four to nine. She came home one night to find him gone, and she never saw him again. Betty's life was wrapped up in raising the children, and she knocked herself out working nights to be sure that they had a roof over their heads, food in their mouths, and clothing on their backs.

One of Betty's talents was writing poetry. She could make up rhymes and poems by the hour. It may not have been good poetry from a literary standpoint, but it was from her heart and said what she wanted to say. During the night, she would often dash off a few lines and leave them in my box. You could always tell from her poetry how she was feeling and what emotional problems she was having. I usually got a kick out of the poems, and I kept a few of them. One year I was getting ready to go on vacation and found the following poem in my box:

"Before Dr. G's Vacation
The steps get steeper,
The halls get deeper,
The days seem long,
The nights go wrong.

"The phone sounds dreary,
The patients are weary,
The end of the script,
Have fun on your trip."

When I got back, I found the following poem in the box:

"After Dr. G's Vacation
The steps seem easy,
The halls are breezy,
The days start brighter
The night calls are lighter.

"The phone sounds cheerful,
The patients less fearful,
Though talent I lack —
We welcome you back.

"This verse should arrive
When your vacation is past.
But to tell you the truth
I don't think it will last."

When Betty was blue and things weren't going right, and she felt the responsibilities of her job, she would write one like this:

"Security
At morning when I hit the sack
I think of all the things I lack.
I go to work with spirits high
And blunder through even though I try.

"Decisions, decisions, what should I do?
Won't someone please give me a clue?
Should I hang up my coat and put on my cap?
Decisions, decisions, I'm caught in a trap.

"I get a call, what should I say
Other people seem to find a way.
Decisions, decisions, I'm really torn
Should I say this is Betty or Mrs. Horn.

"To tell the truth, I'm in a quandary
My inabilities have no boundary.
I will not say more, I will be brief
I'd rather be an Indian than heap big chief."

One morning she told me something about her father, and it wasn't long after that I found the following poem in my box:

"Who?
In all the world, there never could be
Anyone who meant more to me.
His sense of humor was beyond compare
His way with people was very rare.

"His affection was not shown in a loving way
Instead it was shown in what he would say.
He was a self-made man, he worked all his life
He knew the burden of sorrow and strife.

"He was honest and kind, his friends he did charm
His home was his castle, his pride was his farm.
If you didn't know him, I wish you had
He was the greatest guy on earth, he was my dad."

Betty was always telling me about her children and the usual problems that mothers have. One time I found this in the box:

"My Children
I think that I shall never see
Nicer kids than my three
You made me laugh, you made me sad
But I did my best as your mom and dad.

"Misfortune struck us a few years back
But we didn't let it throw us off the track.
We didn't have things we might have had
But don't hold that against your dad.

"We are all part of a family tree
If it weren't for him, you wouldn't be."

It was a sad day when Betty found out that she had cancer and could not live more than a few months. She underwent chemotherapy and did everything that medical science knew to do for her, but her course was slowly downhill, and the last poem she wrote was as follows:

"No poems of late, no inspiration
Guess it's from poor circulation.

"No verse of late, not inspired
Boy, have I been feeling tired!

"Job's been rough, spirits low
Did I surprise you with a tale of woe?

"Things will improve, have no doubt,
Hope I can survive the latest bout."

She died at the age of forty-six—wonderful nurse, mother, and poet. Her three children are all married. If Betty had lived, she would be enjoying grandchildren from every one of her three children. Betty's mother is still living at ninety years old and was a patient of mine until I retired. I understand that she is still mentally sharp and remembers very well the many office visits we had together when we talked about Betty's problems.

Fred

Fred died two days ago, and today I was his pallbearer. As the funeral procession passed the Phillips Park Golf Course on its way to Lincoln Highway Cemetery, memories of Fred went through my mind. Many times he and I played this golf course, and we never imagined that some day I might be escorting his body as a final farewell.

My contacts with Fred and his family are a prime example of how doctors become so integrated into their patients' lives that they become almost as one. My first meeting with Fred was one night in May 1946. We had just finished a late dinner, at about 8:30 P.M., when the phone rang and the voice at the other end of the wire said, "This is Fred H........ You don't know me, and I have never met you, but I have a sick son. He has been sick for a number of months and is not getting any better. He is worse tonight, and I wonder If you could come over and see him." I said, "Sure." I slipped my shoes and coat back on and went over to see Allen, who was six. When I examined him, I found him to be indeed very sick. We needed blood tests, which we had done the next day at the Clinic, and found that Allen had lymphatic leukemia. He had been followed for some months by another physician, and for some reason the diagnosis had not been made. Over the next few weeks I saw Fred, his wife, and Allen many times and became well acquainted with them. There was also a smaller child, John, who was too young to understand what was going on. In 1946 there was no proven treatment for leukemia of this type. Fred took Allen to California to see if the research being done there could help him, but to no avail. Allen died before the year was out and took a little bit of Fred and Edith with him.

Following Allen's death, Fred went into a chronic depression, became morose, did not talk much, and just sat at home. He could not seem to snap out of it. The following spring, his wife came to see me and said, "Dr. Greeley, what can we do for Fred? He just can't seem to forget Allen, and it makes it awfully hard for John and me." I said, "Edith, what Fred needs is to get out and find some new interests, meet other people, and get away from his memories for a while. I have just learned to play golf. Maybe if I asked him to play golf with me it might get him started." I called Fred the next day and invited him to play. He hesitated at first and then said yes, he thought he would like that. I had been playing with two other people from Kiwanis, and Fred joined us for a game. Thus began a lifelong friendship. Fred, Waddy, Ed, and I played golf twice a week from then on for many years. We played every course within twenty-five to thirty miles of Aurora and always had a wonderful time. Fred came out of his shell and began to enjoy meeting people and doing things again. All golfers have their idiosyncrasies. One of Fred's was that every time he got up to putt, he would start wiggling the toes of his left foot. When you saw the toe of his shoe move up and down, you knew he was about ready to putt, and he was an excellent putter. We kidded him about it a lot.

Fred joined our Kiwanis Club, became a loyal and faithful member, and was a good worker in the Club. He made many friends in the community and was well liked. He was always doing things for people but never publicized anything that he did, so few people knew how kind he was, especially to older people. No record was ever kept of his gifts of time and money to needy people, but they were legion. Fred was helpful to everyone in the same way, with no thought that he might get anything in return.

An interesting incident resulted from one of Fred's many contacts. He was a close friend of an elderly Aurora couple and was always helping them at home. I took care of that family, also. When the husband died, Fred went over to the house as often as necessary to keep up the yard and garden. The widow lived alone in a very large house in a middle-class neighborhood. I made many house calls there and treated her in the hospital a number of times. When she died, she left what she had to Fred, but it wasn't the bequest that was interesting, it was where the money was found. When the lawyer and Fred went through the house they found several thousand dollars in cash. There was money in the Bible, in practically every book in the house, in the dishes and pans, under the mattress, in the pillowcases, under the rug, in coats, in the attic, in the basement. Wouldn't a burglar have had a field day if he had known that this woman did not believe in banks and kept all her money hidden at home?

As the years went on, Waddy and Ed died. Fred joined the Country Club and we played golf there together for a number of years, but when he retired he relinquished his membership and I didn't see so much of him any more.

During the last few years of his life Fred had the added burden, emotionally and physically, of a very sick wife. Edith developed Alzheimer's disease. Fred took care of her at home as long as he could. He cooked for her and was her private nurse. Once a week he had a visiting nurse come in to care for her while he attended to business and, occasionally, played some golf. During his last year, Edith was in a nursing home, and Fred visited her faithfully day after day and spent many hours with her, even though she did not know he was there and could not communicate with him.

A few months before he died, he asked me to play golf with him at one of the smaller courses, in North Aurora. The two of us played that morning and had a wonderful time recalling past experiences. On the last green I noticed that Fred still had his old putting habit. I said, "Fred, I see you still wiggle your toes before you putt." He answered, "Yes, and I am going to make this putt." The ball was about thirty feet from the hole. His toes wiggled, and he made the putt. With a sly grin on his face he said, "Harry, I just couldn't putt if I couldn't wiggle my toes." I didn't realize at the time that this was Fred's last putt and last golf game.

We had now reached the cemetery and the grave site. We laid Fred to rest, and I said goodbye to a good friend and a great person.

XLII/The Legal Profession and Medicine

The court system in this country receives some deserved criticism from the public. There has to be something wrong when it takes three to five years to get a case onto the court dockets. It makes for such a backlog that by the time a case does come up, the details are vague and inconclusive. A legal system is inconsistent when criminals can go scot-free on technicalities or a person can embezzle millions of dollars and be put on probation, while someone else can steal a few dollars and go to jail for years. There is something wrong when a person can be arrested for drunken driving and the lawyers can get continuance after continuance until the case is so cold that facts cannot possibly be remembered. It makes for a terrific increase in costs and for an inefficiency that is unheard of in any other profession. With the increase in crime during the last fifteen years, there are not enough jails to hold every lawbreaker. I do not offer any solutions but only a review of the problem.

I will confine my remarks mostly to the legal profession's dealings with the medical profession. During my years of practice, I have known many lawyers, most of whom are honest, upright citizens trying to do their jobs and raise their families just as doctors do. There are always some that spoil that image and stir up antagonism between the professions. This, of course, has been aggravated by the malpractice situation, which during the past fifteen years has become a major source of income for some lawyers. Some of these lawyers make statements like: "If doctors don't want malpractice cases, they shouldn't commit malpractice." That is unfair, as doctors do not purposely commit malpractice. The very nature of medicine makes it difficult always to be completely right. The many large malpractice awards have caused malpractice insurance to go from about $300 a year for an internist in 1970 to $4,000 by 1980. Orthopedists and some surgical specialties have premiums as high as $30,000 a year. It puts a doctor in a very vulnerable position. He is criticized for not doing enough tests, and he is criticized if he does too many. There is no question that doctors have to practice defensive medicine and be sure to cover all tests that could possibly bear on the case, including X-rays, because just one slipup can subject them to a million-dollar malpractice suit. One factor that has made doctors more vulnerable to malpractice is that in this modern age they are continually making complex diagnoses by correlating many test results and clinical examinations. They lose that close personal contact with patients and their families which, in many cases, would help them in solving a lot of the patients' problems.

In some malpractice cases, lawyers get unscrupulous doctors to pose as experts, and lay juries don't know the difference. Doctors are subjected to frivolous suits in which there was no malpractice and in which the lawyers have attempted to prove something that wasn't there. A few times doctors have countersued the lawyers for frivolous harassment, but this is rarely successful as you are working with a group of professional people who will not usually testify against each other. There are certainly many cases in which lawyers sue doctors thinking the cases will be settled out of court for a few thousand dollars, of which the lawyers get 30 to 40 percent. An example was the case of a doctor in our group who was sued for a million dollars. As time went on, the patient's lawyers wanted to settle the case, and they kept coming down until they asked to settle for five hundred dollars. Our doctor said he would not settle for ten cents as he had done no wrong. The suit was then dropped entirely. That is an example of a lot of wasted energy in a case that never should have been filed.

One of the things that has annoyed me most over the years is lawyers' abuse of the power of subpoena. I will cite two examples. In 1976, one Friday night at 9 o'clock, the doorbell rang and a man delivered a subpoena for me to appear in court in Chicago on Monday morning at 9 o'clock and bring all my records. I didn't even remember the patient whose name was given on the subpoena, nor had I ever heard of the lawyers. In looking up the case, I found that the accident had happened seven years before, and the only thing I had done was to see him in the emergency room and refer him immediately to a neurosurgeon, as there was some brain damage. No lawyer can build a good case and get cooperation from a doctor when, with no previous contact, he serves a subpoena at 9 o'clock on Friday night for him to appear in a Chicago courtroom at 9 o'clock Monday morning on a seven-year-old case. A lawyer might have the common courtesy to phone the doctor and at least go over the case with him.

The second incident happened just a few days ago, eighteen months after I retired. I had been in New Mexico for three months doing volunteer medical work and had been home only a week. Violet and I were going to Champaign to see our son and grandchildren for about a week, and she had gone on ahead of me. I received a certified letter in the mail on Friday with a subpoena for me to appear in court the following Wednesday with all my records. No attempt was made to contact me by phone beforehand. My medical records all belong to the Dreyer Medical Clinic; I have no personal records. Why should I be expected to cancel my vacation without notice? There should be some verbal contact between the two professions, not dictatorial action just because the lawyer has the power to do it. I have testified in court many times. The cases that have worked out the best were the ones in which the lawyer discussed the medical facts with me before the court date. Many reputable lawyers are trying to abolish these dictatorial practices. I repeat, most of the lawyers I know are of solid character, honest, and of good standing in the community. However, there are enough of the type I have described to give the whole profession a bad name.

XLIII/Insurance Companies and Medicine

There is no question that health, hospital, and medical insurance, especially group insurance, has been very beneficial to patients, doctors, and hospitals alike. It has also been profitable for the insurance companies. I have filled out thousands of insurance forms for my patients and have found that there are both good and bad insurance companies, not always related to the size of the company. Many insurance companies are guilty of misrepresentation and dishonesty covered by the fine print in the policy, which is impossible for anyone but a lawyer to interpret. I will give several examples.

Early in my practice, I took care of a man who was disabled because of chronic congestive heart failure. He said he had disability insurance. He was able to sit in a chair and to walk around the house and sit out on the porch. The insurance company sent a man to spy on him, and when he was seen on the porch, his insurance was canceled. In the fine print, it said that a person, in order to be considered completely disabled, had to be continuously confined to bed and seen by a doctor at least once a week. That, as you can see, is an unrealistic definition of disability. How many people would fit those criteria? Not many, and the insurance company knows it. Yet they advertise widely, making people think they have good disability coverage when they need it, but they really don't.

A similar case was that of a woman who had tuberculosis. She was able to sit outdoors in the sun, which was good for her. Still her disability policy was canceled.

A few years ago, I cared for a schoolteacher who had a myocardial infarction. He was critically ill and even had a cardiac arrest and was resuscitated. After a long illness, he had bypass heart surgery. He was certainly completely disabled. I filled out all the insurance company papers in detail, but that wasn't enough for them. They sent an investigator who inquired of all this man's neighbors whether he had been seen outdoors and how much he seemed to be able to do. They cut off his disability payments. The school was upset by this action and canceled their group policy because of it. This kind of insurance is tricky and all too often is sold to the public by high-pressure salesmen. It is no wonder that insurance companies have done so well financially.

I realize, of course, that there are two sides to the coin. Policyholders try everything they can think of to get insurance settlements that they don't deserve. But that does not justify the tricky fine print in many policies. Auto insurance is a no-man's-land in which policies can be canceled on the least provocation even though the policyholder has paid premiums for years.

Insurance is certainly something that we cannot do without. Everything we have is subject to robbery, damage, or catastrophic loss. Insurance for our lives, houses, cars, for accidents and disability are all important parts of the industry and fill a need in modern society. However, people should research companies and policies carefully before buying insurance of any kind.

XLIV/Medicine and the Press

I would like to preface my remarks on this subject by saying that I believe in freedom of the press. Certainly, I don't want a controlled press. I do, however, deplore overzealous use of this freedom in the name of the First Amendment. There are too many examples of the media going roughshod after news, not caring whom they hurt, just to get a good story. I certainly deplore the woman correspondent in Washington who falsified a story and won the Pulitizer Prize. However, is that any worse than *Newsweek*, which put the picture of a poverty-stricken, malnourished child on the cover and implied that that is the America that Reagan stands for? I call it yellow journalism at its worst.

When the press is represented by all kinds of people, there are bound to be abuses, but sometimes the abuses are promoted by the higher-ups of the profession. Medicine has been a whipping boy for the press for many years. On the other hand, they praise advances in medicine and are always one jump ahead of the doctors in publicizing new scientific discoveries in their efforts to be first. They often do this at the expense of accuracy and arouse the public needlessly. On the other hand, they criticize the medical profession mercilessly and picture doctors as money-hungry vultures who have no regard for their patients. Most doctors are ethical and caring persons and do not deserve the bad press they get. Following are some examples of press coverage that I have found obnoxious.

After World War II there was a lot of publicity about leukemia. There were theories that the advent of the nuclear age would bring new cures, especially for leukemia, which was singled out as a disease that would be controlled through nuclear knowledge. This was played up extensively by the press, and whenever a case of leukemia was diagnosed it received national publicity. In 1946 the seven-year-old son of a friend of mine developed leukemia. At the time the University of California Medical Center was the mecca for leukemia victims, since much research was being done there. My friend Fred took his son Allen to California to see if anything could be done for him. He wanted to get him there as quickly as possible, so he took a commercial flight that made a number of stops between here and California. He did not want any publicity about his son, and the boy did not know he had leukemia. The press got hold of the story and ran it in papers all over the United States, unbeknownst to

Fred and Allen. When they arrived and the plane door was opened, the reporters barged aboard and yelled, "Where is the boy with leukemia?" Allen knew what leukemia was, and when he realized that he had the disease he knew he was going to die soon. He broke into tears and was almost uncontrollable. Allen was checked at the University of California, but he had a type of leukemia that they could not help. He was brought home and made as comfortable as possible, but he died within a few months. I cite this as an example of cruel conduct in which the reporters gave no thought to human feeling in order to get a story. Of course, such behavior is stimulated from above by competitive managements that push their reporters to get stories at all cost.

I remember another case of leukemia that I cared for in one of the Aurora hospitals and that somehow got national publicity. Reporters called me at two o'clock in the morning wanting to know about the case and asking a lot of questions that could only have been asked by a lay person who didn't understand medicine. Why should a busy doctor be called in the middle of the night for that type of thing? It is pure thoughtlessness on the part of the reporters in their overzealousness to get a story.

Another example: In the early 1950s I was called to see the local police chief, who was having chest pain. He had been under criticism by many people in Aurora and by the press. When I saw him, he was a sick man and in danger of a serious heart attack. I hospitalized him and forbade visitors. Not once did the press call me to ask about his condition. Instead, they ran an editorial accusing me of using the hospital as a refuge for a man under severe criticism. That was not true. He was hospitalized solely for medical reasons.

Over the years, *Reader's Digest* has run articles on wonder drugs and cures, many of which were premature or not factual and came to conclusions by innuendo. Some of the articles were advance publicity for drugs that were completely unproven. Many times drugs that were described in glowing terms were later found to be ineffective. After every article patients asked for medicines that were not available and wanted to know about discoveries that were not proven. It became almost a standing joke among doctors that if you wanted to keep up with medicine you had to read the *Reader's Digest*. Medical articles in the *Reader's Digest* are often unreliable. I feel that they sacrifice truth to get a glamorous story.

Both krebiozen and laetrile resulted in slanted articles, not scientific reporting, by magazines and newspapers. Many people suffer thereby. Both drugs have been proven to be without merit in the cure of cancer, yet the public believed what they read in papers and magazines, not in scientific articles. This misplaced confidence made a lot of quacks rich. For instance, I had a patient who came to me with free fluid in his chest. He gave a history of having had surgery for cancer of the lung some years earlier. He was hospitalized, but while we were trying to make a diagnosis, he suddenly signed a release and left the hospital. He went to

Mexico to take laetrile because he was sure that he had a recurrence of cancer. Two or three months later I saw his obituary in the paper. If he had let us go ahead with our workup, we would have been able to make a definite diagnosis and, through chemotherapy, we might have given him a year or two of useful life. This example can be duplicated over and over again by doctors all over the United States. It is frustrating to see cancer quackery written up in such glowing terms that even state legislatures pass laws permitting the use of laetrile.

The New England *Medical Journal* is one of the better scientific medical publications and is probably read by most doctors. Its articles are outstanding and factual and report the latest that is going on in medicine. Many of the articles, however, report research that has not been concluded. Every few weeks the press takes one of these articles and publishes it in newspapers all over the country as a medical breakthrough. They take quotations out of context and lead the public to believe that there may be a new cure for hypertension, heart disease, or some other condition. Then the next week, physicians are flooded with patients who want to know about the new wonder drug. The reporters who write these articles are laymen and are not scientifically knowledgeable enough to report accurately. It isn't that we do not want the publicity where it is due, but we would like to have it factual and not give the public false hopes.

I would like to cite one more example of the press's attitude that bothers me. Violet for the past six years has done volunteer work in a juvenile correctional facility, in which she teaches arts and crafts to boys, thirteen to nineteen years of age. She had developed a good program, and a local newspaper wanted to run an article about the work. They sent a reporter, and by the nature of the questions Violet could see that she did not understand the program. When the interview was over, Violet asked if she could see the article before it was printed to be sure that it was correct. The reporter was indignant and said, "Of course not! That would be interfering with freedom of the press." The article was printed the following week and was so full of inaccuracies that it gave a completely wrong impression. I understand this is common practice. Once a reporter interviews a person and writes an article, the person can never see it until it is printed in the paper. Even though the story may contain important facts from the standpoint of public information and should be accurate, it often isn't.

Over my thirty-eight years of practice I have known many good reporters—accurate, honest, and fine people. I am sure that the good far outweighs the bad. I only wish that the powers that be would direct their reporters to avoid being so overzealous that they hurt people and make needless mistakes. I feel there has been considerable progress in accuracy of reporting over the years, but there is still much room for improvement.

XLV/The Doctor as a Patient

It is common knowledge that doctors make the worst patients in the world. They are even worse than nurses, and that is pretty bad. Doctors are individualists who like to think they are in control, but when they become patients they are stripped of their dignity and are at the mercy of others. Sometimes this is difficult for them to accept. I have been hospitalized twice in my life, and I think I was a good patient. I would like to relate my experiences during one of my hospital stays.

In 1960 a left inguinal hernia, which I had had for several years, was progressing to the point where it was causing a partial bowel obstruction. I knew I had to have it repaired. If this had happened when I was young and did so much lifting and hard work, it wouldn't have been surprising, but now that I was no longer engaged in strenuous work it was impossible to explain the condition.

I was scheduled by Dr. Milbacher for a herniorrhaphy. I was used to hospital procedure, knew all the nurses and doctors, and was accustomed to giving orders, but all of a sudden I realized that the shoe was on the other foot. I came in street clothes to the room assigned to me and was met by a nurse, who told me to undress and put on a gown. The hospital gown she gave me was so short it hardly reached my thighs; it opened in the back and was barely large enough to go around.

"Do you mean I have to put on this thing?" I asked. "I have pajamas here, and they would be much more comfortable."

She replied, "Hospital orders. You have to wear this gown."

So little of me was covered by it that when I got up to go to the bathroom, I used my right hand to hold it closed in the back and my left hand to pull it down in front to cover my nakedness. I was to have surgery the next morning and thought I was all prepared. However, about nine o'clock in the evening a nurse came in with an enema can, saying, "Dr. Greeley, you have to have an enema."

"Why do I have to have an enema?" I retorted. "I don't need an enema; I am in good shape."

"Doctor's orders," she replied. "Turn over."

I began to realize it was useless to object. I was given the enema, much to my embarrassment, and it worked. Pretty soon she came in with a sleeping pill.

I objected again, "I don't need a sleeping pill."

"Doctor's orders," she insisted. "You have to have a sleeping pill."

"What if I can sleep all right without it? If I don't, then you can give it to me," I suggested.

"No, you have to take it now."

So without further argument I took the sleeping pill. In the morning I was prepared for surgery and shaved, which didn't make me very happy. Just before the surgical nurse came for me with a cart, the floor nurse came in and, seeing the wedding ring on my finger, said, "You have to take off that ring."

"I never take my wedding ring off," I protested. "It has been on my finger ever since I was married."

"Hospital orders. You have to take it off. We will put it in the safe for you." And she removed the ring. I hoped I would see it again.

I was then wheeled to surgery, where I saw more nurses whom I knew and also the anesthesiologist. I had glimpses of Dr. Milbacher scrubbing to do the surgery. An IV was started in my arm, and as I lay there, still awake, I realized how helpless I had become. I was stripped of all dignity and no longer had control over my life. I was at the mercy of the operating-room nurses, the surgeon, and the anesthesiologist. I hoped they knew what they were doing.

Pretty soon the anesthesiologist said, "We are going to start giving you sodium pentothal now. Try counting and see how far you can count."

I didn't get far before I was out like a light. When I woke up I was in the recovery room and the operation was all over, but I did have a very sore side. I was up the next day, and my recovery was uneventful. My ring was returned to me, and I was permitted to wear my pajamas. I didn't have to take any more sleeping pills. My diet was increased so I almost felt like living again. Visitors began to come and go without restrictions. By the time I left the hospital I had recovered most of my dignity. I was again in control of my life and could look back with great appreciation for everything that was done for me, even though at the time I protested a great deal. I now knew what my patients who were referred for surgery had to endure.

Doctors do not always follow the advice that they would give their patients in similar circumstances. I will cite the case of a doctor who had a heart attack while playing golf. He was an internist and knew all about heart attacks, but when he recognized his pain as a probable myocardial infarction he kept on and played another hole of golf. His orders to a patient would have been to lie down on the golf course until an ambulance could be called and he could be taken to the hospital. However, this doctor rode his scooter to the clubhouse, stopped to take a shower, and then drove his own car to the hospital emergency room. He walked in and said, "I am having a heart attack; send me up to the Coronary Care Unit." He did everything wrong. Everything he would have had his patients do, he didn't do himself. Luckily, he got away with it and made a good recovery. These two incidents are just examples of how doctors react to their own illnesses.

XLVI/Alternate Life-styles

I can't finish this book without a few words on alternate life-styles. My remarks will be confined primarily to homosexuals, both male and female.

During the past twenty years the news media have discussed homosexuality in great detail as if it were something new. Homosexuals, both male and female, have always been with us. They represent a life-style that is hard to analyze and the etiology of which has not been entirely clear even though it has been researched extensively by the medical profession. The public acceptance of homosexuals, however, has shown a marked change.

When I started in practice, homosexuals did not reveal themselves, even to their doctors. They lived with the knowledge that their feelings were different and that they would be treated as curiosities if people knew. I learned early that homosexuals cannot control the way they feel, that something either innate or environmental has caused the variation. Most of them are productive citizens, and they are found in all walks of life. They need to be accepted and not looked down upon.

One cannot help wondering why some people vary so much from accepted norms. Some psychiatrists theorize that it is their childhood environment, with emphasis on sexual stimuli from the same sex. From my observations, this is not a valid theory. The country school I attended had a girls' side and a boys' side of the school yard, each with its own outdoor toilet and separated by a board fence. The pupils knew more about sex than the average child because they lived on farms, where reproduction was observed in farm animals and was consequently no secret. It was common practice at noon or recess for six or eight boys from eight to thirteen years of age to meet in the boys' outhouse and masturbate together. They would all get erections and then see who had the longest penis. They would also masturbate each other and have a gay old time. My mother had impressed on me before this that if I ever "played with myself" it would ruin my brain and I would be an "idiot." I believed her, so I didn't participate. However, my purpose here is to point out that not one of those boys became a homosexual or an idiot. It wasn't long before they were noticing the girls on the other side of the fence. They would stick their penises between the cracks in the fence to get the girls to giggle and squeal. It also wasn't long before some of the ten-year-old boys began taking the girls out into the woods and down in the basement and attempting intercourse with them. Believe me, they became heterosexual in a hurry. Not one of them had any interest in other boys once they had established heterosexual patterns. Kinsey reported this type of activity, and the results were the same as above.

The 1960s and 1970s brought liberalized thinking about homosexuals, which I think was a good thing. It is foolish to be intolerant of another human being for something over which he has no control. I feel that the press, movies, and television have gone overboard in representing homosexuals as something special and almost glamorous. One can respect them for their abilities and accept them as human beings with different life-styles, but I cannot accept the premise that they are normal or variations of normal. I am sure that God never gave man a penis to put in an anus—the cesspool of the body. Anatomically and physiologically, the penis was made to put into the vagina. By the same token, two women trying to make love to each other, rubbing their body parts together, caressing, is also not normal. The female body was not made anatomically or physiologically for this kind of activity with each other.

I realize that homosexuals cannot control their sexual preferences, and I certainly feel that people should be tolerant of them and let them live their own style of life. They are the victims of something that has not been explained adequately and for which there is very little help. Even though they do not represent a normal life-style as we know it, I hope we never revert in our thinking to a generation ago when a homosexual had to "hide in a closet."

The discussion above deals primarily with pure homosexuals. There is a large gray area in between that is difficult to analyze and will require a lot of psychiatric research to delineate. Some people are both homosexual and heterosexual and can enjoy either life-style. A male homosexual may marry and raise a normal family, and the same is true of the female. However, there is a condition called "latent homosexuality" in which a person who has been living heterosexually for a long time will revert to homosexuality. For example, a woman patient said that her husband had walked out on her and had gone to Chicago to live with a man. He confessed to her that he was really homosexual and that he did not want to live as a heterosexual any longer despite the fact that they had four children in grade and high school. It is simple just to condemn this man and say, "Well, if you could live together and have four children, why do you have to go to homosexuality now?" I have no answer, except that there seems to be a compulsion that a person cannot control.

Another example was a wife with a ten-year-old child who left her husband to live with a lesbian, leaving him with the child. To try to explain the workings of the mind in these two cases is impossible. It is our hope that psychiatrists and medical men in the future will find out what causes these changes and be able to do something about them.

There are other sexual aberrations that are not seen as often. Early in my practice, a young woman patient married for a few months complained that her husband was unable to have intercourse unless he put on high-heeled shoes and silk stockings. Naturally, she was upset, as she had never been aware of such aberrations in male behavior. She was counseled that they can occur in a few men and that little can be done about it; it should not interfere with a happy marriage if she could just accept it. The family went on to have a number of children, who grew up normally, and the man was successful in business and able to provide well for them. This is a typical case of transvestism, of which I have seen several cases over the years in my practice. Here, again, there is no logical explanation; it remains one of those mysteries of the human brain and personality that are not understood.

Another aberration is quite different. A male patient, married a few months, told me that his wife had an insatiable desire and wanted to have sex five or six times a day and probably more often if he could have complied. Because of her desires, he would have sex when he woke up in the morning and again when he came home at noon from his business, which was a short distance away. At night he would have sex before dinner and again at bedtime. If he woke up in the middle of the night, she would want to have intercourse again. Even this did not satisfy her. As time went on, he was unable to adjust to his wife's demands, and he eventually got a divorce. This, of course, is a typical case of nymphomania. There is no logical explanation for it. Studies have not shown that it is due to an unusual amount of female hormones. It is probably psychological, but psychiatrists have never been able to analyze and treat it.

In the same category of sexual aberrations is exhibitionism. I remember a case in which I was called to the police station one noon to see a man who had been arrested in a downtown store for exhibitionism. He had entered the store wearing a long coat that concealed his open zipper and his genitals outside his pants. In walking the aisles of the store, all he had to do was throw his coat open and exhibit himself. He had evidently done this a number of times before but had never been caught and arrested. This time there happened to be a policeman handy, and a woman to whom he had exhibited himself was able to identify him. He had a long history of exhibitionism in several cities. Here was a man who was successful in business and had a happy home, with grown children who were all normal. There were no major conflicts at home. He was active in community work, attended church regularly, donated generously to charities, and was considered a model in the community. How does one explain a person like this who seems socially normal and yet has a compulsion every so often to show off his genitals? Cases of exhibitionism are very difficult to treat.

[146]

Maybe all of the conditions that I have described are influenced by environment and are amenable to psychiatric treatment. That does not explain the many people who have similar backgrounds in development and environment and who do not develop these aberrations. There remains a lot of research to be done, both organically and functionally, to try to determine why a small segment of our population develops these alternate life-styles.

XLVII/Retiring from the Board

In 1975 I began to realize that I was growing older. I had attained the age of sixty. I had worked all my life with no letup, and there was really no letup now, but I realized that I was in an older age group. According to custom, when a doctor is over sixty he does not have to take emergency room call at the hospital or be on call for the rest of the doctors in the Clinic. Although I worked just as hard and collected and booked as much as I ever had, it was a relief not to be on call every fourth or fifth night for the other internists and also not to be on emergency room call at both hospitals. The years from sixty to sixty-five were satisfying but hard years.

According to Clinic policies that we had laid out many years before, a doctor was expected to retire from Board work at the age of sixty-five. It was felt by the senior doctors, who formulated the basic Clinic policy, that at sixty-five a person should step aside and give the younger men a chance, as they, too, have an interest in the Clinic's future and perhaps some new ideas that need working over and integrating into our policies. Accordingly, I reached sixty-five on March 9, 1980, and my last Board meeting was in February. The meeting went as usual, and then I gave them my retirement letter. I had served on the Board of the Dreyer Medical Clinic for twenty-four years, as long as there was a Board, and the longest that any doctor had ever served. For seven of those years, I was Chairman. I figured out that I had attended 288 meetings of the Board, averaging three hours a meeting, for a total of 864 hours. Special meetings took up another 136 hours, for roughly 1,000 hours of Board service. Dividing this by 24, it comes out to 41 days, 16 hours, that I sat in the Board Room of the Dreyer Medical Clinic. For the first 17 years, we received no money for our service on the Board, but during the last seven years we received fifty dollars per meeting.

As I look back over those twenty-four years, I have many pleasurable memories of the Board achievements and of our Clinic's growth—first in the business building downtown, going from one floor to two, to three, to four floors, and then to our own building, which had to be enlarged within three years, and then again another major addition at the end of ten years. The building and equipment that we had in 1980 when I retired could not have been replaced for $10 million. During my thirty-eight years at the Dreyer Medical Clinic, the gross income increased from $160 thousand to over $10 million a year. Our medical staff increased from five to forty-four doctors. As I conducted my last Board meeting, which was attended by the whole group, I had a great feeling of satisfaction at having done a good job. As my part of the meeting ended, Dr. Blackburn took over and presented me with a $1,100 Rolex watch inscribed, "Dedication, Leadership, Service, Harry Y. Greeley, M.D., 1942-1980, Chairman of the Board 1973-1980, Dreyer Medical Clinic." In his speech of presentation, he reminded me that I had driven Cadillacs for thirty years and still wore a Timex watch. He said he thought it was time for me to graduate to a watch to match my Cadillac. There were a number of other complimentary speeches by other doctors. I had recruited many of them, and their talks reminded me of the persistent work I had done in getting them to join the Clinic. It was an emotional meeting for me, knowing that my life as one of the policy-making doctors in the Dreyer Medical Clinic was over. I knew it would leave a big void in my life, but I also realized that the policies of the Clinic were sound, and that at sixty-five I should step out and let younger men have a chance.

I missed Board meetings very much, but I never had any desire to go back. It was just one of those things where you have to write "Finished," and start anew.

XLVIII/Plans for Retirement

Old age is insidious, but it comes to all of us if we live long enough. The worst part of it is that we can seldom see the gradual deterioration in ourselves. This puts an aging doctor in a particularly bad position, because his responsibilities are so vital to other people's lives. Older doctors may make mistakes in judgment that they wouldn't have made earlier. It is shocking to the physician and embarrassing for those who have to tell him that he is becoming forgetful and uncoordinated.

I remember a famous teacher I had in medical school who had written several books and had been head of his department for many years. In his seventies his work and judgment began to slip; this was evident to all his colleagues, but he could not realize it himself. He became worse and worse but could not see that he should retire. His colleagues did not want to hurt his feelings and said nothing but tried to help him in every way they could. His department and work continued to deteriorate so that by the time he had a stroke and died in his early eighties, great damage had been done to many people. It was this type of deterioration over which we have no control nor ability to judge in ourselves that made me resolve to retire at sixty-five, or soon after, before someone came around and said, "Harry, you aren't practicing good medicine any more."

Many physicians do not take time to develop hobbies or other interests. Their whole life is medicine, and they do nothing else. That is fine as long as no one gets hurt in the process. I certainly recommend that all doctors try to develop other interests and hobbies so that when physical and mental abilities deteriorate they have something to take the place of medicine.

Two weeks after my last Board meeting, I reached sixty-five, and the facts of the situation made me feel more than ever that the time had come to make a major change in my way of life. I was still working seventy hours a week. I had one of the largest practices in the Clinic and probably in the city of Aurora, and I was still trying to work at the pace I had set many years ago. I knew something would have to give—I couldn't keep up the pace much longer. Some people said, "Why don't you cut down?" Well, that isn't as easy as it sounds. First, to whom are you going to say "No"? Second, suppose you did cut down to half of your usual practice. You would still have to go to the hospital every day, including Sundays and holidays, still go to the office every day, and take your phone calls at night. You are still tied down. No, that isn't the answer. Some doctors said, "Why not cut down and be a medical director part time?" Our clinic needed a medical director, and the idea was attractive; however, that still was a day-after-day responsibility.

My philosophy had always been, "After sixty-five, no one knows how many healthy years are left before one contracts a fatal disease, becomes disabled, or dies. I have many interesting hobbies: travel, golf, electronics, and if I am ever going to enjoy them, I had better do it before it is too late." I always thought it would be fun to do volunteer medicine maybe four to six months out of the year and have the rest of the time free.

Golf rain or shine: Harry Greeley and Al Wulff.

After much soul searching, I decided to retire at the end of that year, December 31, 1980, in the last part of my sixty-fifth year. I informed the Board and told them that they should hire another internist to take up some of my practice. Actually, there were two internists who were not completely busy, and the addition of one more should fill the need very well. The Board concurred, and I recruited an internist to take my place. The doctor was a Board-eligible internist, a local man, who had worked his way through medical school and whose recommendations were top-notch. We hired him to start September 1, 1980.

As the summer wore on and I began to realize the dimensions of what I had set up for myself, I subconsciously tried to find ways to avoid completely severing my relations with the Clinic. I thought about covering for doctors when they took vacations, but that wasn't very practical. As September came around and I was reaching the point of no return, I knew I had to decide whether to make a complete break or hang on in some capacity if they would have me. The September Board meeting was coming up, and I had requested time at the meeting. A few days before, I wrote a proposal suggesting that I become a medical director for a nominal fee and retire from medical practice. That way, I could still maintain connections with the Clinic, which had been my life and which I loved very much. I wasn't sure the Board would go for it but thought that at least they might offer a counterproposal. I spent a sleepless night before the Board meeting. Many things went through my mind. This Clinic had been my lifeblood for thirty-eight years. In many ways, I wanted to be a part of its further development, and yet there were many other things I wanted to do. The following day, as has happened so many times in my life, things began to come into focus; shortly before the Board meeting I tore up the proposal and wrote an official letter of resignation as of December 31.

Once the decision was made, there never was any question that it was the right one. I presented my letter to the Board and told them I would phase out my practice over three months and see that all my patients were referred to the three internists who were taking new patients. I thanked them for all past favors and left.

As I walked out of the Board meeting that night, it was as if a veil had been lifted and I could see new light at the end of the tunnel, new things to do. I always had a little missionary in me, and right away I began planning for my four to six months of volunteer medical work. I knew there were many possibilities. One could spend a few months in Africa or Thailand. Indian reservations and Appalachia always needed doctors to help out. I began to lay plans and write to these various places to try to find a way to do volunteer work with enough pay to break even. During our travels, we had been in American Samoa, and I knew that they needed doctors. I wrote to them and was accepted for four months; they would pay our way there and provide housing. I did not expect to retire in any of these areas but only to work part of the year and perhaps serve two projects of this type each year. In the other six months, I wanted to play golf, travel, see my grandchildren, write a book, and work on electronics. It was with great anticipation that I planned my retirement.

Once I had made the decision, it became necessary to make everything terminate as of December 31. I never realized it would be such a job. You can't just shut the door and say, "I'm through." I had many patients that I had taken care of for thirty to thirty-five years, and some from my first summer in 1942. I didn't realize what an emotional experience it was going to be to leave all those wonderful people. I had gone through joys and good times, heartaches and sorrows with all of them, and it wasn't going to be easy to tell them goodbye. A notice was sent out with the billing that I was going to retire on December 31. In October I started to tell patients that this would be their last office visit. Many of them would hold my hand or hug me, and the tears would come. Then I would break down and shed a few tears of my own. Invariably they would recall some experience in the past, some crisis, some sickness, some death that I had shared with them and by so doing had become very close to them. On leaving my room, they had to pass the telephone secretary outside my door. She would see them crying and maybe hear some of their remarks, and she would cry, too. Then the patient would stop to visit with the receptionist and pretty soon she would be crying, also. This was repeated over and over again, day after day, for three months. It was the saddest three months of my life: I shed more tears than I had all the rest of my life put together. I had never thought it would be that hard to retire.

On the 31st of December, at 5 o'clock, I saw my last patient. Luckily, he was jollier than a lot of people had been and joked about my retirement and his loss of a doctor, but you knew down inside that he really felt bad. After he had gone, I went to the reception desk, sat down, looked at my list of patients for the day, and said to the girls, "It is all over now; I will not be back anymore." I then went back to my office, took all Violet's paintings off the wall and loaded them in the car, took all of my belongings out of the office, turned in my keys, and went home, knowing that I would never see another patient at the Dreyer Medical Clinic.

XLIX/Parties and Farewells

As I went into my last month, I was completely unprepared for the expressions of appreciation that I received from many sources. I didn't realize until confronted with it how difficult it was to change a routine. I also did not realize the high esteem in which I had been held by so many people. I didn't expect anything special when I quit, for I had just done my job. I began getting many letters and phone calls of thanks and best wishes. In addition to the letters, cards, phone calls, and farewells at the office, I was given a series of retirement parties.

Physicians in the Dreyer Medical Clinic in 1980: (first row) Thomas Gifford, Lawrence Evans, Theodore London, William Blackburn, C. L. Gardner, Harry Greeley, Edwin Haus-mann, John Abell, Arthur Abbott, Kenneth Lindahl; (middle row) David Clark, James McAninch, Fred Kemp, William Scanlon, Kenneth Albrecht, Phillip Jacobson, Richard Angell, Stephen Baldwin, Marc Schlesinger, Michael Loebach, Richard Nelson, Thomas O'Shea, Richard Foth, Tom Stemper, Robert Nudera, James Hofer, Paul Herwick, Patrick McNellis, William Donovan, James Sandrolini; (back row) Irineo Acacio, John Potter (administrator), John Palmer, David Davis, Leonard Snyder, Chang Man Kang, Soo Oh, John Blair, Govind Chandra, James Pedersen, Daniel Susmano, John Landes.

My nursing home practice was always an integral part of my work. In 1980 I had about eighty patients in nursing homes, and it was routine for me to see them monthly and more often if needed. I loved and enjoyed these old people; however, I was one of few doctors that the homes could count on for regular service. It was always hard for me to understand why doctors do not as a rule enjoy taking care of elderly people. It is sad to see people who were once the active generation deteriorate and become sick and helpless, but they greatly appreciate good care and concern. As I said before, old age is insidious, but none of us escapes it if we live long enough. I was overwhelmed by expressions of appreciation and gratitude that I received from nursing home patients and staffs. At my last visit to Hillside Nursing Home, they had a special surprise party for me that included all the employees and the administrator, with whom I had worked for many years. They gave me a plaque expressing their thanks and signed cards wishing me well. Some of the patients made gifts for me. I had never expected it, but it certainly made me feel good.

At their yearly Christmas party, Elmwood Nursing Home gave me a present and praise. I also had special gifts and cards from many patients, expressing their love and appreciation.

At Four Seasons Nursing Home, the patients and nurses presented me with a barometer and humidity gauge to tell me goodbye and to thank me for past services.

St. Charles Nursing Home also gave me messages of gratitude and a gift.

Aurora Manor sent me a lot of cards from the patients and from the employees, expressing their thanks and farewell.

The Medical Records Department at Copley Hospital held a special luncheon, with cake and coffee. I had many good friends in this department. As you may know, medical records are a very important part of a doctor's work but are often neglected. It is the difficult job of the Medical Records Department of the hospital to keep urging the doctors to complete their records promptly. I was one of very few doctors who were always up to date. I kept my records completed so well that they never had to put my name on the list of doctors who were behind. The Department appreciated my efforts in this respect, and for this they gave me special honors, a party, and a gift.

The medical floor at Copley was almost my second home. More of my patients were treated on that floor than on any other for many years. I knew all of the nurses and nurse's aides very well. The last week before I retired, they also gave me a party in which they let me know that they were going to miss me, as I would miss them.

When I first went to work at the Dreyer Medical Clinic, there were approximately four lay employees. When I retired there were about 180, most of whom were women. One day at noon they called me into the women's lounge, where they had prepared cakes with my name on them, cards, and a gift to express their appreciation for all I had done for them and for the Clinic. I was deeply touched.

During the last years, my practice was mostly geriatrics. These people were in the prime of life when they became my patients, and they were the active force of the Aurora community. Their only fault is that they are now thirty to thirty-eight years older than when I started to care for them and their families. Of course, I am also thirty-eight years older, so I grew old right along with them. I received many letters and retirement cards from these wonderful people.

On January 7 I was given my final retirement party, which certainly turned out to be a fitting climax to everything that had come up to that time. My good friends, the nurses in the Intermediate Care Area and Coronary Care Unit at Copley Hospital, planned a dinner and program for me at the Lincoln Inn. I was given the impression that it was going to be only a few of my close friends, possibly fifteen or twenty people. Violet and I were surprised when we arrived and found that tables were set for two hundred. I couldn't believe there were that many people who cared enough to come and wish me Godspeed. Most of the people were Copley-oriented—nurses, doctors, nurse's aides, technicians from both laboratory and X-ray, medical records, administration, and of course the doctors from the Clinic and the community. As I greeted them at the door, I began to realize that each and every one of these people at some time or another had had a special part in my life. They represented my professional colleagues in Aurora and over long years had become very close and special friends. We had a wonderful dinner, but that was the least important part of the evening. Many complimentary speeches were made, and it was difficult to respond to them because I wasn't prepared. What I did say certainly came from my heart as I tried to express my gratitude to all of those present. Pat Peterson, from the Intensive Care Unit, read a poem that she had written using "The Night Before Christmas" as a model. It went as follows:

" 'Twas a day just at sunrise
    When all thru the place
The nurses were stirring
    Gearing up for the shift they must face.

The charts they were hung
    In their racks by the pair,
Awaiting new orders
    For the giving of care.

The patients were nestled
    All snug in their beds,
While hopes for a discharge
    Danced thru their heads.

The assistants in blue
    The nurses in white
Had just finished report
    And began with the lights.

When out on the street,
    In the same parking space,

Came Dr. Greeley, as always
　　To be the first in our place.

He was dressed just as usual
　　From his head to his foot
In his clothes always dapper
　　He always wore a suit.

A bundle of coffee
　　He carried in a sack,
And tickets for pancakes
　　He sold by the stack.

His eyes how they twinkled
　　As a diagnosis he'd bestow,
'She's just 95
　　But she's active you know!'

A quick cup of coffee
　　With his favorites he'd seek,
With the steam of it circling
　　His head like a wreath.

His droll little mouth
　　Was drawn up in a grin,
As the latest 18 hole tale
　　He would spin.

He was gentle and kind
　　A right jolly old elf,
And we'll cry 'cause we'll miss him
　　In spite of ourself.

He always had time
　　For understanding and caring,
He always had time
　　For listening and sharing.

So as he leaves to enjoy
　　Some of life's leisure pleasures,
We bid him farewell
　　With a love that's unmeasured.

But it won't be goodbye
　　At the end of this rhyme,
We'll just say hurry back
　　Come up and see us sometime.

Pat Peterson, 1981
(signed) With love,
　　　Pat"

Many friends knew of my interest in electronics, and they had bought me a home computer with their donations. Nothing they could have given me would have been more appreciated. I have spent hours with this gift since that time, and there is no end to its possibilities. I took it to Kentucky and New Mexico with me, and it certainly was a big help in passing the time in the evenings. The photographer there that night took many pictures that were later given to me by the nurses in a memory book. Sometimes doctors who work in clinics do not have the best rapport with outside physicians, but I always considered most of them my friends. This was confirmed that night when I counted twenty-seven doctors from outside the Clinic who were there to celebrate with me. It was a very good feeling. Mrs. Ruth Lester masterminded the party, and I can't say enough good things about that tremendous person whose life has touched so many other lives in her work as an Intermediate Care and Intensive Care nurse. The same goes for all the other nurses at that party. They are a wonderful group of women—capable, professional, and A-1 in my book.

As I left the party that night, I realized more than ever before how many friends I have in Aurora, professional and otherwise. The party was really the termination of my medical practice in Aurora. The next week I was to leave for American Samoa, and from then on my life would be entirely different and exciting. I was going to get a chance to do many things I had always wanted to do. My thirty-eight and a half years in the practice of medicine were now wonderful memories.

L /My Life in Medicine

This book has been an attempt to portray my life in medicine. It has been a very rewarding life, and I feel privileged to have been a part of the American medical fraternity. I have always been proud of my profession and have never been sorry that I went into medicine. As I have said before, I lived through more medical discoveries and developments than occurred in the entire history of medicine previous to 1940. It has been very exciting to be a part of this great profession and to see the great strides that have been made. The average length of life has been extended twelve to fifteen years during my lifetime due to the combined knowledge and research of many brilliant men. I have worked hard trying to keep up with those developments so that my patients could benefit from them.

Besides my work and joy in the actual practice of medicine, I had two other great interests. One was the Clinic, of which I was a part for thirty-eight years and which grew from five to forty-four doctors. These young, dedicated doctors were all well trained and contributed new knowledge and know-how. I never drive by the clinic without a feeling of satisfaction from knowing that I had a large part in its development. It is one of the finest multispecialty clinics in the Midwest. I predict it will continue to grow and be a great asset to the Aurora community.

Finally, I want to pay tribute to my wife, Violet, a great humanitarian and a wonderful helpmate in everything I have been able to do. She had two great interests in life—first, to be a good mother, and second, to be of help to other people. In her first interest, she succeeded admirably. When I was so busy practicing medicine that I didn't have much time for my family, she took over and devoted all her time and skill to the children. Our children are married and all have done well. Richard earned his Ph.D. in organic chemistry, did special work in laboratory medicine, and has charge of all the chemistries in a large hospital in California. Donald is an internist with a pulmonary subspecialty and is a member of a large clinic in central Illinois. Barbara is a special education teacher and lives in central Illinois. John Hohm, our foster son, taught industrial arts for two years and now has his own automobile body shop. From these children we have eight grandchildren, six boys and two girls. It is very gratifying that all our children like to come home to visit.

Violet's second interest, helping people, is demonstrated by the following examples. When the children were all in college and away from home, she went back to teaching. For ten years she taught home economics in Naperville High School; most of her classes were senior boys, and she taught them food planning and preparation. She loved her students, and they loved her. Whereas most teachers now have unlisted phone numbers, Violet would give her students her phone number the first day of the semester and say, "If you ever need me in any way, call me." She meant this, not only academically but for other problems. Many of her students visited us in our home even though we are twelve miles from Naperville. One time, one of her students called in the middle of the night and said he was in jail—I don't remember the charge. She went over, sized up the situation, and bailed him out for 75 dollars. He later repaid her in full. After Violet retired from teaching, she started volunteer work at a correctional institution fifteen miles from Aurora. These are boys aged thirteen to nineteen. She teaches them arts and crafts and has spent two afternoons a week there for the last six years. Violet is a professional artist and always accompanies me on my trips to do volunteer medicine. While I am working, she paints the local scenery. Usually we have very few paintings to bring home. Local people who see them buy them almost as fast as she can paint them.

Violet is the one person without whom my life would have been quite different and this book would never have been written.

Addendum

The following Chapters are accounts of experiences in volunteer medicine, after my retirement, that were sent back to friends and relatives.

The Samoan Experience

January 1981

On January 13, 1981, we finished our packing, locked the door of our house, and started for the airport on an experience that we had anticipated for several months. Now that the time was at hand, we were not at all sure that we wanted to go through with it. However, we got on the "big bird" at O'Hare. I couldn't help thinking of what I had read in the paper a few months ago about this 747 that flies nonstop to Hawaii, which weighs 750,000 pounds and barely takes off by the end of the runway. I timed the takeoff, 51 seconds, with very little runway left. We had a beautiful flight and reached Hawaii right on schedule.

We stayed overnight in Honolulu at the Holiday Inn, close to the airport. Our plane was not to leave for Pago Pago until 5:30 P.M.; however, we had to check out of our motel by noon, so we went right on over

The Greeleys at the Safua Hotel on Savaii, Western Samoa.

to the Continental check-in station at the Honolulu Airport. To our surprise, there were already some other passengers checking in for this flight. We checked our bags and then sat back and watched the people, who were mostly Samoans. The thing that made it most interesting was that these Samoans, brought to the airport by their friends or families, had all their belongings in great big cardboard cartons and crates of various kinds that were taped and tied together. We wondered if they would get to Samoa all right. One of the Continental employees informed me that this was the usual thing for this flight, that it was always Samoans and that they, being very close family people, were going home, or else some of their children were going home, to Samoa, and that they always came with huge cartons and no suitcases.

As we neared Samoa, we had a feeling of apprehension for we were approaching the unknown. We got off the plane, went through customs, and found Dr. Turner, medical director at LBJ Tropical Medical Center, and his wife there to meet us. We had to wait over an hour for our bags as all the cartons and crates came first and the suitcases last. Dr. Turner told us that often this plane was so crowded with cartons of the Samoans that they couldn't get them all on and would leave baggage in Honolulu until the next plane three days later. We were happy ours arrived with us.

While we were waiting for the bags, Dr. Turner introduced me to two engineers who were his golf buddies and happened to be at the airport that night. Before we even got our bags, he had already signed me up for a game of golf the next Sunday. He said that they play early in the morning because of the heat, and he would pick me up at 6:30 Sunday morning. After our bags came off the plane, we were driven to our apartment in Dr. Turner's station wagon. We had to carry these heavy bags up steps and grades approximately twenty-five feet. When we got into our apartment, about 11:30 P.M., we took one look at it and were dismayed. Another couple with children had just moved out a day or two before and had not had a chance to clean it up right. Although there were clean sheets, they were not on the beds. The walls were bare and marked up with chalk and crayons. There were no curtains or shades on the windows. One of the air conditioners wouldn't work. One of the toilets wouldn't work. We thought to ourselves that we really had lowered our standard of living considerably. We even started counting and figured there were only 119 days left.

The only bright spot in the evening was a note on the kitchen table from the LBJ Hospital Auxiliary, which said "Talofa (which means 'hello'). Whatever you need, give us a ring and we will help you." This was signed by Marilyn, who we later found was the wife of one of the doctors. The note also said, "In the refrigerator we have left bacon and eggs and bread and milk for breakfast." We felt rather low when we went to bed that night, but we were committed and there was nothing else to do about it.

The next day dawned bright and clear and hot. I went over to the hospital and was taken around by Dr. Turner and introduced to various doctors and got some idea of what was expected of me. Then I had the rest of the day off, and Violet and I went out and bought $71 worth of groceries. We started cleaning the place and getting the shades and drapes up; and the hospital maintenance staff fixed the refrigerator and unstopped the toilet. By night things looked a good deal brighter.

The following day, I made ward rounds in the Medical Department with several of the family practitioners and internists and saw a series of extremely interesting cases. I learned that 85 percent of the Samoans have gout and many have elephantiasis. One of the internists in the clinics called me in to see a fourteen-year-old boy who had leprosy; it was diagnosed in 1975. He was given medication for it, which he did not take, and he did not come back for follow-up. Now he is in serious condition. He has degenerated joints in his hands, skin lesions, a hard, prominent auricular nerve on the left side, and multiple affected body organs. His father died of leprosy at the age of thirty-one.

I saw my first patients in the clinic and hospitalized one woman who was brought in from a neighboring island, who had chronic obstructive lung disease with bronchiectasis and arteriosclerotic heart disease with congestive failure. I saw that my services were very badly needed.

In the meantime, Violet got the apartment pretty well cleaned up. We have two bedrooms, two baths, and a living room, all in a row. We also have a kitchen with electric refrigerator and electric stove. We are not in bad shape, although the apartment is minimally furnished and each room has two full walls of windows with few draperies. The appliances work fairly well when the electricity is on.

I am into the spirit of things now and think I am going to have a wonderful experience. Samoa is a beautiful island. The people are gentle, kind, and very friendly and appreciative of anything that is done. The hospital itself is certainly not another Copley. It is all on one floor, and the wards are all open to the outside. They are not air-conditioned, but the breeze blows through the screens pretty well and the patients do not complain. Both X-ray and laboratory are quite limited in what they can do, but they could be a lot worse. I hate to think what this area would be without this hospital.

As to the staff, they are a very dedicated group, but they are constantly changing. A number of doctors are two-year employees who are given nice houses to live in and are the bulwark of the hospital. Volunteer doctors come and go all the time and are in the same category as I am. I have met most of them, and I just cannot say enough good about them. We all live in a compound within a short distance of each other, and there is a lot of camaraderie among us. On Sunday we are having a get-together so that all the new doctors can get acquainted; several of the older ones are leaving.

It looks like it is going to be a wonderful experience for both Violet and

[165]

me. Violet is converting one bedroom into a studio where she can do some painting, and, believe me, there are some beautiful things here to paint. I am looking forward to the work in the hospital and also looking forward to Sunday, when I get my first crack at the Lava Lava Golf Course. I understand from people who have played it that it is a very good course and that the reason it is called the Lava Lava Golf Course is because there are chunks of lava here and there on the fairways. They say that when you tee off on the first hole, if your drive goes right down the middle, it will hit a bunch of lava rock and go "BOING!" and disappear forever.

February 1981

Since the last letter, many things have happened to the Greeleys. We did have our get-together party the Sunday after we arrived here and met a lot of wonderful people. The chief surgeon and his wife are retired from the practice of surgery and teaching in the States and decided to spend a year of their retirement here.

As time went on, it became obvious that we needed something for entertainment and some way to get around the island. We bought a black-and-white twelve-inch television set, with which we were able to see the Super Bowl and other programs, all a week late. We finally bit the bullet and rented a Toyota four-door sedan for $450 a month, and we will probably renew it as long as we are here. The high cost of rental made me think three times. The hospital has a car that is supposed to be available after 4:00 P.M. for the doctors, but the clutch went out. Too many doctors wanted to use it anyway.

The short-wave radio that I bought before I left home picks up Australia very well. I get London sometimes and also the American Armed Forces Station. We get the latest news this way, but that is about all.

People are constantly coming and going here. Dr. Harrison and his wife left today. He is an internist, who had been here since Thanksgiving. Tonight, coming in on the plane will be a family practice specialist and his wife from Missouri to spend several months. Also, we have an internist from the Army Air Force Hospital in Honolulu.

Violet is doing some painting; however, it is more difficult than she expected in that the 90 percent humidity affects the acrylics and watercolor. She is getting some sketches that she may paint when she gets home.

As to golf, I have been playing at least once a week. The first two weeks I didn't do too well and got a ninety-five. The second game, I hit four balls out of bounds, including one that lodged in a coconut tree and would not come down. My partners gave me a choice of climbing the tree and retrieving the ball or taking two strokes. No way could I climb the thirty-foot, slippery palm tree, so I lost the two strokes.

The second part of this letter will deal with medical experiences since I last wrote. My hours are rather short here. I go to work at approximately 7:30 in the morning, and I am home an hour at noon. The office hours in the afternoon are supposed to be over at four, but are often over by three, so I am not on duty too long at a time. On my day on call, I may have two or three hospital admissions and a night call once in a while. I have seen a number of cases of elephantiasis and a leprosy case, which I will never forget. This is a case of a thirty-year-old man who has not taken care of himself or taken his Dapsone as prescribed. He came into the hospital with erythematous, nodular leprosy, high fever, and anemia and was really a mess. He had clawlike fingers with osteomyelitis caused by leprosy and disintegration of many of his joints. He had nodules all over his body. He looks like the typical case you see in the textbooks. Dr. Matangi, who has charge of all the leprosy cases here, put him on steroids, and within forty-eight hours he was markedly improved. Of course, he is also taking Dapsone and some other medications.

An ophthalmologist from Harvard, Dr. Weiss, flew in last week, and one of his colleagues came a few days ago. I think they had a Samoan adjustment to make, as this is not anything like Harvard. There is a lot of cataract surgery to be done here, and an ophthalmologist who comes for a month, like Dr. Weiss, will probably do twelve to fifteen besides some corneal transplants, which are not ordinarily done here. It is an interesting experience for them, as well as a cultural shock.

I had an interesting case of ciguartera fish poisoning a few nights ago. Two whole families ate a barracuda and within eight hours became very, very ill. One of the patients had to be put in Intensive Care. Ciguartera fish poisoning causes hypotension and bradycardia. Often the pulse will go down to about thirty and the blood pressure down to around fifty. It is reported that this poison also occurs in red snapper here, and there is about 12 percent fatality for cases of this kind. Luckily, all these patients recovered.

THE ISLAND ITSELF

American Samoa is a beautiful island. It is volcanic and mountainous with some flatter areas covered with lush vegetation between the mountains and the ocean on the south side. The Samoans, for the most part, live in the low areas, although some of them have built houses up on the hills. We took a drive over the length of the island's only roads, about thirty miles along the beach. It was really beautiful. Occasionally a hurricane tears up the island quite badly. None have struck for several years, and none are due this year, I hope. The island is overrun with African snails that were brought in accidentally several years ago and are the intermediate hosts to the rat lung worm, which causes eosinophilic

[167]

meningitis. I see about twenty of these snails on the fence just outside our window right now. They are very pretty but so dangerous.

THE PEOPLE

The Samoan people are a beautiful Polynesian race. They are brown-skinned, very pleasant people, always smiling and not belligerent. They have a culture all their own that they have had for centuries. Their diet is largely carbohydrates and fish. There are 31,000 Samoans on this island and 800 white people. The Samoans had 1,200 births last year and 80 deaths, so you see what is happening. They are extremely fertile, and most families have eight or nine children. The children, when they get to be adults, migrate to New Zealand, Hawaii, or California. I understand there are more Samoans in California than there are in Samoa, and also there are more in New Zealand and Hawaii than there are here. They are very close families, and they are constantly making the trip back and forth as soon as they save enough money to do it.

It is amazing how large these people get. The average weight of a Samoan woman is 204 pounds, and that of a Samoan man is 228 pounds. As you may have noticed from sports reports, eligible Samoans are sought by college teams and pros because they are so heavy and short and make excellent football players. One can easily see how they get to be heavy when one looks at the lunch the hospital serves every day—about 2,000 calories—and that is only one of the three meals.

Approximately 20 percent of the Samoans are diabetics, and about 80 to 85 percent have gout. Hypertension is also rampant, and a good deal of our outpatient clinic work is diabetes, gout, and hypertension.

THE WEATHER

The weather has been hot and humid and always rainy. The total yearly rainfall is about 220 inches. Sometimes it will rain an inch within ten or fifteen minutes, and in another twenty minutes it is all dried out and the sun is shining again. The golf course is on porous lava soil. Ten minutes after an inch of rain you can play golf using scooters, and the course is not even muddy. It is quite a different type of vegetation and soil than in Illinois.

March 1981

The thing that is uppermost in our minds today is the big storm. If you remember, in my last chapter I said I didn't want to get caught in a hurricane if I could help it. Last week was just fantastic weather-wise; the sun shone every day and the weather was not too hot. On Sunday, March 1, in the middle of the afternoon, an announcement suddenly

came on the radio that there was a typhoon or tropical storm building up about five hundred miles northwest and heading straight for American Samoa. At its present speed it would get here sometime Monday afternoon. Everyone became quite excited, as the oldtimers can remember the big hurricane of 1966, which just about wrecked the island. By Monday morning the winds were blowing very hard, and it was beginning to rain vigorously. People boarded up their houses and took all the precautions they could. As far as we were concerned, we live in so-called "hurricane-proof" quarters with precast concrete rafters and concrete reinforced steel supports all the way through the building.

I stayed at the hospital until approximately one o'clock. There were no patients coming in, so all the clinic nurses went home, and I left also. Even though I had to walk only one hundred yards across the street to our apartment, I got soaked. I never saw it rain so hard in all my life; it rained about seven inches in just a few hours. As we were sitting in our apartment watching, the lights and water supply went off. It was almost dark, the clouds were so black, and the wind was violent. We lit a candle and tried to play double solitaire, but somehow at a time like that you just don't feel very competitive. Finally, we just sat and watched. The winds blew down a number of banana trees, but that was about all the damage that was done. The main force of the hurricane turned shortly before it got to our island and went east and north and hit one of the other islands of American Samoa, called Manua. That island was completely devastated; all of the trees and most of the buildings were blown down. I don't know if there was any loss of life, but it almost obliterated the island vegetation. We were very thankful that it missed us. The following morning the sky was clear, and everything seemed all right again.

Our living quarters now are fine and we are well settled. We have most of the comforts of home. We still have some trouble with big cockroaches, approximately three inches long, that drive Violet to distraction in the kitchen. She has some Raid, which kills most of them. The thing that really bothered her was that one night she was going to bed and found a three-inch cockroach in her nightgown. We have a rather wide crack under one of our doors, and at night we put a towel over the crack to keep out the cockroaches and toads. Occasionally we forget to put the towel down, and we may wake up at three o'clock in the morning with a big toad in our room, which we have to escort out the door with the aid of a flashlight. Usually they are pretty cooperative and just jump right out without any trouble.

The Samoans have closely knit families. Many patients in the hospital are accompanied by their families, and one or two of the sons or daughters stay all night and sleep on the floor by the patient's bed so that mother or father will not be left alone. I admitted a seventy-year-old woman yesterday who had pneumonia and was quite sick. Her two grown sons asked if it was all right if one of them stayed all night and slept on the floor by her bed so that she would not want for anything.

The floors are hard, but these people are well padded and they seem to sleep just about as well as if they were in a bed. After all, they don't have beds in their own houses.

Maybe you would like to hear about a couple of interesting cases that were seen in the emergency room. The pediatricians had a ten-year-old boy come in with pain in his ear. He had been to the emergency room twice, and they had looked in his ear and seen nothing. When the pediatrician looked in his ear this time, he saw a worm coming through the eardrum. It was an *Ascaris lumbricoides* worm, four and one-half inches long. The amazing thing is that this worm came from the stomach, up through the nasopharynx, through the eustachian tube and back of the eardrum, and finally made its own hole through the eardrum to get out. The other interesting case was a young fellow who was brought into the emergency room with a six-inch fish in his throat. The Samoans are great reef fishermen, and when they catch fish they often bite their heads off. This man got the fish stuck in his throat and couldn't get it out. It was removed successfully in the emergency room.

While we are talking about medicine, I might as well tell you about the bush doctors to whom some of the Samoans still go. I had a fifteen-year-old boy in the hospital with hepatitis. He left suddenly without a doctor's permission. When the Public Health people sent an ambulance and a policeman out to get him, he saw them coming and ran off into the bush, and they never did find him. He went to a bush doctor who treats illnesses with herbs and leaves. The last I heard, the boy was getting along fine even though he didn't get regular medical care. Quite often parents bring in small babies that have been treated by a witch doctor and wrapped with all kinds of irritating leaves. Sometimes these babies are acidotic and die from exposure as a result of the treatment.

My golfing group includes some Samoans, who are pretty good golfers. They are in approximately the sixty to sixty-five age bracket. A couple of weeks ago, Lene Yanell invited all his golfing friends, which included me, to a Fia Fiar, a Samoan feast, at his home after our game. He has a beautiful home overlooking the Pacific Ocean. Lene showed us his umu, which is an outdoor cooking shed in which they heat rocks on which to cook the dinner. This is a custom of centuries. Many Samoans cook that way every Sunday morning, so that often the island is well covered with smoke from the umus. After visiting awhile, Lene started to bring around the food. The first was a very large plate of mixed types of raw fish. I have never been able to enjoy raw fish, but when the dozen men started eating it with such relish I thought I should at least try. One takes a big chunk of fish on a kind of toothpick and dunks it into hot sauce. The sauce was much hotter than any I have tasted. I got the first piece of fish down. The second piece caught in my throat for a little while, but went down. The third stuck and I just couldn't eat any more. Everybody else seemed to be enjoying it to the last. The main course included five kinds of meat, including chicken, spareribs, pork, beef, and

[170]

various kinds of fish. Also, we had taro, pineapple bananas, breadfruit and papaya. It was a regular Samoan feast, a fia fia.

Lene is one of the high chiefs and owns quite a bit of land. He came to me for a complete physical later and liked it so well that he had one of the other chiefs come for a checkup, also.

Violet is having good success with her painting now. She has painted some of the most beautiful pictures I have ever seen. I am not sure if we will get home with any of them because the doctors, and the Samoans, also, just can't get over how nice they are and want to buy them. She probably will sell most of them, but she will bring home the sketches so that she can probably redo some of them at home.

A woman came to see me recently and told me that her sister had died the previous week. In describing the funeral and burial, she told about how all graves are located close to the family residence. Her sister's husband had died several years ago. They dug him up, took all the meat off his bones, oiled the bones with Samoan oil, and put them in with her sister so that they could be together and also take up only one grave. I understand this is common practice with Samoans.

There is a place on the coast about three or four miles from here called "The Turtle and the Shark." It is a very rocky area, and the waves come tumbling in with great vigor. According to legend, two hundred years ago a woman and her granddaughter were starving to death, so they went out on this rock and jumped off. She was turned into a shark and her granddaughter into a turtle. Ever since then, if you chant the right song, the turtle and shark will appear. We went to this place and asked a poorly dressed, older woman who was walking by where we could see the turtle and the shark. She said she would show us, and she got out on the rock and chanted this beautiful song. In several minutes a six-foot shark came swimming in and then disappeared. After she chanted a little bit longer, a big sea turtle came in and swam across directly in front of us. It was hard to believe. We often doubt the truth of legends, but when this woman sang and the turtle and shark both appeared, it made a believer out of me.

I believe it might be helpful if I tell you a little more about the island and how the people live. There are about seventy small villages on Tutuila. Most of them are on the south, east, and west sides. The north side is so rugged that roads cannot be built there, and the few villages can be reached only by boat. A blacktop road hugs the seacoast and goes approximately half way around the island. The road does not have one straight place in it, and at no time can you go over twenty to twenty-five miles an hour. The view along this road is beautiful—the rain forest up on the hills and mountains on one side, and the surf and waves coming in from the Pacific Ocean on the other.

I mentioned there were seventy villages. Each village has a high chief, who is the big boss. Under him are several chiefs and talking chiefs. All the land from the village to the top of the mountain belongs to everybody. It is not recorded in the courthouse, and much of the island has not been surveyed. It passes from generation to generation of the families living there.

The beach that fronts on each village belongs to that village and is not a public beach. An outsider must get permission from the chief in order to swim. As a general thing, the villagers are very harmonious in their relations with each other, but this is not always true. About three weeks ago, one of the villages had appointed a new high chief because their former chief had died a year or two ago. A Samoan who thought he should have been appointed promptly took his gun and murdered the new high chief and also one of his relatives. The murderer is now in jail, so he really isn't gaining much. Some feared it might cause tribal war, but so far nothing has happened.

To confuse you more, five to twenty villages form a county, presided over by a paramount chief and at least two talking chiefs. Five to six counties comprise a district, and they also have paramount chiefs and talking chiefs. I am not quite sure what the talking chief does, except that he is the spokesman for the big chief. If this has you all confused, don't worry. I have lived here now for three months and I am more confused than when I came.

A good many of the people live in open fales (houses). You have seen pictures of them on postcards, and I will bring you some pictures when I come home. They are single, open rooms, and the families sleep on the floor on very thin mats. As you drive along the highway, especially in the afternoon when it is hot, you will see many people lying in the fales because that is the coolest place around. A few of the people in the last generation have built more modern homes, but still by far the largest percentage of Samoans live in open fales.

One has to be careful about driving at six o'clock. At 6:00 P.M. everybody has vespers, or religious services, which last from fifteen to twenty minutes. The villages post guards at the village entrances so that cars cannot drive through during services. If you happen to come along at that time, you just have to wait until the vespers are over.

I think there are at least twenty religious denominations on this island, including all of those that we have at home, like Mormons, Methodists, Presbyterians, Congregationalists, Catholics, Baptists, Seventh Day Adventists, etc. Church services are mostly in Samoan, so there is not much point in going except out of curiosity. I have never heard any prettier voices than the Samoans' choirs. We plan to go to services in several different churches before we leave.

When it comes to athletics, the young Samoans are very competitive. They play rugby and cricket with such intensity that fights sometimes result. A week ago there was a rugby match between two of the villages, and the losers beat up the referee, injuring him quite badly; then the fans and the players of the two villages got into a free-for-all, and a number of them ended up in the emergency room at the hospital. I guess that's not too much different from what we have at home in baseball games and football games.

As you have guessed from my other chapters, this is strictly government medicine. It is such a contrast to the type of medicine we have at home that it makes me appreciate much more the quality of medicine I was able to practice. Because of the shortage of doctors and the constant turnover, these people never have a personal physician. I am very much impressed with how they crave someone to be their friend and their doctor over a number of years. They come to me as patients two or three times and then want to know how long I will be here. When I tell them, they just shake their heads and say, "It would be so nice if doctors would come here and stay. We no sooner get to know one than we have to go to another one."

Just a word about how government medicine is financed here. The hospital turns in a budget to the American Samoan government, which in turn submits a budget to the Department of the Interior of the United States. That department furnishes Samoa with around $36 million a year, with which they pay a good many of their bills and also budget so much for the hospital. The American Samoan government has local income from the fisheries here and other businesses. Also, the people are charged an income tax, as in the United States, the only difference being that the money collected from income tax in American Samoa stays there to help run their island. If it weren't for the help that the United States has given Samoa, especially since World War II, I think it would be a much poorer island. It has given them a taste of civilization as we know it. Many of the younger people like it and go to California, Honolulu, Australia, and New Zealand, breaking away from their Samoan culture, which is pretty much as it has been for centuries.

World War II really brought the changes in the island. Every half mile you see the remains of a concrete pillbox along the coast. American Marines were trained here for the landings and island-hopping that they used so successfully against the Japanese. One can still see many remains of World War II ships and concrete gun emplacements.

Cruise ships come into Pago Pago Bay at least two or three times a month and stay one day. The passengers take tours around the island and do sightseeing. After all, this is probably one of the most beautiful islands in the world. If we have time, we sometimes go down to the bay and go aboard some of the big cruise ships. They are always very interesting. Two of the people with whom I play golf are pilots and run the tugboats that bring these big ships into the harbor.

I had two patients with ciguatera fish poisoning again last week, one of whom was a nurse who worked in the intensive care area. She ate the fish at two o'clock, came to work at four o'clock, and at five o'clock she suddenly got so sick that her blood pressure dropped to seventy and her pulse to thirty. She had to go to bed right in the intensive care area where she was working. We gave her all kinds of stimulants and oxygen to keep her going. It took a week for her to get over it. Her husband had eaten the same fish, but not as much, and he was in the hospital for two days. It scares us so that we are afraid to eat fish here.

My golf game is getting along fine. I play at least once a week, sometimes twice, with the nicest people. I haven't lost any more balls in the coconut trees, but I have knocked some out of bounds. When they are out of bounds they are gone, because they are in a rain forest and there is no way you can ever find them.

As far as our living conditions are concerned, they are quite satisfactory. I haven't seen many cockroaches lately. We do have several six- to eight-inch lizards in the kitchen that I understand get rid of the cockroaches. Through the daytime they stay up in the rafters where you can't see them, and then at night they come down and find the cockroaches. They really don't bother us much, and they are supposed to be harmless, so we don't worry about them.

A scene in Pago Pago, American Samoa.

The electricity often goes off, sometimes several times a day and sometimes for several hours. The other morning I had half my face shaved with my electric razor when the power went off. It didn't come on again for several hours, so I had to go to work with my face rough on one side and smooth on the other.

Violet and I bought some lava lavas (wrap-around skirts) the other day. We thought that if all the natives wore them we ought at least to have some to take home to show you. Some of the doctors even wear lava lavas to make their rounds and do their hospital work, but I haven't come to that yet.

I will tell you about one more interesting custom and then will close. When a family on this island has many children, most of them boys, they need a girl to help do the things that women do. They purposely make one of the boys into a girl. They dress him like a girl and teach him to do women's work completely—like washing and cooking. He grows up to be a regular transvestite and is accepted everywhere. Some break away from it and become heterosexual and have a normal marriage, but most go through life as a person who does not marry and who is a transformed male. They wear their hair like a woman, wear clothes like a woman, and act like a woman in most respects.

Time is going rather rapidly and it won't be long until we leave this island and return to the United States.

April 1981

This chapter is being written in Honolulu after having flown from Samoa the night before last.

To bring you up to date, we have had about two weeks of continuous rain, at least two inches a day. I don't know how the Samoans can stand this much water. It doesn't seem to bother them. They go out in the rain the same as if the sun were shining, and if they get wet, so what? It's always eighty to ninety degrees.

April 16 was Flag Day, a celebration of the day in 1900 when Samoa became a protectorate of the United States. They have had a very good relationship with the United States and have been subsidized to the point where they are better off than the neighboring islands. On Flag Day they hold all kinds of parades and contests. One of the most interesting events has always been the longboat race in Pago Pago Bay. By longboat, I mean a boat that carries forty-six people, twenty-two men rowing on each side, and one with a drum at each end. As the drummers beat time, they all dip their oars in rhythm. This year the race was won by Tonga, not by Samoa, but it was still a very picturesque occasion.

Three more internists have come and gone; each stayed a month or less. Two of them were residents, and although they were thorough in their workups of patients, they were inefficient in getting work done. I think you have to practice a while to acquire those skills. The other internist was a well-trained army man, but he stayed only three weeks. He was not really interested in his patients and in some ways was not much help to us.

We have many types of personalities among the doctors here. For instance, Dr. Holloway and his wife, also an M.D., sailed here a year ago from San Francisco, a distance of approximately five thousand miles, when baby Sam was only two months old. Now that their year is up, they are going to sail back to San Francisco. This seems a little bit foolhardy, but maybe it's just my age and their youth that makes the difference in viewpoint.

Violet closed her studio about two weeks ago because of lack of materials. Altogether, she finished about twenty paintings and sold all but three. Everybody seemed to like her work.

Knowing that we were going to be leaving before too long, we decided to take at least a two-day holiday and go to Savaii, one of two big islands in Western Samoa. We made the trip as a package tour with two of the other doctors and their wives. Western Samoa has had its independence only a few years and is what you might call an emerging nation. The average income per worker is approximtely $400 per year. They subsist off the sea and land—from the fish they catch, the coconuts they pick, and the taro and breadfruit that are available. They subsist, but that is all. In contrast, American Samoans have plenty to eat and are very well nourished. The United States furnishes them every year with a sum equivalent to about $1,000 per person. It is easy to see why they are so much better off than the Western Samoans. Though American Samoa has a difficult time getting doctors to stay and staff the hospital, and does not have good medical care as we know it, it is still better than Western Samoa.

Our small plane landed in Savaii on an old lava-rock runway that looked more like an old road. Tall trees on each end of the runway made it somewhat hazardous, but we landed safely. We were met by the owner of the Safua Hotel, an Englishman, who took us approximately eight miles to his hotel in a pickup truck and van. The Samoan-style lobby was completely open. Our rooms were separate fales, small but adequate and wide open on all sides. We slept under mosquito nets to avoid the swarms of mosquitos. There was also a small bathroom with shower, lavatory, and stool attached to the fale. It rained hard one night, and the thatched roof leaked like a sieve. The proprietor of the hotel is white, but his wife is Samoan. When we asked him how many children he had, he said he wasn't quite sure; he had some by his first wife, she had some children by her first husband, and the two of them had some of their own. I gathered that there must be at least ten or twelve. It was very interesting to hear this man talk about the troubles of the people there. He said they are very hard workers but there is no industry in Western Samoa. The only jobs they can get are picking coconuts or helping with fishing, neither of which brings in much money.

The people of Western Samoa, even though they are of the same race as those of American Samoa, are lighter in weight and more muscular because they work hard and often do not have enough to eat. It was obvious that the children were hungry, and some of them appeared to be malnourished. In inquiring further, we found out that their medical care and public health work, such as immunizations, are probably twenty years behind American Samoa. They are attempting to build hospitals and attract doctors but can offer little remuneration. The doctors they are recruiting come from Australia, New Zealand, and Germany. We met a pathologist who had retired from practice in Australia. We also met a young doctor and his doctor wife from Germany. They had been there about six months and are planning to stay the rest of the year. He said that for two years before this he had been in Africa. When I asked him if he was going back to Germany to practice, he said, "No. My wife and I expect to do this kind of work as long as we live. This is our life." When I think of the many people of Western Samoa who are benefiting from these dedicated doctors' care, it makes me proud that there are people of this caliber in the world.

The proprietor of the hotel drove us around the island in the back of a truck and an old station wagon. We traveled many miles over the roughest kind of roads. We saw pyramids and lava beds, and we swam at the beautiful sand beaches. As I left that island and went back to American Samoa, I couldn't help but contrast the two Samoas. One had been helped by the United States, and the other was trying to make it on its own. It has a long way to go. I understand that 40 percent of the people of Western Samoa have filariasis from mosquitos, and there is practically no mosquito control. There are over four hundred cases of leprosy. American Samoa is very fortunate. They have the same culture, but what a difference!

As our plane took off for Honolulu, our minds were full of thoughts of the past three and one-half months. It has not only been an educational experience for both of us, but I feel that I was able to do some good where I was needed as a doctor, even though I often felt frustrated and wondered it it was all worthwhile. We both made many friends, both Samoan and American. I cared for quite a number of patients, and they were all sad when I told them I was leaving. I had good rapport with the nurses and the medical officers, who were also Samoan. The white people on the island were exceptionally good to us, and we made many friends with whom I am sure we will correspond the rest of our lives.

I have described the culture of the people of Samoa, and I will close by citing two examples that point up what I have said before. The first case was a woman in her late 70s, who had a serious stroke just after I came to the island. She was not my patient, but I did care for her several times when her doctor was absent. She was on a ventilator for quite a while, and she has been tube-fed ever since. She is completely unconscious. Her family, of whom there are many, have spent every hour of every day with her ever since she became sick. When it was hot, they fanned her to keep her cool; they turned her frequently so that she got no bed sores, and they sat up with her all night, night after night, taking turns among members of the family. This kind of love and closeness of family relationships is something that is not always seen in the United States.

The second case was a young secretary who worked in the hospital, who came to see me as a patient. During the interview our conversation went something like this:

Dr. Greeley: "What is your trouble? Where do you feel bad?"

Ana: "I'm tired all the time. I have some numbness in the fingers, but mainly I am just tired."

Dr. Greeley: "How old are you?"

Ana: "Twenty-eight."

Dr. Greeley: "How many children do you have?"

Ana: "I have nine children. I have five of my own. I have two that my husband had by a previous marriage. Another one is a child of my sister-in-law, whose husband died and she had to give some of her children away as she couldn't raise them all, and then I adopted one that belonged to an unwed mother. You know, in Samoa, we think that every child should have a parent and have a family life, and it is not uncommon for Samoans with big families to adopt more if it is necessary."

Dr. Greeley: "I certainly admire you for your attitude in trying to raise these nine children. At your age, you probably could have nine more."

Ana: "Not if I can keep my husband from catching me, I won't."

Dr. Greeley: "Well, that is quite difficult sometimes."

Ana: "Yes, that is what happened when I had the last one. He did catch me."

Dr. Greeley: "I don't see how you can get all your work done at home and work full time as a secretary. Do you have help?"

Ana: "My children help me quite a bit. We do all our own washing. We do all our own cooking. We go to church three nights a week, and we don't eat until after we get home."

Dr. Greeley: "Where do you go to church?"

Ana: "At the Assembly of God Church."

Dr. Greeley: "You live in Pago Pago, and the Assembly of God Church is handy, so at least it doesn't take you long to get there."

Ana: "We do not go to that church. We go over the mountains, about five miles, to the Assembly of God Church in Fagaso. We used to go to the church in the next block, but some people were jealous of us and would not attend because we were in the church. We thought that if we joined the church on the other side of the mountain, those people would come back to church so their souls could be saved, too."

Dr. Greeley: "Ana, you certainly live and exemplify the Samoan Christian spirit."

And with that, Violet and I close the fifth and final chapter of "The Samoan Experience."

The Appalachian Experience

November 1981

On October 28, 1981, Violet and I returned from California, and between that time and the early morning of October 30 we packed all our things and prepared to leave for Appalachia. We left home at 7:00 A.M. on October 30 and drove approximately 450 miles the first day, arriving in the hill country of Kentucky. We still had 150 miles to go to get to Appalachia. The mountain country of southeastern Kentucky really started when we turned off Interstate 75 onto the Daniel Boone Highway. We then traveled through some beautiful hill country. The road was new, slicing through the mountains to Hazard, which is the principal town in our area of service.

When we arrived in Hazard, we found it to be a sleepy town of about five thousand people, nestled in a valley with low mountains all around. We finally found our way to Hindman, where the June Buchanan Clinic is situated and where I would be working. We arrived at the Clinic at approximately 11:00 A.M. and were met by Joyce Smith, a nurse from the emergency room. She made us welcome and showed us the clinic. This facility has three examining rooms for each of the two regular doctors, a small laboratory, an X-ray room, business areas, and the emergency room. There are two rooms off the emergency room that are used for obstetrical deliveries. Most of the deliveries are done here unless they are complicated, in which case they are sent to Hazard Hospital. The patient who delivers goes home the same day or may possibly stay over one night if she needs watching. The two doctors in the clinic are Dr. Barker and Dr. Watts. Dr. Barker is sixty-five years old and has done family practice all his life. He was born and raised in Hindman, so he knows the people and their needs. He loves medicine and is a delightful person. He is one of the most respected men in the community. It has been said that practically everybody under forty years of age in that area was delivered by Dr. Barker.

Dr. Watts also is a native of the area. He is around fifty-five years of age and has a tremendous practice. He is a workaholic and often sees patients until eight or nine o'clock at night without stopping for dinner. His patients love him, and he is also one of the pillars of the community.

[179]

Unfortunately, Dr. Watts became very ill with diverticulosis and diverticulitis. Repeated attacks made it necessary for him to have a hemicolectomy, and he is recuperating now. It is because of Dr. Watts' illness that I was asked to go to Hindman to help out.

Getting back to the events of the day, Joyce Smith introduced us to Pat Sloan, the pharmacist at the clinic. Pat led us by car to our apartment, approximately fifteen miles away, near Ary. It is part of what is called the Homeplace Settlement. The Homeplace Clinic is also operated by the Appalachian Regional Hospital System and has two doctors. The apartments there house the medical staff. The first ten miles, we followed Pat along the new superhighway, which had just been finished and was not yet officially open. Then we turned off onto a narrow mountain road following the valley. We passed many mountain homes separated from the road by the creek. Suspension footbridges connected the houses to the road. After about five miles of beautiful scenery and winding road along Troublesome Creek, suddenly the area opened up into a broad valley, and we could see our apartment house on the side of a hill about a half-mile away.

Our small apartment has a wonderful view of the whole valley and the mountains across Troublesome Creek. We have a bedroom with closet, a bath, kitchen, small living room, and utility area. There is electric heat, electric stove, refrigerator, and minimal furniture. The superintendent of the grounds came up and supplied other things we needed. We found out that he is from New Jersey and has been here about ten years. He is the minister for the interdenominational services in the community house, where he preaches every Sunday to about twenty-five people. On Sunday, November 1, we attended his small church. The people are certainly very religious and friendly.

We bought groceries and explored Hazard and Hindman and were ready to start work on Monday, November 2. I got up early and drove through the valleys and mountains to Hindman, getting there about fifteen minutes before eight. I went into the emergency room and was immediately confronted with a patient who was in congestive heart failure and was critically ill. Dr. Barker had been there with her since six o'clock. He had also been on emergency call the night before and was about worn out. I took over for him with the patient while he got some breakfast and did some other work before coming back to the clinic. As soon as the patient became more stabilized, we sent her by ambulance to the Appalachian Regional Hospital in Hazard. That is the procedure that we follow with patients who need hospitalization or have problems we can't handle here. I was with this patient until about ten o'clock, and then I started in the clinic for the day. I saw patients in Dr. Watts' office all morning and all afternoon with only a short break at noon. I was through at approximately five o'clock and had seen twenty-seven patients the first day. That's not bad!

Dr. Barker, who had been up almost all night, saw more people than I did. I certainly have a lot of respect for him who, at the age of sixty-five, carries such heavy medical and community responsibilities. Dr. Watts came over in the late afternoon to see how things were getting along. He has recovered from his surgery quite well but will not be able to work for a while. He is exceedingly pleasant. I just can't say enough about these two men who shoulder most of the medical needs of Knott County. The cases I saw on my first day were generally run-of-the-mill—a few pneumonias, strep throats, hypertensives, and minor accidents. Some took only a few minutes and some much longer. There was a Dictaphone in my office on which to dictate medical records, not much different from the Dreyer Medical Clinic.

Les Rogers, the clinic administrator, talked with me for a while and challenged me to a game of golf with him this weekend on the nine-hole Hazard course. He says a number of the greens are blind and you have to shoot from down under and hope that you land on top. I guess it is a pretty hilly course, and it should be quite a challenge.

Everybody at the clinic seemed to be glad to see me and were so nice that by the end of the day I felt quite at home. Many of the patients were exceedingly poor and certainly needed care. Hindman is a town of approximately one thousand, on Troublesome Creek. It is interesting that we also live on Troublesome Creek, only fifteen miles downstream. It is a typical southeastern Kentucky mountain town. The streets are narrow, the cars are old, the houses cling to the sides of the hills. The only industry is coal mining, including deep mining and strip mining. With their big machines, coal companies actually start at the top and completely knock the mountain down with dynamite charges and strip mining equipment. Big drags will dip up sixty-five yards of coal at a time. There is one such rig working across the valley from where we live, twenty-four hours a day. At night we see the lights of this big crane, ten stories high, swinging back and forth, removing the overburden. The thirty-ton coal trucks are then driven over public roads to the Hazard tipple, where they empty their coal and go back for more.

On my first day of work I was given a Ram Charger with four-wheel drive, so I won't have to use my own car. It sits up very high off the road, and it took me a little while to get used to it, but it runs very well. I don't know if they anticipate that the roads will soon be full of snow and ice, or what, but they sure gave me a mountain car.

On that first day, as I drove through the mountains, down by Troublesome Creek, and up over the passes, with the fog rising over the mountain tops, I couldn't help thinking back how exactly forty-nine years ago on the morning of November 2, 1932, at the same hour, I left home with two dollars in my pocket and only the clothes I wore—no coat, only a red sweater, which I needed because it was kind of chilly that morning. I walked the first ten miles and then hitchhiked for many more miles. As I look back on these memories, I realize what a good life I have had. God has been very good to me.

Violet is adjusting to her new life very well. She has the apartment all cleaned and has located a number of things that we needed. Luckily, she has our car, in which she can explore—with due respect to the coal trucks. I think she will soon be doing some watercolor paintings. She has already looked up the local extension service, and she may be helping them before long, also.

I am writing this at the end of my second day of work. It was not as busy today as yesterday, although I saw between fifteen and twenty patients. We did have one interesting case. A twelve-year-old boy was bitten by a copperhead snake. He was brought immediately to the clinic with a tourniquet on his leg. The area below the bite was quite dark, swollen, and exceedingly painful. You could easily see two puncture wounds from the snakebite. He was given Antivenin, three ampules, at ninety dollars an ampule, and IV fluids and then was moved to Hazard Hospital. I was told that five such bites had been treated this summer and all had done well with little residual effect. This was a new experience for me, as I had never seen a poisonous snakebite before.

The Appalachian Regional Hospital System is a nonprofit group that works throughout Virginia, West Virginia, Kentucky, and part of Tennessee. It owns eleven hospitals and has a number of clinics that provide the only medical care these people have. The June Buchanan Clinic, at which I am working, is operated by the System, as is Homeplace Clinic and the hospital at Hazard. There is a clinic about fifteen miles on the other side of Hazard by the name of Yerkes Clinic, the same as my middle name. It was named after a man who was president of the local railroad. I suppose he probably was a relative of mine. It would really have been a coincidence if I had worked at the Yerkes Clinic. The Hospital System is doing a lot of good for the mountain people of Kentucky, Tennessee, and Virginia. All of their doctors, including Dr. Watts and Dr. Barker, are salaried. There are about six doctors in all of Knott County, which has a population of seventeen thousand. You can see that the people are not overly served by medicine, but the doctors that are here try to do a good job. I feel that Dr. Barker and Dr. Watts are well prepared in family practice and are providing excellent medical care as far as the facilities will allow.

The culture here is quite different from Northern Illinois or Samoa, but I believe that our stay will be very pleasant, and we look forward to it.

Last Saturday I played golf on the Hazard course. I have never played on such a hilly course. It seems rather odd to stand on a tee and know your ball is going to land 125 feet below and about 175 yards away, if it makes it. In spite of the Kentucky River, the railroad, valleys, and hills, I was lucky and shot an 87 for my first game. We have had bad weather on

On Troublesome Creek, Ary, Kentucky.

Saturdays ever since, so that is probably the only game I will play. Now it is too cold.

We drove out to the Yerkes Clinic one day last week. The road is very narrow and winding, one way in some places, up and down hills and around mountains for seven miles. It was quite an effort, just to get my picture taken by the sign of the Yerkes Clinic. For the most part, the nurse practitioner runs the clinic and takes care of all the patients who come in. A doctor goes out for a half day each week. The nurse has been there three years and knows the mountain people. She certainly is a valuable asset to Yerkes and represents the only nearby medical care available.

We have been to the Homeplace church at the foot of the hill three times. The preacher, who is also the caretaker, presents the whole service. There is no piano so he leads the singing, and one Sunday he played one of the hymns on a harmonica. He reads his own text and preaches the sermon and doesn't take up a collection. Even though there is not all the ritual of our churches at home, one could not help but feel that God was there. Another Sunday we attended the Presbyterian Church in Hazard with Les Rogers, the administrator of the Buchanan Clinic and several of the other clinics. Today we went to the Hindman Methodist Church. It is quite different from the Methodist Church at home. There was a place in the service for the congregation to relate experiences for which they thanked God for helping them, or in which they asked for special prayers for themselves or their friends. One woman with three children said that her husband drove a coal truck and was going down a steep mountain with thirty tons of coal on his truck when the transmission went out and he lost control. Luckily, his truck bounced into a bank and did not turn over. It finally came to a stop without hurting him or anyone else. After seeing these trucks go up and down the mountain roads, I think she was justified in thanking God for her husband's safety.

There are five miles of mountain roads between Ary and the super-highway. One meets many intimidating coal trucks, both empty and loaded. The dropoffs are abrupt and the road is winding, uphill and downhill. On my way to work one morning, about 7:30, I came around a curve and saw a coal truck and some other cars stopped in front of me and realized that there had been an accident. A woman who was driving home from working all night in a nursing home had fallen asleep and slammed into a branch of Troublesome Creek. Her car was jammed in so that the front end was against one bank, the back end against the other, and the left side was against the side of the road. The whole car was below road level, and the poor woman was still at the wheel. I stopped to see if I could be of any help. There were several strong men already down in the creek trying to get her out, but it was a job because she had a broken hip and a badly broken leg and was semiconscious and heavy. To get her out of the car, we would need to slide her out and then take her up a steep bank. I got down in the branch and was able to get into the back seat of the car and to straighten out and hold her head. We didn't know but what she might have a broken neck, so we put blankets around her to keep her warm and waited for the ambulance, which came in ten or fifteen minutes. We were then able to slide a stretcher board underneath her body and get her out of the car and into the ambulance. Although she was in shock, she was conscious, and when I asked her what happened she said she just fell asleep. Well, you sure can't go to sleep on those mountain roads. She was taken to Hazard Hospital, and I understand that she is getting along well, although she had to have surgery to set her hip.

It just happened that that morning I was supposed to meet Bill Francis and Les Rogers, who were going to take me on a tour of the coal mines in the Hindman area. I was over a half-hour late, but I guess my excuse was good. That day I learned facts about coal mining that I had never known before. At the main underground mine, the guide showed us the tipple where the coal comes out on conveyor belts, is graded and washed, and then is shipped out. The tunnels go back underneath the hills about three miles in this particular mine. We did not go back to where the men were working, although we went into the mine shaft for a short distance. I never realized it before, but when it is so far to the coal face, it takes about three hours of travel time each day from the opening of the shaft to the face of the mine where the men are actually working. Those three hours and a half-hour lunch period are part of the miner's eight-hour day, so he actually puts in only four to four and one-half hours of work; he is paid from portal to portal.

I was talking to one miner who worked over near Whitesburg, Kentucky, where the mine face was seven miles under the mountain. In that mine they had railroad tracks, so they traveled faster than in the first mine I saw. It gives me the shivers to think of being that far under the ground in a small shaft. The veins of coal may narrow down to as little as thirty-two inches high, which means that a miner may have to work on his knees all day. Some veins may be seven or eight feet thick and the miners can work standing up, but most of them have to work in a crouched position. Yet very few coal miners complain about their work.

We also visited a strip mine on top of one of these small mountains where they were blasting and clearing to get down to the veins of coal and were loading it into the trucks with a loader. They would load a thirty-ton truck in just a few minutes. Then the truck would have to go down steep mountain grades on roads where it couldn't pass another truck or car for several miles, to get to the bottom of the mountain onto a road that had a good solid base. I wouldn't want that job for anything.

Many of the miners get black lung disease after twenty-five to thirty years in the mines, but they accept it as something that is inevitable and part of a miner's life. I asked my nurse, Joyce Smith, whose brother has worked in the mines for years, why these men continue to work there when they know they are going to get black lung if they keep at it. She said, "Dr. Greeley, this is the only industry we have in the whole Appalachian area. It is the only way the working men have of making a living; coal mines or coal trucks—that is their whole life, and they have to accept the fact that they will probably live ten years less than the average because of it." Miners get ninety dollars a day, and the men who run the coal trucks probably get even more. The men feel fortunate if they have jobs in the mines or connected with them, as there is 20 percent unemployment in the area and many families are on relief.

Part of the miners here are unionized, and part are nonunion, and there is a great deal of friction between the two. There is no question that the unions have done a lot for the miner. Before they were unionized, a miner could break his leg on the job and be disabled for life and that was just too bad. Also, wages were very low and there were no safety regulations in the mines. The nonunion miner produces an average of fifteen tons of coal a day, while the union miner averages about seven. Of course, you can see which the mine owner would like to have working for him. Regardless of which system is used, the mine owner does very well. He is a millionaire in southeastern Kentucky, a land in which the contrasts are great. There are many very poor people who have insufficient food and clothing and very little education. All in all, my visit to the mines that day was educational and gave me a fresh and, I hope, enlightened view of the area in which I am living.

Since the oil crisis a few years ago, the coal mining industry has been revitalized, and the economy in this area is better than it has been for many years. However, that is still not saying that it is good, as evidenced by the high unemployment rate.

In the practice of medicine, I see the usual run of cases as I described previously, with perhaps more black lung disease than I have ever seen before. I see more poor people who have never had an education and whose future looks bleak. A twenty-five-year-old mother of two children, ages six and seven, came to see me the other day and was very nervous, agitated and upset. She said that her husband had been shot and killed three weeks before. He had been visiting his sister-in-law in Hazard and was standing out in the yard when a car drove by and somebody shot and killed him. This is not a rare occurrence in southeastern Kentucky. There are many homicides as a result of friction between families; however, this violence is accepted as inevitable. Even though many times the person who did the shooting is known, there is little attempt to bring him to justice, mainly because witnesses are afraid to testify.

The other day a man came to my office for a disability exam. He was thirty-two years old and had not worked since 1968. In the process of the examination it was revealed that he could neither read nor write. That presented a problem for me. How was I going to test his eyes for vision when he couldn't read the eye chart? He couldn't even read the big letter because he didn't know what it was. My nurses came to my rescue and produced an eye chart on which there were pictures of animals of different sizes that are familiar to everybody. I was able to ascertain that his vision was 20/150 and he was entitled to disability.

Last week both Dr. Watts and Dr. Barker were back in their offices, so it was arranged that I could take two or three days off for Thanksgiving. Violet and I drove over to Hendersonville, North Carolina. When we arrived, we looked up Don Spray and Clyde Hewitt, former Aurora residents whom I have known for many years. They both seemed to be enjoying their retirement here, but they have both had quite depressing events in their lives the past year. Clyde had to have triple bypass heart surgery about a year ago, and he is just getting to the place where he can do everything he wants to do. Now he is in fairly good health and is able to work around his mountain cabin and small farm. Don has a beautiful home on top of a high hill overlooking the Smoky Mountains. He showed us the homes, the mountains, and the city of Hendersonville. Don's and Marian's thirty-one-year-old son had been sick with kidney trouble for several years and on renal dialysis for the past year and one-half. He died last September, and his death has left a very sad spot in their lives. We did have a lovely visit with these two families, and we had Thanksgiving dinner at the Sprays' home. Marian is a wonderful cook—the only trouble was that I ate too much, Violet ate too much, and we are already too fat. We came back to Ary the Friday after Thanksgiving, and now I am ready for my final two weeks of this east Kentucky service.

The settlement schools of southeastern Kentucky developed in this area from about 1910 and were started because there were no schools. There are at least a dozen of them scattered over the area, and all of them have excellent records. An example is the Red Bird Mission and Hospital and schools, about sixty miles from where we are living. Yesterday we spent most of the day visiting this hospital, seeing the area, and learning about the services it provides. The Red Bird Mission and Hospital are run by the United Methodist Church and serve five counties. During the last few years, the state of Kentucky and the counties have helped to finance the Mission School. The school has classes from grades one to twelve and an enrollment of about three hundred students. Dormitories were built to provide housing for students from remote areas. The county does run school buses now, but some families live in such inaccessible places that the students live in the dormitories in order to go to school in the winter. There is not another hospital or clinic within thirty miles. Red Bird Hospital is a beautiful twenty-eight-bed hospital with three doctors, who live on the grounds, and three dentists. They see altogether about 35,000 to 40,000 patients a year.

At least sixty to seventy families do quilting and make crafts of various kinds, which are on sale at the local mission store, but they even appear in New York and Chicago stores that deal in Kentucky crafts. These settlement schools, of which Red Bird Mission is an example, have provided experimental farms, churches, schools, community activities, and craft industries to this underprivileged area. I just can't say enough good about them.

Violet will be leaving for home on the fifth of December and will start our Christmas shopping. I will follow in about a week or ten days. We will both look back on our work here as an educational experience and also one in which we hope we have been able to do a little bit of good.

December 1981

The week before I left Appalachia, there was a terrible mine explosion about ten miles from Hindman, in which eight men were killed. I am sure you all read about it in the papers. Some of the victims were patients of the clinic, and the nurses knew them and their relatives. The next day the sister of one of the men who were killed came to the office to see me. Only a couple of days later there was another mine explosion in Tennessee. The mining of coal has many hazards, but the miners accept them in a stoic way and just hope accidents will never happen to them. Whenever there is a disaster, it affects everyone in the community. People are grief-stricken and talk in subdued voices about the tragedy and about the young men who were killed. It is a very sobering experience. Even though I have lived among these people for only a few weeks, I feel a certain closeness to them and their problems that I didn't have before. They are really a brave group of people.

I had a chance to go to lunch with Dr. Watts the other day, and I was entranced as he told of his experiences in the practice of medicine. He came back to the Hindman area in 1957 and set up practice. Even though that was only twenty-five years ago, most of the deliveries were done at home. He said that many times he would go out in his four-wheel-drive Jeep on very bad roads as far as he could along the creeks and into the hollows. At the end of the road, people would meet him and take him either on horseback or on foot, carrying his bag, to see a patient who might be in labor at the very far end of the hollow. Sometimes he would be gone two days in particularly bad weather or when the patient was very sick. He would spend the whole time waiting or helping with the delivery and be paid about thirty-five dollars. About half the time the patient was on welfare and would be unable to pay him at all. After a few years of this type of practice, he realized how inefficient it was. He started delivering babies in rooms adjoining his office and quit going to the homes. When a patient was in labor, she was brought to his office; he would deliver the baby, and the patient would go home in two hours. He delivered about two hundred babies a year this way. If the patient had complications and couldn't go home in two hours, a nurse would stay with her overnight. This saved him a lot of time during which he could be practicing medicine and doing other things for people instead of being tied up for one to two days on one delivery way out in the mountains.

Dr. Barker, who at that time had offices across the street, did the same thing. Both of these doctors are very efficient and well-trained physicians and have an excellent reputation in obstetrics. For years they both have delivered all their babies in the office, except the more complicated ones, which they sent to Hazard. Then June Buchanan donated the land, and the community, with the help of a grant from the government, built this clinic building. The two doctors, who had never practiced together before, combined their practices under the auspices of the Appalachian Regional Hospital System in the clinic. Since the patients know both of them, they go to either doctor if one is away or ill. The infant and maternal mortality for deliveries at the office are no greater than in the hospitals where mothers stay for several days before going home with their infants. Dr. Watts also told me about many other interesting things that happened in his practice—accidents, illnesses, and long hours, eighty to ninety hours a week, sometimes going forty-eight hours without sleep. In spite of all this, he has enjoyed his medical practice very much. He loves people and people love him. What I have said about Dr. Watts applies equally to Dr. Barker. I have never seen two more dedicated doctors in my life, and they practice excellent medicine.

On the fifth of December, I took Violet to Lexington to take a plane home. I did not look forward to a week by myself and I was also afraid that the winter weather might close in. I was apprehensive about the roads between the Homeplace Clinic and the new Route 80, as the area is mountainous, the roads are narrow, the coal trucks are plentiful, and I just couldn't see myself driving on them in ice and snow. The morning before I was supposed to leave for home, I was driving from Homeplace to Hindman and noticed a few flakes of snow. When I reached Route 80 it was snowing so hard I could hardly see to drive. By the time I got to Hindman, there had been a snowfall of three inches. On some of the hills the cars were slipping and sliding in every direction. Lucky for me, my four-wheel-drive vehicle took the roads in good stride. The schools were closed, and many patients couldn't get to the office. It was then I realized why most people in this area have four-wheel-drive vehicles. By night, the snow was pretty well melted. I had had all the taste I wanted of the icy roads in the wintertime in the Kentucky mountains.

On December 11 I went to work as usual. I had everything packed in the car, as I was going to leave directly from the clinic. I planned to drive part way that afternoon and thus make it home easily the next day. I saw fourteen patients in the morning and was finishing up about one o'clock. I went to the vending machine to get a bag of peanuts for lunch and was talking with Dr. Watts when both of us were paged to come to the emergency room at once. We hurried down there and, to my surprise, when we opened the emergency room door, all the employees were there with a table set with Kentucky Fried Chicken, potato salad, slaw, and all the trimmings. It was a surprise farewell party for me. They had driven twenty-two miles over the mountain roads in order to get the chicken and the other things. They gave me a beautiful going-away card with all their names and notes of appreciation for my helping them out. They also presented me with a handmade model coal wagon, with a driver and donkey, mounted on a wooden base about two feet long and seven to eight inches wide. The man, donkey, and wagon are made of coal. It must have taken many hours of work to carve this out of a chunk of coal. I don't know of anything that these good friends could have given me that would have been more appreciated. Dr. Barker is back from his vacation and also attended the party.

As I drove down the main street of Hindman for the last time, and up the long hill, over the mountain to the main highway, I had a feeling of warmth in my heart and a great satisfaction at having had the privilege of meeting all these nice people and sharing their problems, joys, and sorrows for the six weeks I was there. One becomes attached to that mountain country and the wonderful people who live there, and I fully expect to go back some day to see them again.

The New Mexican Experience

January 1982

When we were getting ready to leave home, we were apprehensive about the snowy weather. We left early and drove as far as Bloomington, where we stayed all night with our daughter, Barbara. We had some snow in Bloomington but were able to get out of it the next morning, and as we traveled farther south we drove in rain instead of snow. From then on the trip was no problem. We stopped in Tahlequah, Oklahoma, to see the doctor and his wife who had lived next door to us in Samoa. It was fun recalling our experiences together in the South Pacific.

We didn't know what to expect in the New Mexico area. The first thing we noticed was that there were endless flat plains, very few towns, and large ranches. We got to Tatum about 2:00 P.M. on January 2. We had been told by letter that we would be living in the Methodist parsonage, so that was our first stop. The parsonage was unoccupied because the new minister would not be coming until June. It is a well-planned, three-bedroom home, very handy to the church. This is the first time in my life that I can go to church without having to walk more than thirty to forty feet.

When we arrived, several church women were there measuring for drapes, cleaning up, and laying new carpet, not only for us but for the new preacher. We met Dr. Morse, who had preceded me at the clinic and who may return and take my place when I leave. She showed us around the house, the town, and the clinic.

The people of Tatum welcomed us with a reception, and it wasn't long before we felt as if we belonged here. They put up a sign at the intersection of two of the main streets that said "Welcome, Dr. Greeley."

I went to work on Monday, January 4, and have been working five days a week ever since. I have not been exceptionally busy, but business is gradually increasing as people find out that the clinic is open. This corner of New Mexico is semi-arid, with many large ranches. It is difficult to attract doctors to the area even though there are about one thousand people in Tatum and more in the surrounding area. Lovington, twenty-two miles from Tatum, has about ten thousand people and four doctors and a small hospital with twenty-eight beds. Twenty miles farther on is the 130-bed hospital in Hobbs, a city of thirty-one thousand. It has an active emergency room and is equipped to practice pretty good medicine. The cases we can't handle in Lovington we send on to Hobbs. The cases that can't be handled in Hobbs are sent on to Albuquerque or other distant medical centers.

During my first four weeks I sent the surgeon in Lovington three bad gallbladders, all of which required cholecystectomies, an appendectomy, a pilonidal cyst, and some other minor surgical procedures. One of the gallbladder patients was a twenty-two-year-old girl, the mother of five children, who had been having attack after attack of vomiting and abdominal pain. She had been to the emergency room in Hobbs several times, and she had seen a number of doctors when she had attacks, but because of her age nobody thought to take a gallbladder X-ray. The X-ray showed her gallbladder to be full of stones. After surgery she made a rapid recovery, and for the first time in a year and a half she is now completely free of pain.

The culture here is entirely different from Kentucky, Samoa, and Aurora, Illinois. The ranchers are independent, rough, honest, and genuine people. One patient, a rancher, said he had forty-two sections, which is approximately 26,000 acres. I said, "You certainly have a big ranch." He replied, "No, mine would be considered a small ranch. Some around here have 800 sections—that's 500,000 acres." He said that when he was branding calves in the spring he would invite me to come out to watch.

The other big thing around here is oil. There are several wells within a few miles of Tatum, but the biggest oil pools are a little farther away. Approximately twenty miles west is an area where you can stand in one place and count at least seventy-five pumpers working day and night. There are other areas just south of Lovington and east of Tatum.

Lea County is four times the size of the state of Rhode Island and has a population of 59,000, a thinly populated area. One is impressed by the flat, dry land, the tumbleweed, the cattle, the windmills, and the roads. The few roads are very good, and distance means nothing to these people. The school buses that pick up the children for the school at Tatum go as far as seventy miles away. Can you imagine a child riding seventy miles one way to school, a round trip of 140 miles every day? He almost sleeps, eats, and studies on the bus. When the schools play basketball games, they normally go one hundred to two hundred miles. One school in their football schedule is 240 miles from here. The hospital in Lovington is twenty-two miles away, but the road is absolutely straight and flat and well maintained. You set your cruise control at sixty miles an hour and you are there in twenty-two minutes. It used to take me about twelve minutes to get from my house to Mercy Center, so it is only adding ten more minutes to get to the hospital here.

The weather here is something else. People told me when I came that they had very little snow, maybe two to five inches, and the temperature would always be up around sixty in the daytime and maybe in the twenties or thirties at night. The first week we were here, we had a snowfall of fourteen inches. It paralyzed everything. There are no snowplows, so they couldn't plow the roads. The people just sat at home and waited for the snow to melt, which it did in three or four days. The temperature gets cool at night, but it always warms up in the daytime. Today, January 31, it is approximately fifty degrees and sunny. It was twenty-four degrees this morning, but few people wear coats. They say in March and April they have strong winds and sand storms. I hate the wind and dirt, but it looks as if I am stuck with it for three months anyway. Summer temperatures go over one hundred degrees ten days out of the year; but more of the time it is in the low nineties with low humidity, so the heat is not so noticeable, and it is always cool at night. Rainfall averages about fourteen inches a year.

This is a great big plain that they call "the cap rock," about 4,000 feet elevation. This high plain extends about one hundred miles north, about one hundred miles east into Texas, and south to the border. It is the land of the big sky. At night from the city limits of Tatum we can see the lights of Lovington twenty-two miles away, and they look as if they are only a few miles off.

My little clinic here has an X-ray, a small laboratory, a number of offices, an emergency room, and electrocardiograph. I can get blood chemistries done in twenty-four hours, since a courier from the hospital in Lovington picks up any lab work every day.

Violet is painting windmills and oil wells, old houses, fence posts, and sky. We are going to take some trips west to the mountains in the next few weeks where she may find more subjects.

March 1982

Time is getting short and we will be going home in two weeks. It has been a different experience from anything we have ever had, but it has been very rewarding. These people are not poor, but they need medical care just as much as the poor people of Appalachia. It is difficult to portray what it is like here from the medical standpoint. For instance, I had a patient recently who had a piece of steel in his eyeball. It was right over the pupil, and I didn't feel that I should dig down deeply to try to get it out. The nearest ophthalmologist was in Roswell, eighty miles away; he was able to get the foreign body out without any trouble. That is only one specialty that isn't available locally. There are no urologists, dermatologists, or neurologists. Though the area is prosperous, it has few doctors and no specialists.

The people of Tatum have been very good to me, and I am going to miss them. Many of them have come to me as patients, and I have had some interesting cases. I am seeing only twelve patients a day in the office, and I usually have one or two patients in the hospital in Lovington, which makes a round trip of forty-four miles a day to see them. I have been called out at night only three times in three months. I have had very little Saturday or Sunday medical work.

After the first snowstorm and freezing cold, the weather has not been bad. I have been able to play golf several times. Frequently the temperature is around twenty-five degrees in the morning and sixty-five to seventy by noon. The last two weeks have been exceptionally nice, with temperatures up to eighty degrees. The trees are beginning to leaf out; the grass is beginning to grow. I am still waiting for the big winds that people tell me will come yet in March and April. These winds come out of the west, usually about forty to fifty miles an hour, and carry a lot of dust and sand.

In early February there was a fire in a chemical plant in Lovington that necessitated evacuating many residents. A number of firemen were overcome by fumes. I received a rush call from Lovington, via the police department, that they needed extra help at once. I was going to drive my car, but the Tatum policeman told me he would take me. That was the fastest trip to Lovington I have made. He had his flashing lights on and drove about eighty-five miles an hour on slippery roads. I was very glad when we got there and back safely. At the fire department at least five firemen were laid out on the floor on blankets. They were being given oxygen and first aid to counteract the toxicity from the chemical fumes. I checked them out, sent the most serious ones to the hospital at Hobbs, and reassured the rest. It was an exciting afternoon, but if I had to do it over again, I think I would drive my own car.

Three weeks ago we drove 130 miles to Carlsbad Caverns. Eight hundred feet underground there is a network of caverns so big that one has to walk four miles to get around the explored area. I can see why it has been called one of the Seven Wonders of the World.

We are going to leave on Saturday to go to Alamogordo and the White Sands National Park. Then we will drive part way back and stay overnight in Ruidoso and see the mountains and ski areas there. Our new pharmacist in Tatum lives in Ruidoso and hasn't moved to Tatum yet. He and his wife are going to meet us on Sunday and show us the sights of the Ruidoso area.

Last week the president of the local bank invited Violet and me out to his ranch to watch the branding. Phillip Frier and his father own adjoining ranches about fifteen miles from Tatum. Altogether they branded about one hundred calves that day. The cowboys herded the calves into the corral, roped them by the hind legs or neck, and dragged them into the branding area. Then about three men would hold the calf down and four others carried out specific procedures. One man branded the calf; in this instance, the brand was on the side of the jaw and on the back. Another gave the calf a shot for three diseases, black leg disease, brucel-

Round-up time at the Frier Ranches, Tatum, New Mexico.

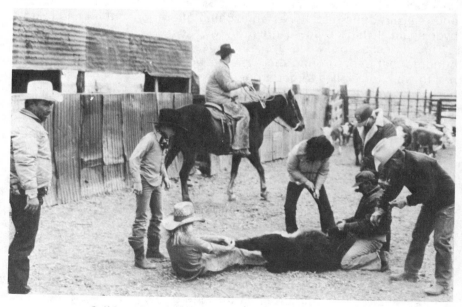

Calf branding time at the Frier Ranch, Tatum, New Mexico.

[194]

losis, and hoof and mouth disease. The third person castrated the male calves, and the fourth dehorned the male calves and put a mark in their ears. The poor little calf didn't have a chance. It was a brutal thing to watch, but that is the way it has been done for the last hundred years. One has to remember this is part of the way that our meat is produced.

Phillip Frier was the main roper. He had a well-trained horse and was skilled with a lasso. His wife helped brand the calves. His daughter Angie, sixteen, and two sons, thirteen and fourteen, all helped. Angie castrated about twenty of the calves herself and did it as well as her uncle, who had been showing her how. They call this procedure "flaking." Angie was anxious for us to take her picture, as she had a twenty dollar bet with a friend that she really would flake the calves. She won!

Later we had a fine dinner at the home of Otis Frier, the banker's father. They have a beautiful modern home on their ranch, fives miles from their nearest neighbor. I don't know when I have enjoyed people more than I have the ranchers and the cowboys. They are so individual; they love the life on the ranch and wouldn't trade it for anything in the world.

Today we had a different experience. One of my patients, Mr. Denton, who has worked in the oil fields all his life, took us for a three-hour tour this afternoon. We got a close-up view of a pump jack and a "pulling unit," which repairs oil wells—pulls out the old pipe and inserts new pipe. We also saw an oil rig drilling for oil and gas. It was a good-sized rig, capable of drilling down 10,800 feet. We were able to get right up on the platform, where the various operations were explained to us. The men who work on the oil rigs certainly earn every penny they make. They are not only hard workers, but they have to be intelligent and highly skilled in order to operate this highly technical machinery. This rig was 130 feet high. At the time we saw it, it had drilled down about 3,000 feet and still had about 7,800 feet to go.

The oil workers are a different type of person from the ranchers and cowboys. I have seen a number of both in my practice and also in our church, and I haven't talked to one of them yet who would trade his occupation for any other in the world.

Red Bird Mission

August 1982

Since I wrote about my experiences in volunteer medical work in Samoa, Appalachia, and New Mexico, I am frequently asked, "When are you going to write some more chapters?" Your interest has prompted me to write again—this time about my experiences in Red Bird Hospital in Beverly, Kentucky.

Dr. Schaeffer asked me to cover for him while he and his wife took a two-week vacation. Dr. Schaeffer has been working as a missionary doctor in this area since 1946, after he finished his hospital training and was discharged from the Army. This twenty-four-bed hospital has an attached clinic building with space for three doctors and three dentists and has furnished the medical care for this area for many years. Dr. Life has been at Red Bird for about twenty years and has also dedicated his life to medical mission work. Shortly before I arrived, Dr. Jones, a family practitioner, moved in and will be here for a year. He had just finished his residency in family practice and wanted to commit a year of his life to this kind of work before going into private practice. He will be furnished a place to live and a salary on which he and his wife and two children can live very well, but nothing like the salary he would get in private practice.

Violet did not go with me on this trip as it was to be for only two weeks. I drove as far as Lexington, Kentucky, the first day and stayed overnight, timing my arrival at Red Bird Mission for around noon the next day. I was to stay at the Schaeffer's home and didn't want to get there much before they left on vacation that afternoon. I arrived about an hour before Dr. Schaeffer was ready to leave, and we got acquainted and talked over what was expected of me and when he would be back. They have a very livable three-bedroom house, not elaborate and not air conditioned, but clean and neat. I was to sleep there and eat at the hospital.

I started work in the clinic on Monday, July 18, and saw a number of patients through the day and admitted one to the hospital. I found both Dr. Life and Dr. Jones delightful, and things went very well. I was to be on emergency call on the second day. I told Dr. Life and Dr. Jones that I would not be able to do any obstetrics or surgery other than minor suturing and that I sincerely hoped I wouldn't get any patients with severe accidents or gunshot wounds. The previous night, a twenty-one-year-old man had been brought in, dead on arrival, who had been injured in the mines. Mine accidents are common in this area, and they are often serious.

I reported for duty in the emergency room at approximately 5:00 P.M., and my first patient was a man who had been shot. The bullet had entered on the right side of his nose, going down through the hard palate and out the corner of his mouth on the opposite side. It had knocked out four teeth and cut the corner of his lip pretty badly. It was something we obviously couldn't handle at Red Bird. Dr. Jones came over to help me, and after the patient was stabilized we sent him to a larger hospital in Harlan, Kentucky, where there was an ear, nose, and throat surgeon. While he was still in the emergency room, the police came to question him. When they asked him who shot him, he refused to tell. They did everything they could to persuade him, but to no avail. This is the way Kentucky justice often works. People take the law into their own hands and settle their quarrels by gunfire or by fighting.

It was planned that I would have the two Wednesdays off that I was there, so on the first Wednesday I went to Hazard to see my old friend Les Rogers and play some golf. While in that area I went over to Home-place, where Violet and I had lived for seven weeks last fall, and renewed old acquaintances.

On the way back to Red Bird, the car didn't sound right. It had a strange hum that got worse as I went along. By the time I got back to the Hospital, it was obvious that something was very wrong with the car. The other doctors referred me to Mike Jarvis, who had a small garage and repaired the cars of the doctors and nurses in the hospital. They said he was honest and a good mechanic. Mike found that the differential was worn and needed to be replaced and that the oil had come out because of a loosened bolt. He kept the car until the following Tuesday, so I couldn't go any place. In the meantime I worked daily in the clinics and hospital, and in the emergency room every third night.

On Wednesday, July 28, I started to drive the car again and found that something was wrong with the carburetor so that I didn't have much power. I thought that the carburetor would be more complicated to repair and probably should be taken to an Oldsmobile garage. I drove to London, about sixty miles away, where there is an Oldsmobile garage, and Dr. Jones's wife followed me in her car. I left the car to be worked on and rode back to Red Bird with Mrs. Jones. The garage called on July 30 and said that the car would be ready at five o'clock, so Mrs. Jones took me to London and I drove my car back to the hospital without any trouble. I expected to start for home the next day.

My experiences at the clinic and the hospital were routine but interest-ing. I had as many as six patients at the hospital at one time, and some of them were very sick, but luckily I didn't have any deaths. Two of the most serious cases were a man with a severe heart attack and a woman with acute pneumonia, but I was able to stabilize both of them.

The nurses and nurse's aides were among the most dedicated people I have ever met and very Christian in everything they did. Some were volunteers; others were salaried and had been working at Red Bird for a year or two and were going to stay longer. The dentists, all of whom were women, had been there from one to three years. A dentist from Freeport, Illinois, had been at Red Bird over a year and was going to stay another year.

The emergency room was very busy every night I worked. Sometimes I worked until one or two in the morning and then was almost always called back before daylight.

Many of the local people are uneducated, and about 20 percent can neither read nor write. The younger people, however, will change these statistics, as they all go to school now until they are sixteen. They attend a school sponsored by Red Bird Mission and the Methodist Church. Their culture is quite different, and because of their lack of education, they don't trust doctors very far. A woman patient with lower abdominal pain came to emergency room, and I needed to do a pelvic examination in order to diagnose her condition. She and her husband, who was with her at all times, absolutely refused to have a man examine her. She said that she had never had any man look at her but her husband, and he was the only man who was ever going to look at her. I tried to explain that this type of examination meant nothing to me and that it would help me to know what was wrong with her. They were both unconvinced and left the emergency room without treatment.

On the other side of the fence, a man with a laceration on the anterior part of his thigh came in and, because there was a nurse in the room, refused to take his pants off so we could suture it. I did convince him, however, that I could cover him with a towel and there would be no exposure, so he let us go ahead and do the suturing.

On my last clinic day, a twenty-two-year-old woman came in with her four-year-old daughter. She had been beaten by her husband the night before. In order to get away from him, she had walked seven miles over the mountains, carrying her daughter the entire distance. Fortunately, she had nothing more than bumps and bruises, and perhaps a mild concussion. She said that her husband had done this five times and that was enough. She wasn't going back to him any more.

As if the trouble with the car wasn't enough, on Tuesday, July 27, Violet called, saying that she had been sick through the night with vomiting and dizziness. Knowing that she was alone, I probably would have gone right home if I had had a car. But I phoned her twice a day and also asked Dr. O'Shea to see her and follow her along. She improved from day to day, so I didn't have to return home immediately.

When the people at the Red Bird Mission Clinic heard that I had trouble with my car, they all prayed that it would be fixed properly, and when they learned that my wife was sick, they prayed for her. One of the nurses even offered to let me drive her Chevette to Aurora and said that I could return it whenever I came back for my car. Several of the nurses and nurse's aides offered to take me to London to get my car or to take me any place I wanted. They were just marvelous.

I thought I would work until around noon on Saturday, July 31, and then start for home. Dr. Wilkerson and Dr. Schaeffer would both be back the next day, so the clinic would be covered and they would not need me any further. My car was back and apparently running fine, so I worked in the clinic in the morning, had lunch in the hospital with some of the nurses and dentists, told them all goodbye, and left. I drove out of the mountains onto the Daniel Boone Parkway and was probably four or five miles from the interchange when all of a sudden the car quit. The motor just stopped. I was going about fifty-five miles an hour and coasted to a stop on the shoulder. I was greatly perplexed as to how to find a phone and whether I could get anybody to help me on a Saturday afternoon. There was a house up on a bank, about two hundred feet from the car, and I walked across a ditch and climbed the bank. There I found a wire fence, which I couldn't get over. I yelled for the people in the house, and two boys came out. I asked if I could use their telephone, and they said, "We ain't got no phone." They said if I climbed the fence and took the road back of the house for about a half mile up in the "holler," those folks had a phone.

Sometimes I think things happen that cannot be explained any other way but that they are directed by a higher power. I was standing there by the fence, a little way from the road, trying to decide what to do, when a blue car went by. After passing it slowed down, stopped, and then backed up. I could see there were women in it, but I didn't know at first whether they were backing up because of me or for some other reason. When they were opposite me, they waved, and I rushed down through the weeds and across the ditch to the road. In the car were two nurse's aides and the two dentists with whom I had eaten lunch just an hour before. I couldn't believe my luck! They took me to Manchester, twelve miles away, and saw that I was getting some help before they left. I was able to get a tow truck from a garage to tow my car back to their service area. Luckily, the mechanics work Saturday afternoons until five o'clock, and this was around 1:30. They put a man to work on my car who really knew his business. He took the carburetor apart and showed me where it had not been fixed properly before—a screw was left out, a spring was broken, and the float was bent. He cleaned it and put it back together, putting in new parts where necessary. It took about an hour and a half. When he had finished, he said, "Dr. Greeley, you will have no more trouble,"—and I didn't. I was amazed when I got the bill. They towed my car for twelve miles, worked on it for an hour and a half, put in new parts, and the total bill was only $39.22. It was still fairly early in the afternoon and I was able to drive on to Louisville before I stopped for the night. The next morning I drove to Aurora, arriving home around noon on Sunday, August 1, with no more trouble from the car. I found Violet much better, and I was glad to be home after all the trouble with the car.

That ends my experience in the Red Bird Mission Hospital. I hope that sometime I can go back again, because I thoroughly enjoyed the people and the work.

Hazelden

November 1982

I have always had an interest in alcoholism and drug addiction, two of the major problems in our society today. Starting December 1, I will be teaching some classes in the Alcohol Program at Mercy Center. These will be primarily medical education lectures. I decided that one of the best ways to learn more about the treatment of alcoholism was to go to Hazelden and take the course they call "Physician Orientation to Treatment." This is an unusual way to observe how a large alcoholic treatment center works. Hazelden is a beautiful institution built on a hill beside a lake in the north woods of Minnesota, forty miles from St. Paul. The 160 patients under treatment are divided into six units of twenty-two people—four men's units, two for women, and one unit for extended care. In these units the people live in two-, three-, and four-bed wards. They eat together, pray together, counsel and work together. It was in one of these units that I lived for five days.

I will try to give you a brief description of the program. At 7:45 A.M., the group met in a rather large room, where we sat in a circle and had morning meditation conducted by one of the men in the group. Following this, we went to the main dining room, where all 160 people ate together, but each group had its own tables and was not allowed to fraternize with the other units. Prayers were offered by men in each unit before and after the meal. We then cleared our own tables and walked back to our unit. After a short rest, we assembled in the auditorium, where we heard a half-hour lecture. We returned again to our unit and discussed the lecture for one to two hours. At noon we had lunch together, then attended another lecture and participated in more group discussions in the afternoon. Four to six o'clock was free time when we could play volleyball, basketball, or pool. If the days were nice, we could walk in the woods and around the lake. Dinner was at six o'clock, followed by another lecture and another discussion. By that time it was 9:30 and our day was over. I followed the program right along with the men for five days. They were some of the most interesting and inspiring days I have ever spent. The men knew I was there as an observer and accepted me as a member of the group.

[200]

The patients who go through the program at Hazelden come from all over the United States and, in fact, from all over the world. One was from Iceland. All walks of life are represented, from poor to multimillionaire, but when they are admitted to a unit, they all become one. They have the same problem: they are all chemically dependent and are there to get the monkey off their backs. Nobody is concerned with anyone's profession. All their efforts are directed to their main problem. There were doctors, lawyers, priests, architects, manufacturers, and merchandisers in our unit, in all stages of treatment. The average length of stay is four weeks. Some of these men had been at Hazelden from one to four weeks and some had just been admitted.

One cannot, in a short discussion, do justice to the treatment program at Hazelden, but it is miraculous what they can accomplish in four weeks. I saw patients come in who were nervous, trembly, confused, and obviously had been drinking very heavily. By the time I left, they were entirely different human beings. Their minds had cleared, their tremors were gone, and for the first time in many years they could look forward to the future. During the group discussions, the tragedies of alcoholism came out very clearly. All of these men had lost something very dear to them—their wives had divorced them, their children had kicked them out, their businesses had failed. They had been ostracized by society, and they had blamed their circumstances on somebody or something else, as all alcoholics do before they come to Hazelden. By the time they leave, they realize that their problem is alcohol, that they are powerless to cope with it, and that they will have to abstain for the rest of their lives. During the four weeks they have hours of counseling and peer support in the form of discussion groups. One might say that Hazelden not only gets them off alcohol and drugs but puts their heads on straight.

I think one of the most effective parts of the program is that these men, in their discussions, help each other. I listened to them and tried to be as sympathetic and helpful as possible. One day one of the men and I took a walk through the woods, and he discussed his problems with me and told me the things that had happened to him as he deteriorated from his alcoholism. He said that for the first time in years his mind was clear and he could recognize that alcohol was his problem. He wondered if he would get home in time to stop the divorce his wife was planning and if his children would accept him again. Everybody who goes through Hazelden has problems of this magnitude that have caused tragedies in their lives.

One of the main principles in the treatment is spiritual. There is no concern about a man's religion; that is his business. But it is brought out that there is a spiritual aspect of the treatment in that a higher power can take over and help the alcoholic. Every group session is ended by saying the Serenity Prayer. All the men stand in a circle, put their arms around each other, and repeat together, "God grant me the serenity to accept the things I cannot change, courage to change the things I can, and wisdom to know the difference." Then they pat each other on the back, put their right foot forward, and are ready for other things.

When a man is ready to leave Hazelden, a special session is held for him called the Medallion Ceremony. He is given a medallion inscribed with the Alcoholics Anonymous insignia and the Serenity Prayer. The medallion is passed around the group and everybody wishes him well and tells some of the things that have happened to make the group one. It is a touching experience. Everyone knows that this man is going back to the world from which he came and that it will be a tough job to keep sober and off alcohol. I was surprised when, on my last day, they had a Medallion Ceremony for me; they presented me with a medallion, passed it around from man to man, and all said a few words. I was deeply touched. As I left Hazelden that day and started my drive back to Aurora, I thought of the events of the past five days and how Hazelden helps drug-dependent people solve their problems. I hope that the lectures I will be giving in the near future will help others in understanding and overcoming alcoholism.